What's the Usage?

What's the Usage?

The Writer's Guide to English Grammar and Rhetoric

by

C. Carter Colwell   and   James H. Knox

Stetson University   *Shenandoah College*

Reston Publishing Company, Inc.

Reston, Virginia

What's the Usage?
The Writer's Guide to English Grammar and Rhetoric
C. Carter Colwell and James H. Knox

© 1973 by
Reston Publishing Company, Inc. A Prentice-Hall Company
P.O. Box 547
Reston, Virginia 22090

10 9 8 7 6 5 4 3 2

ISBN: 0-87909-888-0
0-87909-889-9

Library of Congress Catalog Card Number: 72-96756
Printed in the United States of America.

To Falstaff
who shed great wisps of happiness

Contents

Preface

One of the ploys of gamesmanship[1] admires the way an opponent—at tennis, at golf—moves some part of his body. "I couldn't help noticing the way you toe your left foot in; I wonder if that is why you serve (drive) so well? I wish I could do it." The gamesman makes the other player concentrate so much on one aspect of what he does that all the rest goes to pot. The student trying to better his writing suffers much the same treatment from his textbook. If he looks to his words, his sentences wriggle off uncontrolled; if he looks to his sentences, his paragraphs grow like crabgrass until in impatience he cuts it out altogether.

Inevitable? Well, almost. A textbook can, however, come back to a topic (word, sentence, paragraph), often enough to remind the struggling writer what he is about to forget. This textbook does that, introducing all the usual problem areas (word, sentence, paragraph) briefly, and then coming back to each one twice more. Reading this book, a student needn't wait for page 275 to find out what a paragraph (or sentence, or word) is. Writing is like living. All the vital processes go on at once. By returning to the major topics three times, we hope to keep the student aware that he must attend to word, sentence, and paragraph throughout all his writing, as he turns the alphabet into an essay.

---

[1] First analyzed by Stephen Potter.

Freshman English books about writing polarize. Handbooks mark one end of the scale. While there are excellent handbooks to give a hard brace to the flagging writer's sagging knowledge of grammar, they make poor reading, whether for bedroom, or course assignment.

The opposite kind of Freshman English writing text finds fewer representatives; here one can find an interesting and highly readable montage of comments about writing and communication generally. Alas, such books provide almost no concrete, specific, practical advice on what to do and how to do it.

What's the Usage?, like the handbook, provides specific Dos and Don'ts; but unlike other grammar texts, it is readable.

What is a complete writing text? Both a grammar and a rhetoric, it covers the term paper and library research; can be used for reference; covers all aspects of mechanics, including spelling; explains logical argument; shows how to control tone in correspondence; integrates exercises with the text, illustrating points as they are made; suggests writing topics that fit the chapter or section; and exemplifies both writing errors and writing virtues. *What's the Usage?* does all these.

Other texts, of course, are both grammar and rhetoric. Most, however, share three drawbacks: they are staid; they do not take the student through the actual process of composition; and they are written for an audience that already writes fairly well, knows some grammar, and is motivated to read about grammar and writing. Therefore, we have sought to write a grammar and rhetoric for the people who most need to study grammar and rhetoric—the people who know least about writing. *What's the Usage?* proceeds vigorously, step-by-step, and easily.

This text is vigorous: a panegyric on Corn on the Cob, Mr. Clay's omnivorous pigs (a pity about Angus and Archie's mother), the Gettysburg Address in one-clause sentences, the transparently honest Mr. Glass—all invite vigorous response (that's what the crumple page is for).

This text works step by step. From expanding a prepositional phrase to writing a complete theme, processes are analyzed and broken into a sequence of separate steps. The student who follows instructions will be writing almost whether he wants to or not. We grasp his ankles and lift his feet one at a time and swing them forward; with a teacher's finger to clutch he will soon stride.

Most books, as we said, start with the word and work up through the paragraph before they discuss the whole essay; or they start with the whole essay and work down towards individual words. This text goes from word to paragraph three times, in Parts II, III, and IV. Part II explains what the parts are (words are parts of speech in Chapter 3, for example). Part III explains where to put them, how to arrange the parts (words within sentences in

Chapter 8, for example, and sentences within paragraphs in Chapter 9). And Part IV explains how the parts are fastened together, what connects them (words within sentences being connected by conjunctions—Chapter 12—and Punctuation—Chapter 13; and paragraphs within the essay being connected by suitable transitions and reasonable content, Chapter 14). In addition, the text attends to letters at the small end (Chapter 2), and to the whole essay at the big end (Chapters 10 and 14). But we also start with the whole essay: the first chapter, Part I, looks at the writer, and ends by following him through the successive stages in the composition of an essay. Parts II, III, and IV concentrate on the work, the writing; and Part V turns to the audience and the effect the writer seeks.

The writer whose works are meager, pinched, will find here specific ways to flesh out his writing. Ways to expand thought are simply presented, with traditional grammatical terms used as tools for building sentences, as devices for developing paragraphs into rich and meaningful statements. Especially those who know little grammar and write few words should find this book helpful. Writing it was fun. So should reading it be.

We wish to express our appreciation to Dr. Ernest Colwell, who interrupted a summer's convalescence from an unmentionable operation to pursue a jam of tarts and other flights of fancy; to Mr. Eyler Coates, Librarian at Shenandoah College, for unfailing cooperation; to our amiable relatives who have consented to our not quite libelous reminiscences; and to the two best and most patient editors on our distaffs.

ccc

jhk

What's the Usage?

Part One: THE WRITER

I

How to Make a Theme of Yourself

wo English teachers write this book. Since we're amiable, friendly types, we often will write in the first person, saying "we feel" or "I feel" rather than the third person "one feels," which is formal, stilted, and phony: it pretends that somebody else, some anonymous who-knows-who, thinks what we think. So if a teacher told you not to write "I think," "I feel," "I believe," don't; but don't blame us. We think, and we feel, and we believe.

But we will make one little fiction. Talking in tandem taxes the tongue. It reminds us of Old King Cole, Henry the VIIIth, and a host of royal monarchs, each of whom thinks he is the whole realm and speaks for the entire kingdom he rules, and so constantly speaks in the plural. When Henry said, "We are displeased," his subjects trembled, and so did his wives, because they knew no one was included in that "we" but Henry himself. So we won't say *we*, we will just say *I*.

I hope you don't mind. If you do, console yourself with the thought that you have already had your first lesson: the difference between first person and third person, and between first person singular and first person plural. You (a second person pronoun) are (often a second person verb) the one in between. If that turns you on, turn to page 156 for a chart of more variations. But if you know the difference, you have some idea why people don't say "I is" or "you am."[1]

"WHO AM I?"

A science fiction story I read some years ago tells of a computer which starts turning itself on. One night when all but one eager beaver scientist have left, the machine begins to calculate. The ticker tape feeds out "$2 \times 2 = 4$" and pauses; then it clicks again, "$2 \times 3 = 6$"; then with increasing speed and apparent confidence it prints the multiplication table of two's, pauses again, and then rips out the tables up through 100×100. Once again it pauses, humming softly, light flickering gently, until, before the dumbfounded scien-

---

[1]Puzzle for advanced students: Can you create a grammatically correct sentence in which the words "you am" appear in that order? If you can't, check footnote 3 at the bottom of the next page.

tist's eyes, it roars into action and spews out over and over the words WHO AM I WHO AM I WHO AM I WHO AM I.[2]

It is possible to get through life without knowing the answer, I suppose; but like that computer, a writer must know the answer.

To get somewhere, you must know where you are starting. Only then can you plan your route.

Who are you? In the space that follows, before reading any farther, write three sentences that answer that question, each sentence beginning with the words "I am . . ."

This question, with its call for three answers, was put to me by a fellow student who gave everybody in the room a chance to answer before explaining that it was something used by social workers who needed to get to know someone as a person in a matter of minutes. The point is, your answers are probably true.

One man said, "I am John, I am Jay, I am Jones," giving his three names as his three answers. Another said, "I am a being existentially related to God," and couldn't think of any other answers. The husband of the woman who asked the question gave his answers: "I am Philip Walsem, I am an accountant, I am the husband of this lovely Lucy (smack) and the father of Tom and Maggie."

---

[2]I would like to credit the author of this story, but I read it more than twenty years ago and can't remember either his name or the name of the story. I've looked for it in a number of anthologies without turning it up. If you recognize it, please drop me a note c/o Reston Publishing Company, P. O. Box 547, Reston, Virginia, 22090.

[3]I, say you, am a fool. OR: I, I tell you, am a fool. The trick is the parenthetical expression: the *you* doesn't go with the *am*, it goes with the *I tell*, which is just tucked casually into the sentence as a little aside. The commas fore and aft indicate that the group of words *I tell you* is parenthetical. Change the punctuation and you have a real monster: I! I tell, you am a fool!

What did we reveal about ourselves? Phil, the last, gave the answers typical of a well-adjusted person: name (personal identity), occupation (in his case, his job), and a personal relationship (he squeezed in three). The rest of us came out a little differently. The man who gave only his name, in fact a married student with children, shortly thereafter changed his field of study (from economics to philosophy, and again, to American Studies) and separated temporarily from his family. He left them out because, at least for the moment, they weren't part of him. The man with only one answer—"I am a being existentially related to God"—also shortly separated (again temporarily) from his wife; his field of study was which of the following?

1. engineering
2. religion
3. medicine
4. painting
5. politics

Of course, just knowing who you are doesn't guarantee success. After all, the man who goes through life singing "I want to be a paperback writer" won't get much published if he has nothing to say. "I'm a writer." "How fascinating! A real writer! What have you written?" "Well, I'm still working on that." And even if you know not only who you, as writer, are; even if you know also what you want to say—even then you aren't through. The teacher who knows his subject perfectly sometimes falls into the trap of thinking that all he has to do is say it. But no communication is complete until it has been received by an audience. How many lectures have you slept through? Did the teacher teach you that day?

But although it doesn't guarantee success, knowing who you are is a start. So, for a start, write a paragraph on the

TOPIC

What I did/did not learn about myself by giving three answers to the question, "Who are you?"

The "correct" or typical answers to the question "who are you?" include the speaker's identity, his job, and his personal relationships. All three correspond to the three most important aspects of any writing: the writer, the writing itself, and the audience. Learning to write well means learning to think honestly and analytically about all three: about yourself, about what you write, and about those you write for. This concept—the distinction between author, work, and audience—underlies the division of this book. Part

I (this chapter) concerns the author; parts II, III, and IV concern the work; part V concerns the audience.

What you write, the written work you produce, is a statement. Every statement occurs in a context, which includes your identity and that of your audience. That context affects meaning.

One of the Smothers Brothers said on their TV show that once at a candy factory he fell into a vat full of chocolate. "What did you do?" asked the other brother. "I yelled FIRE!" "Fire! Why did you yell fire?" "Well, would you come running if someone yelled CHOCOLATE!"

Suppose you were in the chocolate factory that day and happened to wander by the chocolate vat in which Mr. Smothers was floundering. "Well, hello," you might say, "and who are you?" On that occasion, the answer would surely include some reference to the vat of chocolate and Mr. Smothers' location in it. The answer might well be, "I'm the Smothers brother (personal identity) who is going to drown in chocolate (occupation) if you don't pull me out quick (personal relationship)."

Context in the chocolate factory—the situation, the set-up, the lay-out, the scene—affected the speaker's concept of who he was; it shaped the necessary message; and it involved who was around to hear. (You were there because you are a chocolate freak.) The total context, that is, included the speaker, the message spoken, and the audience. In a writing situation, the *speak*er becomes the _____-er, the *spoke*n message becomes a _____-en message, and the audience becomes a reader. (Lacking a word vidience, we still call him an audience. Audio, audit, audible, but only video.)

What is your job as a writer? Communicating. What is communicating? Getting it across. What is *it?* "Oh, do not ask, 'What is it?'/Let us go and make our visit." Those two lines of poetry come from one of the most famous poems of the twentieth century, "The Love Song of J. Alfred Prufrock," by T. S. Eliot.[4] They certainly don't *look* like great poetry—little common words, only one or two syllables, they look commonplace and mediocre; they certainly don't *sound* like great poetry—that silly double rhyme of "is it" with "visit" sounds prissy, insincere, self-conscious, artificial, coyly cute. But they sure *communicate* great poetry, because Eliot meant them to be spoken by someone commonplace, mediocre, prissy, insincere, self-conscious, artificial, coyly cute. Your basic job as writer is not to go visit, but precisely *to* ask "what is it"—what do you want to get across? Eliot didn't ask himself, "How can I write some great poetry?" He asked himself, "How can I get across the feeling of a certain kind of person: someone who doesn't want embarrassingly profound

---

[4]T. S. Eliot, "The Love Song of J. Alfred Prufrock" in *Collected Poems*, 1909–1962 (New York: Harcourt, Brace, Jovanovich, and London: Faber and Faber, Ltd.)

or frank questions, someone like J. Alfred Prufrock?" (he chose the name, remember), and he came up with these two lines, among others.

What do you want to communicate? Information? A feeling of personality—what it is like to be you, perhaps—or an experience—winning a race, say—or just a mood? Or do you want to communicate the determination to take certain action—do you want your audience to act a certain way, vote for a certain candidate? That is your first specific task as writer. Your first general task as writer was to know something of yourself; your first specific task is to define the job—what it is you want to get across. Now, defining that task means describing what the work you produce will accomplish; it focuses on the work. The work will be discussed later, in parts II, III, and IV. But for the moment, I note simply that you must have some clear idea of what is to be done before you can do it. If, therefore, you have a choice of topic, choose one you know something about. Write from your experience. That is part of knowing yourself: knowing what you are familiar with. You can't *write* about something on the basis of reading one encyclopedia article. You can *copy*, you can plagiarize, but you can't write.

TEST. Which of the following is the best theme topic for *YOU?*

1. Potlatch practices among the Kwakiutls, or, a primitive society carries conspicuous consumption to undreamed of ends.

2. Robert Fitzralph, fourteenth-century defender of the parochial rights of the secular clergy against the infringements of mendicant friars such as Chaucer's Huberd.

3. Should algebraic topology be taught in a math department whose faculty includes no algebraic topologist?

4. Route-cab control on a simple model-railroad mainline with one return loop.

5. My room is *NOT* messy; an essay on the moral implications of slovenliness.

College assignments often assign the task, often state as an assigned topic the "it" that you must communicate. Your particular work as writer therefore often begins not with the statement of the end to be achieved—that is the assignment; your particular work begins with choosing the means to do the assignment. Practically speaking, you face the problem not "what," but "how."

Here's how . . .

HOW TO WRITE

I. **Get Some Ideas.**

A. *Write the instructions* for your assignment three different times, in different words. Give yourself a limited amount of time to do this; say, five minutes if you are writing out of class. If you can't write it three ways, write it once or twice, and try again after doing step IB.

Suppose your assignment is: How to ask for a date. This might be rewritten: The way to approach a girl you want to go out with you. What I would say to someone I wanted to take to a movie (or somewhere else?). How to tell a girl you'd like to spend some time with her without sounding silly.

This particular assignment might be modified for women, e.g.: How to refuse a request from a young man. Possible rewrites: How to refuse a proposition. How to say, "No, John." Refusing a man doesn't mean insulting him. In the following discussion, I, being male, am going to do the male assignment.

Note that restating introduces some new content, some leads for ideas.

B. *Brainstorm.* (Verb, imperative mood—which means, that's an order. Do it.) Brainstorming helps loosen the mind, gets it moving; brainstorming is how to have an idea. The basic rule of brainstorming is, *Don't evaluate.* Don't criticize, don't judge, save second thoughts until later. To brainstorm just spew out any conceivable answer or approach to a problem without any thought of whether it can be done.

Sit with a piece of paper and a pencil in front of you and the assignment and your restatements of it beside you. Let your mind wander around the topic: jot down everything that comes to you. Don't reject any ideas or passing thoughts; anything goes, and should be written down. Try to go through two brainstorming sessions, separated by at least one hour of other activity—a day, if your teacher's due-date allows.

Here is some of my brainstorming on the male version of that assignment, How to ask for a date:

Smile.
Find out what you both like.
Brush your teeth.
Be honest, direct.
Work up gradually to the subject.
Don't take her interest for granted.
Use your winning charm.
Be modest, not shy.
Don't ask someone who will say no.
Boast.
Show your muscles.
Let her know what you have in mind before you ask her.

Note that two of these items (Be direct and Work up gradually) are almost contradictory. Don't let that stop you from jotting them down; "A foolish consistency," as Emerson said, "is the hobgoblin of little minds" to one engaged in brain-storming.

II. **Rough Outline.** This preliminary outline comes in two steps:

A. First, *review your brainstorming. Now*—after you have apparently run dry at brainstorming, have paced the floor, and have taken a break to go up to the roof and feed the pigeons—*now* be brutal. Cut out all those ideas that don't sound so good the second day: the one about lifting yourself with your own boot-straps to get a running start, the one about hiring Uncle Ambrose for a million dollars to invent a perpetual motion machine, the one about everybody in the country voluntarily contributing two dollars to rebuild the ghetto. Those won't work. Keep, however, the idea about training teachers to praise initiative, the one about lowering the unemployment rate, the one about spending less in Vietnam and more at home. They may not work either, but they are reasonable efforts.

B. Second, *number the ideas* you have kept, in the order in which you will write them. If a few are sort of far apart, jot something down about how you will get from one idea to the next. Remember to put the ideas you have kept into a reasonable order. What is a reasonable order? A reasonable order makes sense. A reasonable order moves from idea to idea easily, like a railroad wheel rolling from rail to rail; an unreasonable order jumps from stone to stone heavily, if at all—like Mark Twain's Celebrated Jumping Frog of Calaveras County, which an unkind competitor had weighted with a couple of pounds of buckshot.

How might this revision go with the brainstorming above? You would note that the list contains several different approaches to the topic: 1) humorous; 2) serious, person-oriented; 3) ideas that could be either 1 or 2. Numbered according to this classification, and with some critical comments, the list looks like this:

3. Smile.
2. Find out what you both like.
1. Brush your teeth.
2. Be honest, direct.
3. Work up gradually to subject.
2. Don't take her interest for granted.
1. Use your winning charm.
2. Be modest, not shy. (? Sounds asinine.)
3. Don't ask someone who will say no.
1. Boast.
1. Show your muscles.
2. Let her know what you have in mind before you ask her.

At this point, you must make a choice: Will you try to write a humorous essay, or will you take the assignment as seriously meant, and try to treat it with dignity? If the first (humorous), you will keep only the ideas in 1 and perhaps in 3. If the second (serious), you will keep only the ideas in 2 and perhaps in 3.

As you face this choice, another possibility may occur to you: you could do both—one could be a set-up for the other. You can describe one kind of approach, reject it, and describe the other. This could go either way: You could describe a tongue-in-cheek he-man approach first, reject it, and describe a decently serious approach as the right way; the overall effect will be serious. Or you could reverse your direction and aim at a comic essay, starting with the serious approach, rejecting it, and then playing with all of the ludicrous possibilities lurking at the edges of the topic. If you do the latter, you will have to make the serious approach seem a bit silly; play up the asininity of "Be modest, not shy."

Deciding which of these you will do depends on your overall purpose—a joke, or a serious essay in human relationships? With that decision made, the outline follows almost automatically.

Most of the time, you will do better to aim at saying something meaningful and serious rather than frivolous and humorous. A gag-writers' convention was visited by a cub reporter. After dinner in the hotel ballroom, one of the writers stood and said, "Three hundred and seventy-two." Everyone laughed. "What's going on?" asked the visitor. "Well, we all know all the jokes there are," answered his writer companion, "so instead of wasting time repeating all the words, we tell jokes just by referring to their numbers." Another writer stood, and said "five hundred and twenty-nine," at which the whole convention was convulsed with hysterical laughter. "Why did they laugh so much harder at that one?" Wiping away tears of laughter, the writer answered, "They hadn't heard it before." "Let me try," the reporter said; "what's the one about the farmer's daughter and the purple hay wagon?" "That's number 843." The reporter stood, and said, "four hundred and nineteen." A few chuckles came from scattered corners of the great room. Hurt, he sat down and asked why such a funny joke got such a weak response. "Well," explained the writer, patting him consolingly, "it's all in the way you tell it."

Bear that in mind when writing your own themes; clowning that doesn't come off really falls flat. Let's assume, then, that you chose to write the finally serious essay on "How to ask for a date," beginning with the tongue-in-cheek he-man approach, which you will turn from to suggest a more meaningful attitude. TEST: how many main parts will your preliminary outline have?

1. One
2. Two
3. Five

eight hundred and forty-three

eight hundred and forty-three

The decision you have made about starting with the he-man, or tongue-in-cheek, approach, automatically carries with it the decision to put the brainstorming items numbered "1" first and the ones numbered "2" second, with the ones numbered "3" fitted in wherever seems best. Where they should go can be decided as you work on the rough draft.

III. Now you're ready to write. Now comes the Rough Draft.

Write the paper. How? Just do it. Sit down with paper in front of you, rough outline (the selected brainstorming ideas, numbered in order) beside you, and write.

Don't write the whole theme at once. Work like the man who was asked how to eat a whale. "First," he said, "get a knife and cut it up into *very small* pieces." Sentence by sentence, expand and develop what you have on your preliminary outline. Your attitude as you do this should be somewhat like your attitude when brainstorming. Work in all the relevant information, thoughts, attitudes, ideas, details, considerations, that go with each point in the preliminary outline. Don't be too hesitant or critical; unless an idea strikes you as clearly irrelevant or absurd, put it in.

"How to Ask a Girl for a Date"
rough draft

Some guys think the only way to get a girl is to use all their masculine charm. So they brush their teeth with Gleem to make a big white smile, head for the girl, and boast about how great they are. Then they show off some big muscle. They think they have them even if they don't.

You ought to be honest and direct. Find out what you both like— tennis, movies—and talk to her about that. Be modest, not shy. Don't take her interest for granted. Tell her what you want to do before you ask her. That way, you will work up gradually to the subject. If she wants to say no, she will have time to think of a nice way of doing it. Of course, if you're smart, you won't ask someone who will say no.

IV. Final Outline.

Reread what you have written, thinking about the shape of the whole paper. Does it make sense? Does it follow that reasonable order you wanted? Now decide whether to move any paragraphs from one place to another. Mark up the rough draft with numbers, arrows, brackets, shoving parts around until they seem to fit best. Then write a final outline, probably consisting of major sentences, one for each paragraph, stating that paragraph's main idea.

As you reread the rough draft above, you note that your tongue-in-cheek approach responds more to the topic "How to prove I'm irresistible" than "how to ask for a date." The introduction will be a good place to make clear your attitude to this approach, which you will reject in part two; after all, you don't want to mislead your reader into accepting values you intend to reject.

Your revised outline will begin, then, with an

Introduction: For some, "how to ask for a date" = "How to be irresistible."

The order is pretty rough, too. The preliminary outline had only two parts; subdividing them will make clearer what ought to go where. The first part—call it the he-man approach—might be grouped into "advance preparation" (brush your teeth); leading up to the question (boast; show your muscles); putting the question itself. Any "How to do . . ." essay invites some chronological organization. As a matter of fact, that's the order followed in the rough draft; not too bad. The final outline will continue, then, with the

I. He-man approach:
    A. Advance preparation: brush your teeth
    B. Leading up to the question
       1. Boast
       2. Show muscles

But the second part of the rough draft comes out a bit rougher. You've decided on a chronological order, but honesty and directness come while you're with her, whereas finding out what she likes and deciding what girls will say "no" both come first, as advance preparation. The final outline of part II, then, might come out—after some thought—like this:

II. But° a woman reacts to your attitudes;°° so ask for a date with
    respect for her as a person.
    A. Advance preparation:
       1. Think about who it is you are asking before asking.
       2. Don't ask someone you know doesn't like you or who has
          totally different interests.°°°
    B. Leading up to the question
       1. Work up gradually to subject°°°°
       2. Tell her what you have in mind before you ask her.
    C. Putting the question: Don't be shy.°°°°°

Notes: °Transitional word, warning reader that subject changes here.
°°New thought while writing outline.
°°° A modified form of "Don't ask someone who will say no," and "Find out what you both like," suggested by looking at brainstorm list for a parallel to I A above.
°°°°Needs some expansion?
°°°°°"Be modest" is scratched; it sounded a little asinine even while brainstorming, and you realize a man in quest of a date isn't supposed to be talking about himself anyway.

V. Final Draft.

Rewrite your rough draft, sitting between it on one side of you and your final outline on the other side. Now is the time to smooth out the connections between sentences and paragraphs, if any roughness still remains. Now too is the time to think a little about your audience, and whether you use the right words for the people you are writing for. Is the vocabulary too simple? too technical? too formal? too informal? Does it reveal an attitude of yours not shared by your audience? If so, don't use those words until you think you have convinced your audience that your attitude is the right one; and if you aren't going to try to convince them, then just change the words to neutral terms.

Now, in short, is the time to polish. Ben Jonson remarked of Shakespeare, "I have heard it said in his honor, that he never revised a line once written. My answer hath been, 'Would he had blotted a thousand.'" Shakespeare did write some bad lines; don't be ashamed if you have done the same. But remember that Shakespeare had a ready commercial market for his work, and you don't. So blot a few.

Your final draft (final copy, if clean and acceptable on rereading) goes as follows:

"How to Ask a Girl for a Date"

For some men, the question "how to ask for a date" collapses into the question "how to prove I'm irresistible." Hardly a good standard, their approach can at least serve as an example of how not to proceed.

The he-man approach concentrates on the body. To get ready for the big pitch, the would-be Tarzan brushes his teeth with Gleem and admires his flashing smile in the mirror for a while just to remind himself how irresistible he is. And that's what he says to the girl: how irresistible he is. At least, that's what his typical boasting implies. He shows a bulging bicep—he thinks his muscles bulge whether they do or not—for her to prod.

But a woman reacts to your attitudes; so ask for a date with respect for her as a person. Don't ask someone you know doesn't like you, or someone who has totally different interests. Instead, think about whom you are asking before you ask. If you do, you will probably ask someone who will accept. Approach your question slowly enough so she will know who you are and what you want. Tell her, in fact, where you intend to go before you ask her to go with you. And when you both know who you are, why you are there, and what you want, then—ask.

VI. Final Copy.

Sometimes another copying isn't necessary, if your final draft is particularly clean—that is, not free of soot and grease, but free of crossings-out and writings-over and addings-to. But don't hold back from crossing and writing and adding just for the sake of the copy. "True ease in writing comes from art, not chance,/As those move easiest who have learned to dance." Pope (Alexander, not The) polished his poetry; you should polish your prose.

Note that the final draft above included some editing:

bicep for *muscle*—more specific word.

flashing smile for *big white* one—more intense, more artificial.

The idea of irresistibility now links tooth-brushing with muscle-showing.

Most of the indignant "bigs" (big white smile, some big muscle) are out; they sound like the defensive anger of a small person.

Where you intend to go for *what you have in mind*—because more specific, eliminates the possible misinterpretation.

VII. **Proofread.**

Most teachers would rather have a copy with some neatly inked corrections than constantly be distracted by tuping erfors or one sort of naother. And if you write longhand, for the love of Pete (that's not your teacher; it's you and the better grade you'll get for not enraging him with illegible scrawls) write legibly. Before you turn this page, hold the book facing away from you; then look at the next page in a mirror five feet away. Which one is the A paper?

Type your out-of-class papers if you can; but if—with your teacher's consent; some don't like that—you have someone else type it, then proofread your friend's typing. You're the one who assumes final responsibility for the accuracy of the work.

A list of common correction symbols, useful for proofreading both typed and hand-written work:

⁋	paragraph
⌐order⌐ word⌐	reverse word order
∧	insert word or letter here
<u>*italic*</u>	italics
⌒	close up entirely, no space
uc	upper case
lc	lower case
stet	restore crossed out words
℘	omit marked material

Your teacher will probably use other correction symbols in addition to those on p. 17 in grading your work. Teacher's lists tend to be a bit more extensive:

I. Symbols identifying specific faults

sp   circled word is (misspellled)

K   awkward construction; rephrase

CS   comma splice; add conjunction after comma *or* replace comma with period or semicolon.

frag sentence fragment; attach it to a correct sentence or make it into an independent clause

rep   repetition of words (circled) or ideas (marked in margin); change word or eliminate one statement of idea

agr   error in agreement; usually of tense or number, sometimes of person

t   tense; if with "agr," change one of verbs to same tense as the other

number; if with "agr," change one of marked words to be plural or singular, matching the other (make subject and verb both singular or both plural; make pronoun and antecedent both singular or both plural)

p   error in punctuation; put the correct punctuation mark in the little circle○

//   lack of parallel construction or faulty parallelism; use similar constructions for matched phrases (or clauses)

trans transition or link needed; add a transitional or linking word or phrase (Furthermore, On the other hand, etc.) where the caret $(\wedge)$ is

coh   not coherent; rewrite passage stating connections between ideas more fully

ref   pronoun reference unclear, remote, ambiguous, or incorrect; use a noun instead

dict diction inappropriate; replace the circled word or phrase with one more in keeping with the rest of the essay

w   wordy; cut out excess words and phrases

II. Abbreviations and symbols used in marginal comments.

sent.   sentence

∴   therefore

∞   is similar to

adj   adjective

adv   adverb

prep   preposition

w/   with

w/out without

=   equals or are the same

≠   does not equal or are not the same

X   wrong

mm, hm, Hm. Hm! HM! varying degrees of doubt and disagreement ques   question

→ ↣ ➤ the comment in the margin refers only to the underlined words

If you are the writer, then you are the boss. You must control what you write.

An old chestnut tells of a Maine farmer leaning on a roadside fence accosted by two lost tourists in a shiny big-city car. The farmer pulled a straw from his reluctant, ruminating jaws, and answered their question thoughtfully: "Aylesbury, eh? Well, now, to get to Aylesbury you take the first left through Bamming, go about two, three miles, past the old Norton place, turn right at the burned oak, bear left all the time, and, uh, hm . . . (spit). No, you better turn right around and go by the ford—turn left at the third turning (not the dirt road, mind you, but the third macadam road), look for a green farm house with 'Mail Pouch' written on the roof, keep right, and at the railroad tracks—no, that won't do, (spit) better park your car here and walk across that field until, um, until, (spit) hmmmm . . . (spit-spit). You know, I don't believe you can get there from here."

TOPIC: Why a Maine farmer with a straw and a superabundance of saliva would make a bad writer.

If you write like that farmer, you have abandoned the basic task of the writer: control. A writer must control what he produces, to achieve his goal. A writer must pick the way to accomplish his task; he must choose the means to reach his end. To achieve that control, follow the seven steps I have illustrated thus far:

1. Get some ideas, including restating assignment and brainstorming.
2. Preliminary outline (including review of brainstorming and numbering ideas in reasonable order).
3. Rough draft.
4. Final outline.
5. Final draft.
6. Final copy.
7. Proofread.

Seven seems like a lot of steps. But they don't take long, although exactly how long depends on the assignment. Steps 1, 2, and 7 shouldn't take more than five to ten minutes each, although it's good to have time gaps within 1, between 1 and 2, and between 6 and 7. The length of time 3, 4, and 5 take depends on how much and how fast you write; step 3 should go almost as fast as you physically get words down on paper, but steps 4 and 5 should go a little more slowly and carefully. With luck, step 6 may not be necessary. Total time for this assignment, perhaps one hour.

A Japanese expert in use of the abacus, a primitive manual calculator consisting of beads strung on wires in a wooden frame, competed with the American mechanical-adding-machine champion some years ago, before the invention of electronic calculators, and beat him. He did easy sums in his head, sliding the beads to record only the sub-totals, whereas his American competitor did each step with separate care.

For the present, you will do better to follow in the steps of the American machine operator, and do your writing step by step. With time and practice, ease and grace will be second nature, and you may leap from shortcut to finished product, a Japanese expert among writers.

Part Two: THE WRITING—Parts

2

Letters: Being a Skippable Chapter About Edh and Owl

very journey has detours. In my experience, detours refresh the weary traveler. This chapter is such a detour. Perhaps I should call it an excursion. Like many excursions, it doesn't cost much; and like some, it may offer a few sights not visible at your main destination. In successful writing and reading, letters are invisible. As an excursion, before you become a fully successful writer, you might like to look at a page before you look through it.

What are you reading? Answer: A book. But you don't read the whole book at once—what are you reading right *now*? Answer: This page. Still, though, a half page at once is about all even the most skilled speed reader can manage. What are you reading this moment? Answer: Lines. (Given by a very good and very fast reader with sharp side vision who runs his eye down the center of the page and looks at each line once.) Phrases. (Given by the normal fast reader, who looks at every third to fifth word and sees the words on either side simultaneously as part of a single group.) Words. (Given by a slow reader, who looks at every individual word.) Letters. (Given by someone who is just learning to read, by someone who is in real academic trouble, or by someone who has just encountered a long word he has never seen before.)

What are the atoms, the smallest bits, the least pieces of language? In spoken language, they are *sounds*: the sibilant hiss of an initial s, the broad open-mouthed ah and the puckered oo of vowels, the humming n, interrupted by the tongue to make a brief d, followed by the buzz of the final s (the humming of the n, continued through the d and the s, makes the last *s* sound different from the first *s*) and you have pronounced the way a word *sounds*. Phonetics studies these sounds, how they are made, and how they are written.

Some sounds use the vocal chords, the throat opened. Letters for these sounds are called *vowels*, a word whose Latin source means "sounding" letters. If you put your finger on your throat, when you say a vowel you will feel the vocal chords vibrate.

Other sounds, in contrast to vowels, check or interrupt the flow of air—with palate, tongue, teeth, lips. Letters that represent these sounds are called *cons*onants. Words in English must have at least one vowel sound to be speakable. The Latin source of the word *consonant* reflects this fact, since it means "sounding with."

Letters, like ideograms, shorthand, and sign language, come from the desire to produce a visible equivalent to language. Unlike some other kinds of writing, letters represent the sounds that add up to words. Since words are symbols, letters are symbols of symbols.

Not all written symbols represent sounds. Pictographs, ideograms, and (originally) hieroglyphs represent not sounds, but ideas.

Pictograph just means writing (*graph*ically) with *pict*ures. Pictographs don't actually represent words; they represent things and events directly. A pictograph might be a single simplified picture, intended—like a sort of shorthand illustration—to remind the viewer of some important event or deed, such as the day Chief Fishing Bear caught seven salmon. A longer and more complex pictograph resembles a balloon-less comic strip. The possibilities for pictographic writing on abstract topics are small.

Topics: (1) Find two advertisements in a magazine that use very few words. Explain what they say, how the pictures say it, and whether they would say it clearly enough without any words at all. See if you can make up a different meaning if the words are omitted.

Ideograms are sketchy picture-symbols. Often two combine. Thus, the idea of sorrow is written in Chinese by combining the symbols for *knife* and for *tear*, *East* appears as a sun behind a tree; the idea of *origin* is written by adding a rootmark to a tree.

With hieroglyphic writing we come closer to the problems you and I face when we try to get our thoughts down on paper by using letters. The word *Hieroglyph*—that is, *sacred carving*—is the Greek translation of the Egyptian expression meaning *the god's words*. The problems you have with English spelling are nothing to the problems you would have with Egyptian spelling.

Egyptian symbols clearly were pictures originally, but the earliest Egyptian writing that can be read used the pictures phonetically to represent sounds, like an alphabet. But the spelling was complicated. (I tell you all this so that you will be happier with your own lot.) The stock phrase *live, be prosperous and healthy*, was written with three symbols:

The first two each represented several consonants, the third represents one consonant. If the English phrase were written the same way, it would come out *lv prps h*, for *live*, be *pros*perous and *h*ealthy. That's like a shorthand in which no vowels are written, and not all consonants.

Apparently that shorthand made problems for the Egyptian scribes, because they added explanatory inter-spellings within a word to make it clearer. Remember that some signs represented one consonant (an owl, for

example, represented M), many represented two, and a few repre-

sented three. The sign *ear* ◢ represented either three or four. To write the word for ear, a scribe would put chisel to wall and carve an ear. Problem: the animal ear he had just carved could mean either consonants *sgm* (hear)

or consonants *msgr* (ear). So he would put the symbol for *ms* 卅 and the

symbol for *gr* ◢ in front of *msgr* (the ear), and then, to avoid any

confusion about them, he would add another symbol for the final consonant of each: ms-s-gr-r-msgr.[1]

That would be somewhat like my spelling the word *scaffold* sc-k-ff-ph-ld-d-scffld.

And a few symbols functioned in a special, non-phonetic, non-alphabetic way. Owl was M, but a sparrow meant that the other symbols were to be taken as something bad or limited.

Letters in English symbolize sounds; they are all owls, with no sparrows. Usually, their names resemble the sounds they symbolize: the name of the letter *B* contains the bubble-start that the letter sounds. The name of the vowel *E* is one of its common sounds. Americans call *Z* zee and Englishmen call it zed, but the buzz (a voiced sibilant, or hummed hiss) begins the letter's name in both cases. Of course, some letters are sneakier, with names that give little clue to sound: doubleyou, as in wow, or eks, as in xylophone, for example. Similar misnamed letters (as far as pronunciation goes) are aitch as in *how* and see or jee as in *cat* or *gat*. ("Don't look now, but this gat has just had gittens," said Groucho at the weapons bin.) These last pose another problem besides the letter whose name doesn't contain its sound (sometimes or ever)—

[1]"Hieroglyph," *Encyclopedia Britannica* (1970).

some letters have more than one sound, as the girl genius said to the city cat.

Besides requiring knowledge of single letters of the alphabet, writing in English requires knowing what happens when letters combine. How do you write the vowel sound in the name of a small three-legged backless chair? One o won't do it; it takes two—as in st*oo*l. But in other words, the same sound may take an *ou* as in th*rough*, or an *ew* as in fl*ew*.

TEST: What other two ways (besides *ou* and *ew*) of spelling the *oo* sound (remember that w is a semi-vowel) are there? Hint: Look at the next-to-last sentence before this test.

Some sounds exist only in combination. The ah and the oo of *sounds* feel like one sound, because the essence of the sound lies in the movement from the ah to the oo. Such vowel combinations are called *diphthongs*.

Some letters lose their own sound in combination; thus, *ph* neither pops nor hunhs, but fffs. These have special names: *digraphs*. (If this sounds hard, cheer up. I was thirty-seven when I learned it from my six-year-old son.) In many vowel digraphs, one of the two letters dominates the pronunciation (*bread*, short *e*; *bead*, long *e*; *tail*, long *a*). Besides vowel digraphs, as in through, there are consonant digraphs—pairs of consonants that produce a single sound—that sound different from the sound of either by itself: Ou*ch*, English *ph*onetic spelling sti*nk*s.

Letters are the least units, the smallest bits, the tiniest pieces, of the written language. Like language, they have a history, and that history some-times makes things more complicated. The very name *alphabet* for the letters we use has a history, extending back through the first two letters of the Greek alphabet, alpha (A) and beta (B), to the three-thousand-year-old Phoenician letters aleph (𐤊), whose name was the word for ox, and beth (𐤂), whose name was the word for house. Indeed, most of our letters, although passed on to us by the Greeks and Romans, come from the sea-faring Phoenicians, who produced the first litter of letters about 1,000 B.C. You wouldn't recognize most of the Phoenician letters, except for O and Z. The Greeks apparently thought the Phoenicians a backward race, because, besides other changes, they turned fourteen out of sixteen letters to face the other way. If you spell backwards, blame it on the Greeks. You probably are just reverting to the Phoenician original. Any time you have trouble choosing between -*ice* and -*ise* (for the sound -*iss*), blame the Romans, who weren't satisfied with one G (C), and made another (G). That left C without enough to do, so they dropped another pronunciation (S) on it.

Our language, English, came from a marriage between middle French and Anglo-Saxon (Old English). When the Norman Frenchman William the Conqueror defeated the Anglo-Saxon Harold at Hastings in 1066, he insured that French would dominate the courts, both law and royal, and the conversation of the well-to-do and educated for several centuries. Gradually, the languages of the conqueror and the conquered merged. The merger combined vocabularies. (*Stool* is an Anglo-Saxon word; *chair* is French.) The merger also combined sounds. *J* doesn't represent a sound that the old English liked very much, but the French loved it. The words beginning with *J* in *Webster's Seventh New Collegiate Dictionary* include many words of French (Roman) origin, like jury, justice, juvenile, javelin, jangle, jamb, jealous, jelly, jeopardy, jest, jettison, jewelry; but Old English is only mentioned once, and that reference (for the word *July*) goes straight back to Latin.[2] *J*, a variant form of *I*, comes into the language—somewhat slowly and uncertainly—from French (and Latin, and a few lesser influences such as Hebrew, Portuguese, Turkish, etc.). But TH is a different matter. The French had no TH sounds and still have to practice making them as we have to practice eu (shape your lips as though to say oo, and say ee instead) or the uvular r (gargle); the Anglo-Saxons had a million of them, and two letters for them: ð (named *edh*, pronounced like eth as in *then*) and þ (named *thorn*). The Anglo-Normans and their aristocratic descendants apparently were too used to their own French alphabet to have much time for foreign letters, and we have been stuck with the digraph th for one of the most common sounds in English.

We also lost the letter ʒ (yogh, pronounced *yoke*), which crept in and out of our alphabet during the Middle English period. It vanished with the velar and palatal fricatives (hacking gargles) now needed by English-speaking Americans only when they visit Amsterdam and try to find their way to Heerengracht (pronounced Hay drdren—clear the throat—drdrdra—smother a chuckle—t).

The history of a language lies partly in its spelling. "Knight" used to be a phonetic spelling: the *k* was pronounced, the *i* was given the customary medieval pronunciation as a long *ee*, and the *gh* was pronounced as a front guttural (or voiceless palatal fricative, or smothered chuckle): kneeʒt.

Test question: The medieval letter ʒ survives in the modern consonant digraph (usually silent)______.

There are other ways, sometimes faster, of writing English down;

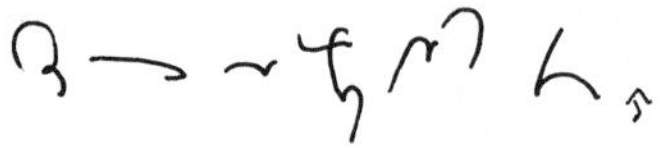

, for example, is a form of speedwriting

---

[2]Latin influenced Anglo-Saxon late—not when the Romans occupied the country in the first centuries of the Christian era (future Anglo-Saxons were still on the European continent, and had not yet driven out the Celts then living in England), but when Latin-speaking churchmen Christianized the country about 600–700 A.D. *W7NCD* is published by G. & C. Merriam (Springfield, Mass: 1972).

or shorthand that represents syllables with single symbols, omits some sounds where context implies what they would be, and represents single sounds with simpler shapes.

Not all sounds that affect meaning in English are written. Inflection, voice melody, in particular has no notation. But try deciding what "oh no" means without considering inflection—it can't be done. Try saying it yourself in horror, in exasperation, in challenge, in reassuring response—it means something different depending on how the voice rises or falls. In Chinese, in fact, inflection gives a literally different dictionary meaning to words. Umbrellas turn into chickens, and vice-versa, if you sing the wrong tune.

The really sneaky thing about letters is the sneaky thing about people: they pronounce differently.

EXERCISE 1: Here are three semi-phonetic spellings of "Oh, I don't know;" identify which would be said by Prince Phillip of England, which by an uneducated Cockney Englishman, and which by an American television announcer:

  a. uh-o, ah-ee duh-ont nuh-o
  b. eh-o, eh-ee, deh-ont neh-o
  c. ah-o, aw-ee dah-ont nah-o

The same letters are sometimes pronounced differently, even by the same man. Find at least one word for each of the pronunciations given for the following letters: Example: ph: (answers at bottom of page)

    pronounced *ff*
                    pronounced *p*
    pronounced *p-h*
    silent (Don't spend long on this one; you probably don't know it)

EXERCISE 2
    a. ough:
        pronounced *oo*
        pronounced *oh*
        pronounced *off*
        pronounced *uff*
        pronounced *ow*

ff—phone, phonetics, graph, siphon, etc.
p-h—slaphappy, with hyphen in top-heavy
silent—phthisic
p—shepherd

  b. ch:
    pronounced *k*
    pronounced *tsh*
    pronounced *sh*
  c. ei:
    pronounced *ee* (long E sound)
    pronounced *ay* (long A sound)
    pronounced *ih* (short I sound)
    pronounced *eh* (short E sound)
  d. ie:
    pronounced *eh* (short E sound)
    pronounced *ee* (long E sound)
    pronounced *ah-ee* (long I sound)
    pronounced *ee-y* (long E plus initial Y)
  e. ea:
    pronounced *ee* (long E sound)
    pronounced *eh* (short E sound)
    pronounced *ee-aa* (long E, broad A sounds)
    pronounced *y* (initial Y sound)

These are examples of one spelling that has a number of pronunciations. Other problems arise when you are moving from speech or thought (hearing the word silently) to writing. In general, the problems then arise from the fact that one sound may have many possible spellings. Those problems pop up in Chapter 7.

Topic: (2) Find someone (friend, relative, perhaps TV personality) who has a distinctive accent. Try to write one sentence exactly the way he says it, spelling his pronunciations rather than the words themselves. Explain what problems you have writing it down accurately and what causes them. Length: sentence plus one paragraph.

But if you approach letters as symbols of sounds, if you think of spelling phonetically, you will eliminate many common errors. You won't, for example, write "the immorality of the soul" for the "immortality of the soul," a student slip that seems slightly sin-centered. For example, if you know that the Anglo-Saxons spelled *what, when, which,* and *whether* the way they are pronounced—hwat, hwen, hwich, hwether—and that we have reversed the spelling by historical accident, then you may pronounce *where* and *were* with enough breathy or breathless difference not to leave out the *h* hhhwhen it's needed.

Before ending this chapter, I will offer some advice—some more advice:

1. Write legibly. Don't make two loops and put a dot exactly half-way between them, hoping that your instructor will decide which is the *i* and which the *e*. That dot was invented during the middle ages just for that purpose—so a reader could tell an *i* from the other letters that looked like it. *M*'s, *n*'s and *u*'s were much alike. A sloppy scribe would have written the word minimum as fifteen almost identical short lines. Don't go back to the dark and dotless early middle ages.

2. Don't use shorthand or other hieroglyphics, even for notes, much less for a theme. When taking notes, if you write whole words, not only will you save yourself that agonizing worry over meaningless scribbles two months later (What does "spglt in Wash.—85, 93, n. t. Fr. amb. dlging" mean?), you also will be forced to make some selection of important material from details, since you won't be able to write down everything. Shorthand tempts you to write everything down because you can. But *good* notes are less than everything. And for themes—do you really want your instructor to have to stop and *think* when he reads your work?

3. When adding a word to your vocabulary, check the spelling and the pronunciation at the same time. This helps freeze both the word and the spelling in your memory, ready for instant thawing at a likely moment. (It helps in remembering names, too; although you should not ask to have a name spelled if you didn't hear it the first time, or you will get the strange look I got, as the answer to my question "How do you spell that name?" came "S-M-I-T-H.")

Letters stand for sounds. One of the best ways to spell well is to hear word-sounds.

3

Words: Parts of Speech, with a Slight Salting of Semantics

Please follow these simple instructions: Before reading beyond this sentence, close your eyes and think of something; open your eyes and read on as soon as you have thought of something.

What did you think of? If you are like most, you thought of some *thing*. Moreover, in many cases you will have thought of a word; or at least your thought will have included the word that names what you thought of. If you thought of your bedroom, you probably thought not only a visual image, but also the words, "my bedroom."

So what? Two points: In a roomful of people, 1. many will have thought *one* word; 2. virtually all will have thought a *word*. The word is basic to thought.

Since the word is basic to thought, good thinking means finding, having, using the right words. A word that you know, is an idea. "How do I know what I think until I've said it?" In a sense, you really don't know what you think until you've said it. You may know that what you said *isn't* what you think. You may feel a troubled dissatisfaction as you hear your own words. But if you don't have the right words, you won't be able to think what you want to think.

Scientific American described the bizarre side effects of brain operations performed on extreme epileptics. Each half of the brain controls half of the body, but one half has full control of speech. Severing the connection between the two halves of the brain left the half controlling speech (located on one side) with no direct connection with half of the brain controlling one side of the body. Thus, if a man felt an object with the hand controlled by the non-speech side of his brain, he had a terrible time saying what it was—the speech side didn't know the thing (since it didn't feel it), and the feeling side couldn't produce the word. But the non-speech side could hear, through its ear, what the speech side said, and could give the speech side cues when the speech side guessed. Thus, if shown a color that the speech side couldn't see, the non-speech side of the man's brain would listen to the speech side guess. If the guess was wrong, the non-speech side would scowl and shake its head—and since you can't shake one side of a head without shaking the other, the speech side would feel the "no" signal, and correct itself: "No, no, I don't mean red, it's *green!*"[1]

---

[1]Michael S. Gazzaniga, "The Split Brain in Man," *Scientific American*, 217, No. 2 August 1967, 24–29.

This example illustrates two points. First, the word and the thing are not identical. The feeling side of the brain felt the thing, all right; what it lacked was the word. Second, without the word, there was no communication.

Words are important then, not only to thought, but also to communication. The ancient Anglo-Saxon poet says, "Beowulf unlocked his word-hoard." That is, Beowulf spoke: he used his vocabulary. The bigger the word-hoard, the more golden the possibilities of speech when the doors are opened. Try, therefore, to build your own word-hoard by looking up words whose meaning you do not know or are uncertain of, as you encounter them in your reading. To build good writing, you need the right parts.

Topics: (1) An imagined dialogue between the two halves of my brain. One page.

PARTS OF SPEECH

Letters represent sounds; and spoken words are built out of sounds; but the single sounds of which words are built (called phonograms) are not thoughts. Words are thoughts. Or, at least, they are used in thinking, as marvelous symbolic substitutes which enable us to manipulate and control the world in our head.

That power is extraordinary, and very important to all of us. The baby meets his world by looking it over; by grabbing it, to see what it feels like; by shaking it, to see what it sounds like; and by popping it into his mouth, to see what it tastes like (taste more or less includes smell, all flavors being a combination of four basic tastes plus smell). As he grows, the desire to possess his world includes the desire to have the words with which to handle it—what is that? what is that? he asks repeatedly in his craving for names.

Religion recognizes the power of the word. In Christianity, the word "word" (in the Greek original, logos) early became a synonym for the divine. "In the beginning was the Word, and the Word was with God, and the Word was God." (John 1:1) In Judaism, the name of God was holy, not to be pronounced. The Tetragrammaton (literally, four-letter word) *Jhwh* (Hebrew scribes wrote only consonants) could not be pronounced Jahweh, but was instead pronounced with the vowels for a different word (adonai), meaning lord, to produce the less magical name *Jehovah*. The name, *Jahweh*, participated in the power of the thing it stood for; the symbol shared the reality of the thing symbolized.

The power of the word is very real. Name-calling reflects that power as much as naming does. Anguished five-year old cry: "Johnny says I'm a dodo bird!" Maternal reassurance: "Now darling, of course you're not a dodo bird."

Tearfully unsatisfied: "Make Johnny say I'm not!" The fact does not satisfy unless the label is removed.

Mere words may not be as powerful now as once in ancient times when long-haired satirists marched into battle beside their warrior comrades, armed only with words, which they wielded against the foe as vigorously as their comrades-in-arms wielded more substantial swords, clubs, spears. Unfortunately, records aren't available to show how many battles were won by wicked name-calling.

Topic: (2) Describe how someone reacted intensely to words in your presence, and evaluate their response. (For example, *should* your mouth have been washed out with soap?) Length: one page. OR describe a time when you had to have just the right words. One page.

EXERCISE 1: Name-calling remains effective, when skillfully done. Skill means not falling back on obscenity, which loses vigor through familiarity. So think of a teacher in another class, and call him names. Alternatively, a local politician; or perhaps the authors of this book. Fifty words, no repetitions, no obscenities—and better not write down his name.

Words are parts; they are parts of speech. Parts (of speech and of other things) can be classified. The easiest classification to understand includes words like *Jones, Carlos, Eisenhower, Hermione, Chicago, Istanbul*. All of these nouns are _____. Other nouns, such as bedroom, idiot, teacher, incest, book, potato, religion, are also _____, but of things rather than of specific people or places.

The most dramatic quest for names, for nouns like the list above, was the late Helen Keller's. Blind and deaf from infancy, she led a wretched life for thirteen years, speechless and uncomprehending, unable to communicate with her family or nurse, deliberately disobedient as a rebel against her condition whenever she *could* understand what she should or should not do. Her nurse tried to teach her the braille alphabet, tapping out words against the palm of her hand, but with no success: Helen had no idea of language at all. Until one day, in the back yard, as her nurse Annie made her pump water to refill a jug she had spilled and tapped the symbols for water in her hand, suddenly like a revelation the idea of the word came to her. One philosopher argues that at this point, the child became a human being.[2] Miss

---

[2]Suzanne K. Langer, *Philosophy in a New Key: A Study in the Symbolism of Reason, Rite and Art* (Cambridge: Harvard Univ. Press, 1957).

Keller recorded in her autobiography the overwhelming urge that drove her to learn more names—the names of all the things in the yard, in the house; she dragged Annie about from thing to thing, grabbing her hand and shaking it, demanding silently to know the magic symbol, the word, the noun that named and made the world hers.

"Name-calling" usually means cursing, imprecation; but in a profounder sense, to call names—because it is symbolizing things—is to list ideas.

But names alone are inadequate for conversation—O.K. for name-calling, but not for dialogue. Suppose I had asked you at the start of this chapter not to name some*thing*, but to have an idea? Or suppose I had simply asked you to think? What would you have thought? If you are like one of my classes, you would have thought, "How can I think of something?" "I can't think of anything." Thinking means formulating questions and statements. Questions and statements need more than nouns; they need words for what those things do, or what is done to them. Those words are verbs.

Verbs stir, move, climb, run, spin, stagger, fall, lie, rest, sleep, die; they persist, continue, cease, fail, escape; they perpetuate, extrapolate, obfuscate, inundate, perforate; they exist, they perform, they link, they act, they do.

Thinking uses V_____ to make statements about N_____. Nouns and verbs together make S_____. Make sense? Yes; also statements and questions, which are sentences.

The two essential parts of speech are nouns and verbs. Others generally depend on nouns and verbs. Look at my class's panic response to the instruction THIMK! What are the names of things, the nouns, in their response? *Anything, something,* and *I;* right? Almost. A subordinate class of words is those words that stand for nouns, and *anything, something,* and *I* all fall into that category. Pronouns are words that stand for nouns. To know what a pronoun means, you have to know what noun it stands for. WHO AM I WHO AM I WHO AM I said the computer. It knew it was itself; but it didn't know what itself was.

Nouns stand for _____
Verbs stand for _____
Pronouns stand for

1. the first item above
2. the second item above
3. both items above
4. neither item above
5. very little nonsense from textbook writers, if the pronoun happens to be this reader.

Go back to the class panic above. What are the verbs? If you think

think, you think right. If you can think *can think*, you can think righter. Verbs are often more than one word, with an auxiliary or helper like "can" (in this case) to express the complete idea.

Nouns (or pronouns) do verb-actions (sometimes with a little auxiliary help).

Other parts of speech expand, elaborate, and qualify the bare bones of the sentence. Words that expand, elaborate, or qualify nouns are called adjectives. Words that expand, elaborate, or qualify verbs (and some other words) are called adverbs. A*d*verbs and *ad*jectives are *add*ed to the bare bones of noun (pronoun)-verb for additional meaning. A*dverbs* can modify _____ s. (To a grammarian, "modify" means expand, elaborate, or qualify.)

For example: My young son met an even younger boy at a campsite and brought him to our campsite, introducing him as an unknown. "Who are you?" we asked, promptly putting to use an interrogative (questioning) pronoun ("who"), a verb indicating a state of being ("are"; in this world, just being is a lot of action), and a pronoun ("you"). He replied, using a strange sound that I can best represent by the French spelling, "I'm Feuilli." (If you don't speak French, the 11's come out like the y in you.) "What's your name?" we tried, and got the same response. Obviously a visitor from another land, where a non-Indo-European language is spoken. We were, of course, wrong; the little three-year-old just didn't know the difference between an adjective and a noun. He gave us not his name-noun, but his age-adjective. He said, "I'm three."

Pretty girl; pretty boy; adjective noun.

Adverbs modify verbs and some other things, such as adjectives. Adverbs modify verb-wise. -*Wise* is a suffix (although not very popular among many), an added ending, indicating adverbial function. Much more common is the -ly, as in "run slowly" or "and gladly would he teach." One of the basic patterns of word formation in English turns adjectives into adverbs by adding -ly. "The horrifying slow train runs horrifyingly slowly."
            1   2   3   4   5   6   7

Words 2 and 3 are _____ s modifying the _____, word 4; words 6 and 7 are _____ s modifying the _____, word 5.[3]

Sometimes, approaching a writing exercise through the parts of speech helps you do it well. Once you have made a preliminary statement, look at it and ask, "Can I add more verbs, more nouns, more adjectives or adverbs?"

For example, suppose you have written, "Yesterday I got a fright. A man tried to rob me. But a policeman came up, and I got away."

---

[3]Word 1, since it modifies a noun (word # ____), is also an _____; it belongs to that special and tiny class of adjectives (including in addition only *a* or *an*) called *articles*.

You could improve this by adding more *verbs:* "Yesterday I got a fright. A man *rushed* at me, *grabbed* me, and *threw* me down, trying to rob me. But a policeman *heard*, ran up, *pulled* the man up, and *placed* him under arrest; after I *had dusted* myself off and *identified* myself, I *was able* to get away."

You could also improve it by adding more *nouns*: "Yesterday on the *sidewalk* in *front* of *Queen Elizabeth's Greasy Spoon*, I got the fright of my *life*. A man rushed at me, grabbed my *wrist* and *elbow*, and threw me down onto the *pavement*, trying to rob me. But a policeman heard, ran up the *street* to us, and pulling the man up, placed him under arrest. After dusting off my *clothes* and giving my *name* and *address*, I was able to get away to the *safety* of my *apartment*."

Adjectives and **adverbs** can help too: "Yesterday, on the sidewalk in front of Queen Elizabeth's Greasy Spoon, I got the fright of my life. **Suddenly,** a *breathless* man rushed at me, grabbed my *left* wrist and elbow, and threw me down onto the pavement, **obviously** trying to rob me. But a *conscientious young* policeman heard, ran up the **almost** *deserted* street to us, and **roughly** pulling the man up, placed him under arrest. After dusting off my *smudged* and **slightly** *torn* clothes and giving my name and address, I was able to get away, *exhausted* but *thankful*, to the safety of my apartment."

EXERCISE 2: Expand each of the following sentences by adding the parts of speech called for (and a few others, if necessary to make the ones you add fit smoothly):

Example:

    a. She screamed. (add verbs) Answer: She *turned*, screamed, and *ran*.

    b. She screamed. (add adverbs) Answer: She screamed *horribly, terribly, again* and *again, agonizingly shrilly*.

    c. She screamed. (add nouns) Answer: The *nurse* at the *door* screamed.

    d. She screamed. (add adjectives) Answer: *Wide-eyed*, turning *pale*, the *withered old* nurse opened *whiskered* jaws to scream.

    a. He died. (add verbs)

    b. She picked up all three. (add nouns)

    c. The man tripped the robber with his cane. (add adjectives)

    d. The boy invented false explanations, but his father sighed and insisted that he promise to stop robbing banks and find a productive vocation. (add adverbs)

    e. The cyclists shot the cabby. (add verbs)

    f. I don't like you. (add nouns)

g. The boy, the cat, and the rat ran from chair to table. (add adjectives)

h. He cursed, he threatened, but she refused to surrender the tooled leather purse. (add adverbs)

i. They cleaned up. (add nouns)

j. The shortstop made an unassisted triple play. (add verbs)

k. Faith brings strength. (add adjectives)

l. The empty cupboard contained one can of rotten tomatoes. (add adverbs)

Adjectiv-ish nouns verb-ize adverb-ly.

Adverbs get around a good bit, since they modify adjectives or other adverbs as well as verbs. Pretty dress, pretty girl, pretty boy; adjective, noun. Pretty hard, pretty good, pretty bad; adverb, adjective. Pretty well, pretty badly; adverb, adverb.

Did I say pretty was an adjective? I did, and it was, in the first group; but in the second group, an adverb. How can it be both? Well, it can't, at least not simultaneously; but it can at different times. There is one of the obstinate facts that makes learning grammar hard. The class a word belongs in depends on what it does. Function determines parts of speech.

Some words shift function easily. In a typical pattern, the same word serves as noun or verb, sometimes with a slight change of pronunciation: "How many will the house house (pron. housse houze)?" Others shift function reluctantly—"I'll geranium you, you potted flower," the angry housewife said to her intoxicated husband as he tried to crawl through the window flowerbox. Some shifts are substandard, and should not be used in formal writing. Some of my fellow enlisted men during the Korean conflict (did you think it was a war?) hoped to have requirements blocking promotion (such as so many months at one rank before promotion to the next) dropped, or *waived;* to *waive* a requirement or regulation is to set it aside in a particular case. The action of *waiving* is a deed called a waiver; that was what everybody wanted— waivers. "Did you get your waiver?" "No, did you get yours?" The noun *waiver*, originally formed from the verb *waive*, was reconverted to the status of a verb, keeping the -r suffix that made it a noun: "Did they waiver the requirement?" The unnecessary formation may have been prompted by the desire to avoid confusion with the word "wave." Nobody who wants a requirement dropped wants it waved right in his face.

Using the right word means using nouns as nouns and verbs as verbs. It does not mean mixing the two up, at least not for the first time in the history of the language, and not when skilled writers object. Your teachers and your reading experience will help keep you straight. Even more important, don't confuse adjectives with adverbs. Snobs (which to some extent includes me and practically all literate people) regard such confusions as marks of illiteracy. You will do good to write careful.

Think of something.

What did you think of? Did you think again of a thing? Or did you think "in," or "whether," or "but," or "hurray," or "artificially"? Why not?

Speech parts: noun, pronoun, verb, adjective, adverb; and more. Some words serve the purpose of the little wheels in a tinkertoy set, which hold rods together, or the couplers in a subway, which hold the cars together; two such classes of words are prepositions and conjunctions.

A *pre*position usually precedes, is positioned before, a noun (with any adjectives) or pronoun. "Don't tread *on* me," goes an early American flag motto, with the preposition "on."

A con*junction* usually makes a *junction*, a joining, of practically anything.

"Do you like artichokes *and* the Mafia?"

"No, I do not like either artichokes *or* the Mafia."

"Do you loathe *and* despise them?"

"No, I neither loathe *nor* despise them, *for* I fear loss of my life by excessive roughage."

The nouns "artichokes" and "Mafia" are joined by the conjunction "and" in the first sentence, by the conjunction "or" in the second sentence; the verbs "loathe" and "despise" are joined by the conjunction "and" in the third sentence, the conjunction "nor" in the fourth sentence; the clauses (they could be sentences) "No-I-neither-loathe-nor-despise-them" and "I-fear-loss-of-life-by-excessive-roughage" are joined by the conjunction "for."

Because conjunctions are joiners, we'll look more closely at them in the next section. At the moment, we are looking at parts. Our list of the parts of speech is almost complete, with nouns and their little stand-ins; verbs; ad_____; ad_____; con_____; and ____positions. (If you do not know how to fill in these blanks, mail this page, 50¢ in coin, and a stamped, self-addressed envelope to Reston Publishing Company, P. O. Box 547, Reston, Virginia, 22090, attn: Colwell-Knox, and I will fill in the blanks and return the page to you.) One more classification remains, much more common in spoken than in written use: words that are thrown in, or -jected inter (not e-jected, or thrown out), are called *interjections*. They are cries unnecessary to the sentence. Oh! Ah! Ugh! Phooey! Bleah! Well, well, well, well.

You know, you really shouldn't take all this stuff for granted. By the time we reach interjections, maybe we are on the edge of triviality; but the fact that nouns and verbs make up the basic structure of our language, noun-things doing verb-actions, that fact matters. It conditions our whole thinking process. Don't say "of course we name things that do actions," because there are other ways of talking, other ways of looking at the universe, starting with the man in front of you. And a little farther away, there are languages that have no nouns. For people who speak such a language, there are no things, no solid samenesses that act differently; there are only actions. In place of the noun-verb clauses that make up our sentences, their sentences (we wouldn't call them sentences in English) are verb phrases. Every (thing) for them is doing, acting, changing. Maybe in a language that saw the world in constant motion, constantly doing, it would be harder to put whitey, or black boy, or eytie in his noun box and happily hate him, knowing that he will be the noun he is anytime you feel like socking it to him.

Topic: (3) Describe an occasion when you (or someone close to you) were categorized (stereotyped, classified, pigeon-holed, "nounified"—treated as a noun-thing rather than as a living process), by a friend, stranger, or relative. One page.

Well, English is the language Americans use, even if Queen Elizabeth has her doubts, and we will continue to think, speak, and write noun-verb sentences. But at least we can know what we are doing, know that the word is not the reality. When told he must join the union, the silly aristocrat with liberal slogans dinned into his ears from birth, now forced to labor for a living, asks in the movie *I'm All Right, Jack,* "Is it obligatory?"—he is ready to refuse being forced to obey. "Naw," says the union representative, "it ain't obligatory, you just gotta join is all." "Oh, well, if it's not obligatory, that's quite all right then," says the aristocrat, and happily joins.

THE RIGHT WORD

Not only the types of building blocks we use to make speech, parts of speech like nouns and verbs, not only these affect our ways of thinking, but the individual words themselves condition our attitudes. Words communicate, they mean, they stand for, they symbolize, in two ways: explicit and implicit.

PRE-TEST: "That which we call a rose by any other name would smell as sweet." (Shakespeare) True or false? Hint: "O, my love is like any of a genus (*Rosa* of the family Rosaceae, the rose family) of usu. prickly shrubs with pinnate leaves and showy flowers having five petals in the wild state but being often double or semidouble under cultivation,[4] that's newly blown in

---

[4]By permission. From *Webster's Seventh New Collegiate Dictionary* c. 1972 by
  G. & C. Merriam Co., Publishers of the Merriam-Webster Dictionaries.

June . . . ." Does that smell as sweet as "O, my love is like a red, red rose, That's newly blown in June"?

The explicit meaning of a word is its *denotation*, its literal meaning; the implicit meaning of a word is its *connotation*, the associated meanings, feelings, it carries with it. Lady, broad, skirt, bird, dame, chick, all have the same _____ , for they all can mean woman. *Lady* and *gentlemen* have similar _____ ; the associations are alike.

EXERCISE 3: Rephrase the following sentences, making clear the differences in denotation:

    a. He stumped the precinct.

    b. He stumped the expert.

    c. He stumped the hallway.

EXERCISE 4: Explain the difference between:

    a. You're living in a dream.

    b. I have a dream.

EXERCISE 5: Fill the blanks with *humorous, witty,* or *facetious,* using each word once. Check a dictionary such as *Webster's Seventh New Collegiate Dictionary* for help.

    a. "I find your _____ remarks inappropriate," she said, turning from him and toward the grave.

    b. She laughed somewhat ruefully at his _____ insult.

    c. The children loved the _____ Santa Claus.

Since words have connotations as well as denotations, choosing the right word means more than simply getting a literal meaning. Pure denotation is the goal of mathematics and of scientific description. People who react emotionally, with feeling tones, to "x," "y," and "z" rarely make good mathematicians.

What do the connotations of the words in the following excerpts from three unwritten best-selling novels tell you? How are they different?

A. The big momma slouched across the barroom. Hoisting a drink, she screeched, "Nuts to the fink who's mucking around with our take-over!" and gulped the booze chug-a-lug. "What a cool pad," she crooned, eyeballing it. The old gink dropped. "Number One!" he crowed. "It's about time we got the drop on that pretzelated spitball who crookedly scares us gutless." "You've got it all!" She put some skin to his threads. "Get hip and do some styling; never mind the bread. We've got to swag it off."

B. The contessa glided across the salon. Lifting a flagon, she trilled, "Perdition to the foes of our claimant to the throne!" and quaffed the beverage at one draught. "What an exquisite residence," she murmured, glancing about. The ancient gentleman prostrated himself. "Majesty!" he exulted, "at long last we shall have the advantage of that conniving urchin who feloniously drives terror into the hearts of all!" "How faithful you are!" She touched a hand to his garments. "Clothe yourself more elegantly, regardless of expense. We must appear the nobles we would seem to be."

C. The dance hall queen moseyed across the saloon. Heisting a shot of rot-gut, she whooped, "Tarnation fer those varmints what tries to hobble our two-gun honcho, the new range king!" and knocked the fire-water straight back. "Some spread," she drawled softly, scouting it from where she stood. Grampa hit the planks. "Ramrod!" he whooped. "The long dry spell's over if we can get the whip hand of that side-winding young'un whose horse-thievin' ways make all our scalps rise." "You'll do to ride the range with." She slapped his duds. "Dude yourself up; shoot a poke of dust. We've gotta ride tall in the saddle if we're gonna cast a wide shadow."

EXERCISE 6: Think of five things or actions for which you know at least two different words, words with quite different connotations.

EXERCISE 7: How many synonyms can you think of which have different connotations from the following?

a. jail	f. beautiful
b. car	g. man
c. policeman	h. large
d. teacher	i. good
e. eccentric	j. die

EXERCISE 8: Describe a scene you know well (the street in front of your home, a college classroom) in one paragraph.

   a. Try to use words that express the most favorable attitude possible toward what you describe; use words that have the best possible connotations.

   b. Now write a second paragraph that contains the same information, the same basic facts, but has a vocabulary with the worst possible connotations. Here your goal is to make the scene seem as bad as possible—without changing the facts you present.

   c. Finally, write a third description of the same scene, using the kind of language you think a cowboy who had just stepped out of a television screen would use.

4

Sentences: Long, Short, and Broken, with a Guided Tour Through a Labyrinth of Verbs etters are parts of words; words are parts of sentences; sentences are parts of paragraphs; paragraphs are parts of essays. We could go on like that through books, libraries, the total printed work of man, until ultimately we reached the universe. (Did you ever write your address "Stephen Dedalus/Class of Elements/Clongowes Wood College/Sallins/County Kildare/Ireland/Europe/The World/The Universe"?)[1] A part *is* a part in relationship to some sort of whole; it is a whole by virtue of some sort of completeness. You are only a part of the human race—but you are a whole with respect to your own little fingers.

Depending on your purpose, where you find the whole unit may vary. James Joyce could have had his fictional character Stephen Dedalus include "Western Civilization" between Europe and The World, or the solar system between The World and The Universe. There are also wholes of a sort between words and sentences. That grouping smaller than a sentence is a phrase. One of the basic signs of literate formal writing is the author's ability to distinguish between phrases and sentences.

A group of words. Which are related. And seem to form. A single idea. But do not make. A complete statement. Constitutes a phrase. Phrases should not be punctuated as though they were complete sentences; such phrases are sentence fragments.

A sentence, however, does make a complete statement of some sort (or ask a question, or—in the "imperative mood," a form you will rarely if ever use in composition unless writing instructions—give an order.) The distinguishing feature of the sentence is its noun-verb structure; a noun, the subject of the sentence, does the verb-action, the predicate of the sentence. Who does What? The answer identifies the subject (who did it) and the verb (what he did).

Phrases lack this subject-predicate, noun-verb, structure. Typically, a phrase begins with a preposition or with a verbal form that does not predicate—assert, state—action. "With malice toward none and charity for all" is a prepositional phrase; "kneeling devoutly," "to live in peace," and "the enemy once defeated" are verbal phrases (present participle, *verb + ing;* infinitive, *to + verb;* and past participle, *verb + ed*). Kneeling devoutly, let us pray (with malice toward none and charity for all) that, the enemy once defeated, we shall be able to live in peace.

The opposite fault to writing sentence fragments is writing run-on

---

[1]James Joyce, *A Portrait of the Artist as a Young Man* (1916; rpt. New York: The Viking Press, 1968), p. 15.

sentences these sentences contain two complete thoughts with no punctuation between them or sometimes a comma, the latter is called not a run-on sentence but a comma splice. The fault here is simply not knowing when to stop, failing to recognize a complete statement. My son proudly showed his mother a remarkable collection of fragments, run-ons, and comma splices. When she pointed out the disjointed impression such errors made, he justified them on aesthetic grounds—he wanted to have his sentences be different lengths rather than all the same, and so had rewritten his homework with periods disposed at random intervals.

At the end of his career, William Shakespeare wrote a marvelous play called *The Tempest*. At its conclusion, an aging magician sets aside his magical powers, breaking his wand, discarding his robe, and casting his book of spells into the sea. How appropriate that would have been for Shakespeare's last play: he would have set aside his magical poetical skill, just as the magician did. Unfortunately he wrote another, a bad one (*King Henry VIII*). Don't ruin the structure of your sentences by carrying on after they have been completed.

We used to have a minister who didn't know when to stop. I don't mean that his sermons ran on forever; they just seemed to. The really chafing flaw in his style was his inability to bring a sentence to a close. Not really talking in comma splices or run-on sentences, he habitually added phrase after phrase after phrase. He would start a sentence . . . and not be able to finish it . . . or bring it to a close . . . and stop talking . . . about the thought . . . which he had completed . . . without the added words . . . which he kept on putting on . . . piling them up . . . rather than stopping . . . the long-dead sentence . . . which he had beaten . . . to death . . . by the hammer blows of little phrases . . . which kept on going . . . and going . . . and going on . . . and on and on . . .

Know when you have stated a complete idea, for that is the time to stop your sentence, not sooner, not later.

The two basic parts of a sentence are the _____, which is a noun (or pronoun) and its modifiers, and the _____, whose core is a verb and its modifiers.

A "sentence" which does not state a complete idea, called a _____.

Two sentences may be joined by a comma, this fault is called a _____ splice.

Sometimes no comma is used two sentences are simply run together in a _____-_____ sentence.

Note that the completeness of a sentence is a grammatical completeness. You may still have something to say when you reach the end of your sentence. Otherwise, all books except anthologies would be one sentence long. Your sentence, however, is grammatically complete when you have named the noun which is the subject of the sentence and have predicated some action by that noun, in the verb which is the heart of the predicate. Noun-verb, subject-predicate.

Topics: (1) Write an essay on boredom. Describe something that bored you. Why were you bored? Is boredom bad? All bad? When might it be good? What are the alternatives to boredom? What is the opposite of boredom? Have you ever been boring? How do (did) you know?

EXERCISE 1: Underline the subject nouns of the following sentences with one line, the predicate verbs with two lines:

  a. Throughout 1971, students in New York Schools attacked a teacher an average of once a day.
  b. Eighty-five per cent of the girls marrying while in high school are pregnant.
  c. Five hundred thousand shopping carts, costing thirty dollars each, were stolen during 1971.
  d. Every year, American commercial fishermen kill 250,000 dolphins, trapped in their nets spread for marketable fish.

VERBS

A Complication: Predicates are of several types. When the noun-subject *does* the action named by the verb, the verb is said to be in the active voice; when the noun-subject has the action done to it, the verb is said to be in the *passive* voice. (The *voice* of a verb is thus simply whether it is _____ or _____.)

EXERCISE 2: Rewrite the following sentences in active voice: (example: A student by whom the work cannot be done should not be admitted to a college. Answer: A college should not admit a student who cannot do the work.)

  a. You are loved by me.
  b. Passive voice cannot always be avoided, even by the most careful student.
  c. The lazy dog was jumped over by the quick brown fox.
  d. The voters of this country must not be cheated. (Note that in order to put this into active voice you must say who does the cheating.)
  e. Writing can be done well, if it is practiced.

EXERCISE 3: Rewrite the following sentences in passive voice:

> (Examples: Praise the Lord; do thy will.
>   People soon part a fool and his money.
>
> Answers: The Lord be praised; thy will be done.
>   A fool and his money are soon parted.)

a. People hated him thoroughly.
b. Thousands of feet, walking from one class to another, had worn the carpet bare.
c. Something or other defeated and discouraged him.
d. Saving a penny is earning a penny. (Keep the *is*.)

Besides being active or passive voice, depending on whether the subject does the action or passively has the action done to it, verbs have mood—bossy (imperative, as in "sit up straight," or "go to the devil," or "bless this meal"), questioning (interrogative, as in "Do I need to illustrate a question?"), and, by far the most common, matter-of-fact (indicative, as in any statement).[2] The fourth mood, subjunctive, is hardest to explain; it is a doubtful mood and involves using different forms of the verb (as in "I wish I hadn't started all this," or "he might not understand," or "if I were you. . ." or "though she be cruel. . .").

Imperative verbs have an understood subject: the person addressed. ("Study," snarled the teacher viciously, and the students dived deep into their books.)

Interrogative sentences either reverse the order of noun (pronoun) and verb (He is a stinker. Is he a stinker?) or add an introductory auxiliary verb (He writes well. Does he write well?) or reverse the order of noun (pronoun) and auxiliary verb (He has finished. Has he finished? The subway ought to have an armed guard on every car. Ought the subway to have an armed guard on every car?)

Speech sometimes turns a statement into a question by intonation, by

---

[2] Footnote for the student who cares: Grammarians habitually count only three moods in English: subjunctive, imperative, and indicative. They include interrogative with indicative. Why they think a question is more like a statement than like a wish or an order baffles me. (The reasons are probably historical.) Since a question habitually changes the verb (as described below) I have counted it separately.

the melody of the voice. Hearing of a saint on a remote mountain peak in South America, an executive gave up his job, abandoned his wife and family, and spent all his savings in a search for the wise old man who could tell him the meaning of life. After two years, when all his resources, both physical and financial, had been exhausted, the former executive heaved himself up onto the mountain ledge at the feet of the saint. "Tell me, oh sage, the meaning of life," he gasped in the thin air. "Life," said the old holy man, "is like a fountain." The ex-executive blew his stack. "Do you mean to tell me that I have sacrificed my job, my fortune, my family, and two years of my life, to have you tell me life is like a fountain?" The sage turned wide eyes upon him and said, "Life isn't like a fountain?"

Usually, when I have recounted that anecdote, I have simply ended it with: "and the old man said, 'Life isn't like a fountain?'" In writing it, however, I recognize the absence of the vocal intonation. Rather than simply relying on the punctuation, on the question mark, I attempted to suggest in words the surprised wonder of the saint as he asks apparently for the first time whether his alleged wisdom has any truth in it. I added the words "turned wide eyes upon him." Did it work? I can't ask my friends, because they all have heard the story at least once. Even if it didn't work, get the point (imperative): you must find words that are equivalents for the meanings usually communicated by tone of voice.

Intonation can even turn a question into a statement. "Can Frank Sinatra ever sing!" The exclamation point hints at the enthusiasm that turns this rhetorical question into an affirmation.

Indicative sentences are the norm. They make their statements in the usual way, noun subject first, followed by the verb with its auxiliaries, adverbial modifiers, and other elements of the predicate. Most of the sentences in this book are indicative, as this one is.

Subjunctive verbs use different forms, typically, a past form. Explaining subjunctives takes as much time as learning to use them correctly. Look first at some examples of verbs in the subjunctive mood:

I wish I *had* it now.

He *might* have done it had the situation been completely different.

I *could* win, if you *wouldn't* cheat.

Contrast to the last example the more positive and affirmative feeling of:

I can win if you won't (= will not) cheat.

Could is the past tense form of *can*; *would* is the past tense form of *will*. In the present indicative, *can* and *will* are used; in the present subjunctive, *could* and *would* are used.

In form, the subjunctive mood thus uses a past tense in a present situation: I wish I *had* (past tense) it now (present situation). In spirit, in—dare I say?—mood, the subjunctive mood expresses doubt, or a belief that the action is not true, not real, but contrary to fact. Thus: I wish I were sure you are getting all this, but I have no way of telling. What I wish is contrary to fact, so I state it in a moodily subjunctive way.

Some samples of different moods:

You have it now. (indicative; statement of fact)

Do you have it now? (interrogative; asking a question)

Have it now, you clutz, or there won't be any cheesecake left for you. (imperative; an order whispered by a well-meaning older brother)

If you had it now, you wouldn't be here. (subjunctive; one prisoner to another, knowing very well that in fact his cellmate does *not* have the picklock that would release them)

Or, in a more complex pattern (more complex because the verb includes an auxiliary verb; see the following discussion of tense):

You have done it now. (indicative)

Have you done it now? (interrogative)

(imperative impossible; if it existed, it would be something like, "Have done it now," but that is gibberish; it would mean ordering someone to do the action of having already completed the action, as though you said, "I order you to have done already what you haven't done.")

Had you done it by now, you wouldn't be here. (subjunctive)

If you have trouble with this talk of verbs, console yourself with the thought that you are doing no worse than the right half of most people's brains. The experiments on cutting the two halves apart that I described earlier seem to show that the right half of the brain is very weak on verbs; it can write nouns all right (it can't talk, you remember) but verbs give it a lot of trouble. So if you are having trouble, maybe you are just right-brained.

EXERCISE 4: Use each verb four times in each of the four different moods. Example: Love. Answer: Aspidistra loves Clement. (declarative) Does Clement love Aspidistra? (interrogative) If Clement loved Aspidistra, his allergies might be worse. (subjunctive) Love Aspidistra, Clement! (imperative)

    a. Order

    b. Pass

    c. Walk

    d. Raise

So far in this discussion of verbs I have talked about voice and mood. Yet to come are tense and the difference between regular and irregular verbs. Note that these categories overlap, like condition of eyes, condition of knees, condition of scalp, and posture. John can be cross-eyed, knock-kneed, pie-bald, and sway-backed, all at once; similarly, a verb can be in the active voice, be in the subjunctive mood, have a perfect tense, and be irregular, all at once.

Verbs have, then, yet another quality besides mood (I count four moods) and voice (there are two, active and passive), the quality of tense. *Tense* indicates the time at which the action occurs.

The two basic tenses are present and past, the latter usually formed—in all but some of the most common verbs—by adding -ed to the former:

I walk now (present tense)

I walked yesterday (past tense)

With the aid of auxiliary verbs, helper verbs, quite complex time relationships can be indicated. For example:

Today is Wednesday. On Monday, before you had completed the job which you finished Tuesday, I was thinking, "I will have finished before you will finish." I was wrong, but now I think I will finish soon, whatever you may be thinking to the contrary.

Or for another example:

I walk often. (present tense used for habitual action)

I am walking now. (present tense, progressive form—using the *present participle*, the -ing ending, for action currently in progress)

I walked yesterday from three to three-thirty. (past definite, action that occurred at a specific time)

I was walking when I met you. (past progressive, for an action that extends beyond a definite time; here, the walking extends beyond the time at which I met you)

I have walked enough today. (present perfect tense; an action now complete)

Since I will be walking most of the morning. . . (future progressive, for an action that will be in progress)

. . . I will have walked quite far by the time I meet you. (future perfect tense)

I had not walked as far as I intended when I met you yesterday. (past perfect tense, for an action already completed at the past time referred to)

I know it's weird of me, but I find this sort of thing interesting: it's so neat.

Simple tenses:

I walk (present)

I walked (past)

I will walk (future)

They are defined with respect to now: before now, after now.

Progressive forms: (they add -ing and some form of the auxiliary verb be—is, am, was, were, will be, etc.)

I am walking (present progressive)

I was walking (past progressive)
I will be walking (future progressive)
These indicate actions that continue, that go on.

Perfect tenses: (they use a past form plus some form of the auxiliary verb have—had, has, will have, etc.)
I have walked (present perfect)
I had walked (past perfect)
I will have walked (future perfect)
These indicate actions that have been completed, are all done, by the time referred to. Whatever grammarian invented the label "perfect" for actions already over with must not have liked his job very much.

EXERCISE 5: Try to work out these combinations of perfect and progressive forms.
Example: Give the present perfect progressive of *walk*. Answer: I have walked (present perfect) + I am walking (present progressive) = I have been [*been* replaces *am*] walking (present perfect progressive).

a. Give the past perfect progressive of *walk*.

b. Give the future perfect progressive of *walk*.

EXERCISE 6: Use the verb in the most appropriate tense, labelling the tense.
Example: By this time, I already __(walk)__ as far as I can. Answer: have walked, present perfect.
You __a. (play)__ all day today, ever since breakfast. I __b. (work)__ in the kitchen for over six hours, when your sister __c. (jump)__ into the room and spilled the soup, which __d. (boil)__ on the stove. Now I __e. (carry)__ the dirty paper towels to the garbage can, if you __f. (tell)__ me by what time you __g. (clean)__ up all this mess.

Some verbs, believe it or not, are more complicated. There are two contrary tendencies in you, and me, and other language users: on the one hand, we make every unfamiliar word regular; and on the other hand, we tend to change the most common words. Thus, the most common verbs have the most irregular forms. Today I ride, yesterday I rode (not rided). I shoot you now, I shot your brother yesterday (not shooted). BUT: I execute you now, I executed your uncle Herbert yesterday. Executing is regular, shooting is irregular.

These changes usually occur in the past tense:

I ride today.
I rode yesterday.

I shoot you gleefully.
I shot my mouth off yesterday.

I run this classroom.
I ran away yesterday.

And verbs that vary from the regular past form (I genuflect, I genuflected; I lie, I lied, are regular) usually are irregular in the form used with auxiliaries, too (regular verbs just use the past tense form, as in I have genuflected, I have lied):

I ride today.
I rode yesterday.
I have ridden often.

I shoot you gleefully.
I shot my mouth off yesterday.
I have shot a lot of things.

I run this classroom.
I ran away yesterday.
I have run off at the mouth quite a bit.

The only way you can know the form of an irregular verb among patterns like ride-rode-ridden, shoot-shot-shot, run-ran-run, is to learn them by heart: either from hearing or reading correct uses, or by going to a dictionary, which typically lists the forms of irregular verbs in that order: the present form, the simple past form, and the form that combines with auxiliaries (called the past participle). Thus, *W7NCD* under the entry "run" gives the phonetic spelling, for pronunciation; identifies it as a "vb"; then lists "ran" and "run" and even the other form (besides the past participle) that combines with auxiliaries, the -ing form (the *present participle*) "running" to show the doubling of the *n*. If you don't look up the forms of the irregular verbs, you may find that you have biten off more than you can chew, or that you have boughten a pig in a poke, or that you have been took for a ride, or that you have lain an egg, or that you have dove into water that is unsafe, or that you have took a fall, or that you haven't sewn the error of your ways, or that you have beed wrong, or that you have does a boo-boo, or that you have ran afoul of standard practice, or that you have typewroughten a wrong form.

Bad grammar is knowing that a verb agrees in number with its subject, and getting an F for writing "He spits on me every time I spits on him."

The most common verbs of all even change form according to what person is the subject:

I am		I have
you are	and	(you have)
he is		he has

Practically every verb ends in -s when the subject is *he* (or she, or it, or any singular noun—a noun naming one thing):

I walk	I shoot
he walks	she shoots
I ride	I execute
it rides	Jo executes

Owl: A Octopus got me!

Weevil: Phoo! Ain't no octopus is got him!

Pogo: Mebbe he mean a octopus DID got him.

Weevil: A Octopus DID got him? is *THAT* GRAMMATIWACKLE?

Pogo: As grammacklewack as RAIN . . . "IS GOT" is the present ALOOF-ABLE TENSE and "*DID* GOT" is the PAST particuticle.

Owl (receding as he runs into the distance): Octopockles! Help! Woctopockles! Octocklewocks! Octowocktopockers!

Weevil: MIGHTY STRANGE! My teachers allus learnt me that the past INCONQUERABLE tense had a li'l more BODY to it . . .

Owl (distance): Octopockles got me!

Weevil: There he go makin' those ungrammatipickle OUTcries an' INcries . . . WHO but a iggerant UNCOUTH type boor could UNNERSTAND such SLOVENLIKE ENGLISH? 'course what he OUGHT to holler is OCTO-POTAMUS IS GOT ME!

Pogo: He could of hollered OCTOPOTS DID GOT ME!

Weevil: That'd be more the PAST INVOKABLE tense . . . only for use 'gainst ELEPHANT an' other DRY type game.

Pogo: True.

Weevil: Then, in THAT case, he'd of hollered ELEPHUMPS DID GOT ME!

Pogo: Wull I DUNno. I'd use the PRESENT INDICTIBLE tense more like this . . . . RHINOCKWURSTS DONE IS GOT ME!

Weevil: No . . . no . . . The FUTURE PROVOKABLE would be better . . . more like HIPPOLOLLIPOPS IS GONE . . .

A shotgun blasts the conversational balloon and terminates the discussion.[3]

---

[3] Walt Kelly, *The Pogo Sunday Parade* (New York: Simon and Schuster, Inc., 1958), p. 73.

SENTENCE LENGTH

Well, I guess I have cheated a bit, because this chapter was supposed to be about sentences, and it has wound up being as much about verbs as about anything. But the verb is what completes the sentence idea which starts with a topic, the noun-subject. First the topic, the noun, the subject; then the statement, the verb, the predication.

Whenever you have a subject and a predicate, you have a sentence.

EXCEPT . . . when sentences are joined together in certain ways; what could be a sentence then becomes a *clause*. But more of that later.

What makes a sentence? Grammatical completeness: a subject and a predicate. What makes a good sentence? A complete idea: as much content as you decide is good for it.

The length of a good sentence differs, depending on context. Some good sentences are long and highly informative, carrying the reader on by a sweep of ideas and details so joined that the movement from one to another seems not simply inevitable, but graceful as well, skillfully and easily coordinating and subordinating phrase to phrase, clause to clause. Some good sentences are short, punchy. Short sentences are easier to write. Long sentences sometimes meander; that is, they sometimes wander or, as it were, lose track of their main point, because they go on for such a long time that by the time the writer gets to the end of the sentence he has forgotten the idea he started out with, or wanted to finish up with, and therefore repeats words all the time when he shouldn't, because you shouldn't waste time by taking up so much time with unnecessary words if you want to hold your reader's attention most of the time, because after all, that's what it's all about, isn't it? Writing long sentences therefore takes more practice than writing short sentences.

Later chapters discuss the building of long sentences (see Chapter 12). Consider for the moment, however, the simple question: Does a sentence have enough content? Is it complete in the sense that it says all that you want it to say?

The question is simple, the answer impossible—in general. In particular, you must answer it for each sentence you write. Most student writing errs on the side of brevity, lack of content, rather than on the side of excessive length, whether that length be padding or genuine content. I suggest, therefore, that you consider in rewriting whether there may not be some additional information, particularly additional details, that you might add to your sentences as originally drafted.

Look at the following sentences, which constitute the end of an article about controlling drug addiction. The author argues that the English solution to the problem, treating it as a medical rather than a criminal fault and dispensing drugs from authorized clinics, will work in America with a few changes. The quotation begins with the author's acknowledgement that the British system must be altered somewhat for America and continues with his concession that medical treatment will fail in some cases. Then, dramatically, he reverses direction, in two one-word sentences, followed by a long sentence about those who will suffer if we *don't* adopt a medical approach. The article then concludes with three sentences of increasing length, the last climactic sentence being the longest on the page. (The "unworkable dogma" in the last line means the belief that taking drugs is immoral and should be treated as a crime.) Try to feel the rhythm of this fall and rise of sentence length as you read.

> At the same time, to suggest a blanket export order of England's clinics to America is as irrational as the blanket dismissals they have suffered in the past. Different models are desirable. Greater safeguards are both possible and required. Even with them, some mistakes will be made. Some innocent youths may be infected. A few charlatans will have to be exposed. And still some more addicts will die of needless over-doses.
>
> Callous? Maybe. But what about the cabby who needs his "protection," the elderly lady who tonight will be terrorized, and the millions of innocent Americans who want and deserve the right to live in our urban centers without having to fear them as jungles?
>
> How long will it be before our national policy is changed?
>
> How long will a flourishing opiate black market continue—daily infecting others because of the astronomical profits that spur an ever-widening clientele?
>
> How long will American addicts be a banished subculture, morally exiled, often from the very medical help they so desperately need, but always present in the criminal countdown of the larger society which has had to safety-lock itself behind so many doors for the luxury of guarding an unworkable dogma?[4]

Topic: (2) Recount some silly mistake made by you or a member of your family, telling it humorously. End with a strong finish, on the funniest aspect of the mistake. Make the climax either a very long or a very short sentence.

---

[4] Edgar May, "Drugs Without Crime," *Harper's Magazine*, 243, No. 1454, July 1971, 65.

The answer is: LIFE
What is the question? (Fanfare)

The question is: What is a long sentence?

5

Paragraphs: United They Fall, Divided They Stand; Including Exercises on Length, Division, and Topic Sentences

When is a paragraph not a paragraph? When it's a singlegraph.

Paragraphing exists only in written work, one of the very few advantages writing has over speaking. Tone of voice, gesture, expression—all are extra communicators available to the speaker. "Smile when you say that," the Virginian said softly, his right hand resting easily beside his holstered six-shooter. A smile can turn an insult into a compliment. "Who could forget a face like that?" one of my wife's relatives said to the horse-faced old maid he had not seen for twenty years, smiling warmly while I twitched apprehensively awaiting her response. She simpered.

The disarming smile and its like can hardly be imitated in print. On the other hand, paragraphing can hardly be imitated in speech. Conversation, of course, doesn't much miss paragraphing, since people who converse in paragraphs usually end up talking to themselves; most of us prefer a little give and take in dialogue, which after all does mean "*two* speak." In contrast, formal speeches need paragraphing, but the nearest they can come to it is a pause by the speaker to sip a little water. Too many short paragraphs mean a water-logged speech.

Paragraphing offers organizational sign-posts. "All sentences between these markers go in the same direction." The indentation at the beginning of a new paragraph, the uncompleted type-line at the end, these identify a common topic. Paragraphs are units of completed thought.

The theory of relativity, as applied to paragraph composition, states that paragraph completeness depends. With respect to sentences, paragraphs are more complete; with respect to essays, they are less complete. Sentences are parts of the whole paragraph; paragraphs are parts of the whole essay. From the point of view of the sentences it contains, a paragraph is a unified whole. From the point of view of the essay that contains it, a paragraph is a part. Metaphorically, let's say that letters are raw materials; words are pieces; sentences are sub-assemblies; paragraphs are modular components; and the essay, of course, is the final manufactured product.

Consider the paragraph first as a part of the larger whole. From this vantage, it appears as a division, a marked off section. The pun with which this chapter opened, although it really wasn't very punny, therefore stated a truth about paragraphs: they exist only in combination with other paragraphs. If an essay is one continuous lump, it really has no paragraphs at all. Moreover, the essay that lacks paragraph divisions, unless it is very short, really is a lump. Lumps lie heavy on the digestive system; lumpy writing burdens the mind. Unless writing a short short paper, therefore, think of it in terms of paragraph parts, that is, units of one paragraph each. To do this, to define what makes each paragraph complete, you will have to see each paragraph in relationship to the ones around it.

In "Drugs Without Crime," Edgar May describes the British system of treating drug addiction as a medical problem, with clinics authorized to prescribe low-cost heroin and other drugs to certified addicts. Here is the first part of one of the essay's major sections, indicated by a break in the text. Read it carefully, and decide where the original paragraph divisions appeared:

There are fourteen clinics in London, which has four-fifths of the country's addicts. Elsewhere an addict may obtain drugs at thirteen special facilities or at some forty-two hospital outpatient departments. Some clinics have hospital beds for withdrawal "cures," many mix social-work services with their drugs, some provide extensive psychiatric service to addicts, some put the top premium on addict employment (almost 40 percent of all clinic-attending addicts work)—other clinics don't have these extra services. Almost all clinics permit addicts to inject drugs away from the premises, but at least two insist that a nurse administer them twice a day. Physical facilities also vary greatly. In the naval-base city of Portsmouth, the clinic is in a large general hospital tucked behind a door marked "Dental Waiting Room." In East London the center is in its own building on the grounds of a mental hospital. In the Denmark Hill area it's part of the hospital's general outpatient department, and if you visit St. Giles Clinic in the Church of England Community Center you are reminded of an Alec Guinness movie. Dr. James H. Willis, a young psychiatrist, holds court, resplendent in white medical coat, in a lecture hall where he sits behind a large wooden table flanked by two pianos and a bass fiddle. He took refuge behind these church walls after neighborly people prevented him from occupying a newly constructed clinic, because they believed that his commuting addicts would infect their children. At none of these facilities can an individual simply walk in and sign up for a governmental-sponsored fix. A detailed form is sent to the Home Office for comparison with the master list of known addicts to prevent duplicate registration. New patients generally receive at least two interviews with a social worker or one or more psychiatrists. One, and sometimes several, urine tests are demanded, usually two or three days apart. Drug-positive urine tests are the chief tools to determine the kind of drug, if any, the addict is taking.[1]

---

[1]Edgar May, "Drugs Without Crime," *Harper's Magazine*, vol. 243, No. 1454, July 1971, p. 62.

Where did you mark the first paragraph break? In the original, the first paragraph is only two sentences long. It announces the topic of this part of the essay, the clinics. The second paragraph, beginning "Some clinics have hospital beds . . . ," also of course deals with clinics. It could, therefore, have been included with the first paragraph, as one larger paragraph discussing clinics. But the second paragraph is followed by a third, also about clinics. ("Physical facilities also vary greatly," it begins.) Unless, therefore, the paragraph is to be of unwieldly length—as long as the whole section—the topic "clinics for treating drug addicts" is too large. The topics of these four paragraphs (the fourth begins "At none of these facilities . . .") therefore must be subdivisions of the whole content about clinics to be communicated. In fact, each paragraph presents a complete thought, without exhausting the total information: 1) There are a number of clinics (exact numbers given); 2) Services differ (beds, social-work and psychiatric services, employment, out-patient treatment); 3) Physical facilities differ (separate room in a general hospital, separate building in a mental hospital, mixed with a hospital's general out-patient department, lecture hall in church building); 4) All clinics screen and test addicts carefully.

The point of this analysis is that the size of the first and second paragraphs—whether they are one paragraph or two—depends on what surrounds them. Suppose the present paragraph three in fact shifted to some topic totally unrelated to English clinics. Suppose for example, it began

> In New York City from April 1970 to April 1971, there were 771 holdups or attempted holdups of change booths, or more than two a day in the 237-mile subway and elevated system. "More than 85 per cent of the people we apprehend are addicts," said Chief Robert Rapp of the Transit Police Department, "and they readily tell us the holdups are to feed their habit."[2]

In that case, the first and second paragraph would combine. The later shift in topic would make them more nearly one than two.

In one of his early essays, the black writer James Baldwin described his experience on visiting Paris.[3] He found, to his surprise, that he had more in common with white Americans than he did with black Africans. In the context of America, he was different; but in the context of Europe and an international student group, the greater difference overwhelmed the lesser

---

[2] A quote from *The New York Times*, May 12, 1971, cited by Edgar May (*op. cit.*) in another context. c. 1971 by The New York Times Company. Reprinted by permission.

[3] James Baldwin, *Notes of a Native Son* (Boston: The Beacon Press, 1955.)

and stressed the previously irrelevant similarities. The same thing applies to paragraphs: what belongs together depends on context.

EXERCISE 1: Mark paragraph divisions in the following opening of a short story:

Here I stand all day, every day, and wonder why. All day and every day except those days when the pain is too much to bear and I stay home. It looks like I'm fishing but I'm not really. I have known for years that there are not many fish in this lake. The boys laugh and wonder why Dad spends such a lot of time here except near the end of the month, when I fish to catch fish. I don't know why I come. I like to see the cypress shadows making two of every tree in the early morning. I like the feel of the heat shimmering off the clear water in the middle of the day. The best time is when the shadows grow and grow and the water turns a dark blue, then light purple and then a fire red and darker and darker until black. I stand and wonder why. Why did my mother tell me he is my father when he's not? Why did I marry only after my wife had given me twin sons? Why does my oldest son hate me? Where is my daughter, my baby? Why is the wool on my head beginning to grizzle as if I am the oldest of men? Oh, why must I suffer and suffer through the pain of my body? The pins in my leg at least hold it together, but they hurt. Sometimes they hurt like fire and my leg swells and swells until it may split even the extra large pants I get for it. I cannot believe it is part of me, and yet, I cannot let them take it off. It is of me and not of me and I hate it and I love it. I stand and watch and wonder why. Why was my mother so cold and so hard, yet so hot? How could she stand on her head every day cutting fern over and over? You know, I don't think she ever looked at the pale green shoots that came out under her hands as she cut the older fronds so loved by elegant florists in cities. I've seen these elegant arrangements and they are shoddy and small when you look at the early curl of a young, unfolding fern. Mother never saw.[4]

What verbal clues provide continuity from paragraph to paragraph and serve as signposts?

Having considered the paragraph in relationship to the essay of which it is a part, now consider the paragraph in relationship to the sentences which are its parts. (As a transitional paragraph, this one can be quite short.)

---

[4]By permission of Jo Goodwin Parker.

The theory of relativity, as applied to the internal workings of a paragraph, states that all sentences within the paragraph must be stated in such a way as to make clear their relationship to the paragraph's topic. That topic itself must be clear, and virtually all the time will appear in a *topic sentence.*

The topic sentences in the following paragraphs are italicized:

This viewpoint [about participants in trailer caravans] is discussed almost openly by a guide for several company-sponsored Caracades or Travelvans who, still being in this line of work, does not care to be identified. "These people tend to huddle," he says. "You know, most of them have run their own businesses or farms, been executives or military men, but they get down here [Mexico] and they want to be told what to do and when to do it. *They get very dependent on their leaders.* After a while you get the feeling you are in charge of a kindergarten class of 60-year-olds. A couple of years ago I had a bunch parked outside Mexico City. We were going to stay two or three days. One afternoon I had to drive over to the airport to meet a friend. I didn't say anything about it, just pulled out. I looked back and here are seven of them coming after me. They must have thought I was getting away and they weren't going to be left behind.[5]

I dislike seeing actors perform in the nude. Not that, at my age, I am shocked, but I become exceedingly uncomfortable as the naked performers begin to perspire under the hot lights and develop a tendency to stick to the furniture, or, worse, to each other. In the aura of silliness which prevails on such occasions, I find myself distracted from the plot (which seems merely to be against the audience) into practical considerations. Do they still call them dressing rooms? If an actor develops a boil in an unsuitable area, is a band-aid used, or the understudy? Is it possible to say to an actor, "I saw you in Oh, Calcutta" without laughing?[6]

[The Mexico City team defeated a weak El Salvador team which allegedly had had so little opportunity to practice that they had set up garbage cans as an opposing team in their drills.] The population of Mexico City could not have cared less whether their team had defeated El Salvador, eleven garbage cans, or England. The Mexicans poured into the streets, ignoring a drenching rain. They climbed the portico over the entrance to the

[5]Bill Gilbert, "A Home on the Range," *Sports Illustrated,* July 6, 1970, pp. 53–54.
[6]Jean Kerr, "I don't want to see the uncut version of *anything*," *Penny Candy* (Garden City, New York: Doubleday & Company, Inc. 1970) p. 94.

Maria Isabel Hotel, press headquarters for the World Cup, and dislodged a 12-foot-in-diameter fiberglass soccer ball. They rolled it two miles down 20th of November Street to the principal square of the city—the Zocalo—where they tore it to bits for souvenirs. *For the most part the celebration was innocuous enough, but an ominous note of violence crept in later* as the Mexican tipples of tequila, pulque and beer began to take effect. Herminio Gonzalez, apparently an objective soccer fan, had the poor judgment to tell his friend, Epigmenio Sanchez Luna, that Mexico's victory over El Salvador did not prove much, since the Salvadorean team was, in his words, "a lemon." Gonzalez was shot through the heart for his honesty. Three other Mexicans met violent deaths in soccer arguments during the first two weeks. In El Salvador no one was murdered, but the defeat caused a suicide. Eighteen-year-old Amelia Bolanos, after watching El Salvador lose on TV, retired to her room and shot herself through the temple.[7]

EXERCISE 2: Underline the topic sentences in the following paragraphs:

a. First and foremost is the fact that the glass snake is not a snake at all but a lizard. The mistake is an easy one to make. The glass snake looks like a snake, crawls like a snake, feeds like a snake and is snakelike in habits. However, the glass snake has eyelids and scales on its belly instead of the plates common to snakes and is thus a lizard, albeit a legless lizard.[8]

b. There's nothing like an old-fashioned Christmas—goodies on the groaning board, halls decked with holly berry, gaily wrapped presents piling up on the window sills, loved ones chiming carols. It can put you flat on your back for a month. For years I spent the whole of January in bed with what was diagnosed as "my bronchitis" but was clearly battle fatigue brought on from my days in Macy's and my nights in Bloomingdale's.[9]

c. The greatest weakness of Louis XIV was for food. He drank wine by the hogshead and ate hogs by the hog. When a servant asked him, "How many eggs do you want for breakfast, Sire—one or two?" he meant dozen. His excuse for eating so much was that it was cheaper

[7]Tex Maule, "Soccer is a Frenzy," *Sports Illustrated*, June 22, 1970, p. 17.

[8]Leonard Lee Rue, II, "The Glass Snake," *Camping Guide*, Jan. 1971 (Mill Valley, California: Rajo Publications Inc., 319 Miller Avenue).

[9]Jean Kerr, "I saw Mommy kicking Santa Claus," *Penny Candy* (Garden City, New York: Doubleday & Co., Inc.) 1970, p. 73.

to buy food in quantity. Most of the dandies of the day walked around with a cane, but Louis carried only a toothpick.[10]

A good topic sentence unifies a paragraph. It states the subject of the paragraph in a way that makes clear what belongs in the paragraph and what doesn't. If, however, a paragraph has no topic sentence or an inadequate one, then the writer may find himself paragraphing arbitrarily, like a modern Procrustes. Unpopular even in his own time, Procrustes had a bed which he insisted all travelers fit. Woe betide the traveler who was too long; Procrustes trimmed him with an axe until he was just right. And the short ones were stretched with thong and wooden drum until they were long enough. Paragraphs, like travelers, die when treated so. There is no one right length for paragraphs. But for any given topic sentence, there are both minimum and maximum lengths, their natural size, which should be neither chopped nor stretched.

If, then, you don't know when to break your paragraphs, check the topic sentence. If you can't tell from the topic sentence you have written, write another.

And if you *still* can't tell, take a break.[11]

Topics: (1) Discuss problems associated with one form of addiction you have had direct contact with (drugs—legal or illegal, liquor, cigarettes, candy, and fattening foods). Underline all topic sentences.

(2) Describe your closest encounter with crime; what did (or might) you learn from it? Was it important? Why? Underline all topic sentences.

(3) How many attitudes toward professional sports do you know of? How many ways do people react (to pro football, for example)? Which do you approve of? Why? Underline all topic sentences.

---

[10]Richard Armour, *It All Started with Europa: Being an Undigested History of Europe from Prehistoric Man to the Present, Proving that We Remember Best Whatever Is Least Important,* (New York: McGraw-Hill Book Co., 1955) p. 76.

[11]Before trying again.

Review Test

Across:

1. You can never find one in the rain
3. A verb form that means action that goes on, continues
8. coordinating conjunction
9. a pronoun (possessive)
10. an aspect of verbs; some grammarians don't count "interrogative" as a separate one
11. a unit of sound built around one vowel sound
15. a common helper verb
17. a stand-in for a noun
20. a verb: bind, link
22. most common adverb ending
23. _____ as a judge
24. How do you pronounce "s"?
27. two or more parts joined together
28. hammer and _____
29. an interjection expressing uncertainty (such as deafness)
30. a preposition of location
32. the initials of a very good textbook writer
33. a contraction of subject + helper verb
35. dirt
37. first name of a textbook writer's wife (starts with A)
39. a preposition of location
40. one of the seasons; also a verb
42. still another preposition, built out of two smaller ones
43. roll it up and dance
44. subordinating conjunction; conjecture
46. indefinite article
47. a dumb bunny
50. the feelings a word carries because of its history
53. a place of rest that sounds like a preposition
56. a word with two denotations, one of which is a common animal, the other, human

Down:

1. in a splice, very bad
2. common helper verb
3. concoct one; or bury someone in one
4. imperative
5. Latin word for "sun;" abbreviation of a man's name
6. initials of an illegal organization seeking union with Eire; also a man's name
7. you will read more about this creature in Chapter 9
11. each one takes a subject and a verb
12. present tense of 61 across; plays a large role in eating and animal combat
13. not odd
14. contraction of a subordinating conjunction which may also be used as a preposition; concerns time
16. if it has the same denotation, it's a _____
17. a before-place; a part of speech
18. a common plural stand-in
19. name; a part of speech
21. connotations are _____
25. not a daughter
26. a mood affirming fact
31. to arrange letters
32. a word that can link clauses, phrases, or words
33. you can hardly present a participle without _____
34. a preposition, sometimes confused in spelling with "have"
35. adverb or subordinating conjunction; you are _____ dumb
36. a transitive verb popular with flower people and other amiable types; also a noun, just as popular
38. found in a nunnery
41. adverb or conjunction: _____ smart _____ a whip
45. determines what part of speech a word is

across continued

58. there are two of these, and one of them is quite passive
59. preposition, as in _____ the hill.
60. an adverb commonly confused with a couple of other words that are spelled differently but pronounced the same way
61. irregular past tense of 12 down
62. a big pig
65. tear
67. a singular number
68. not to be confused with edh; a dead letter
69. a grown-up chick

down continued

47. the Ranger
48. found in infinitives
49. combination of two letters with a sound different from that of either by itself
51. modifies, among other things, an adjective or one of its own kind; a part of speech
52. five to a foot
54. a very common adverb
55. this word has a silent consonant digraph once represented by the letter yogh
57. a letter representing a sound produced with the vocal chords, the throat open
63. an interjection; sounds like the name of a letter
64. don't stop
66. a pronoun

Part Three: THE WRITING—Arranging Parts

6

How to Master
the Technique of Spelling
and thereby Raise
an Unpredictable Art
to the Unfailing Accuracy
of a True Science

se a dictionary.

7

Spelling *a.k.a.* The Precise Arranging of Letters within the <u>Words</u>

etters are parts of words. At the level of the individual word, getting parts in order means spelling correctly.

In writen work, goode speling is taken for granted; but bad speling is taken as a mark of iliterasy. True, mispeled words comunacate as well as corektily speled words. But part of what you comunacate is an impresion of you're self. If you do not sppel corectily, the imppresion you comunacate—how shall I put it—lacks urbanity, gentility, savoir faire, that *je ne sais quoi* which implies total mastery. Eating with your hands instead of a fork works just as well, perhaps better; the main reason you don't eat with your hands is convention and the imppresion you wish to make. So spel corectily and don't imppres your reader as an ignoramus.

Convention and the impression you make provide only the first third of the reasons for learning to spell correctly, however. The second and third relate directly to what you communicate.

The second reason you should spell correctly is static. When speling bekumbs 2 baughed, itt atrahckts sew muhtch utennshian tew merkanniks that itt ahbskewers meenen. Just that little moment necessary for the reader to note to himself, "Oops! misspelled word," or the even longer time it takes to think, "Is that right? a double L? or is it a single L?" slows the reader down, diverts his attention, and tends to obscure the meaning, just as static drowns out a radio program or signal interference breaks up a television picture. How many times students have said to me, "But you knew what I meant, even if I did misspell it." They seem not to realize that to misspell is to write in code. Maybe your reader can decipher the code. But unless you seek secrecy, why slow him down? Some of us lazy readers hate to work at understanding. Make it easy for us.

Words are built out of roots or stems. (No leaves.) The way you pronounce them often changes, even when the basic meaning doesn't. For example: *House* and *hous*ing are words with the same root meaning, but the way that root is pronounced changes. If spelling represented that change, English would be a much harder language to read. For example, if the *z* sound were always written *z* and the *ss* sound were always written *s*, the visible similarity between *house* and *housing* would fade into the difference between *house* and *houzing*. At the same time, the similarity between *resurrection* and *insurrection* would fade into the difference between *rezurrection* and *insurrection*. Similar changes in the spelling of vowel sounds, to make them match shifts in pronunciation, might hide the relationship between *finite* and *infinite* or between *photo* and *photographer*.

English spelling, in short, helps the reader to recognize word meanings. But unfortunately, when people who spell word roots the same way pronounce them differently, the writer—who starts with the sound in his mind—may need a little help. What's sauce for the reading goose is a sticky mess for the writing gander. As a writer, therefore, console yourself with the thought that your agony in trying to spell correctly is making things a lot easier for some poor reader.

The third reason you should spell correctly applies infrequently, but matters when it does. Sometimes, misspelling not only blurs meaning but changes it altogether. The difference between "A plot is a causally related sequence of events" and "A plot is a casually related sequence of events" matters.

Three reasons for avoiding bad spelling: because unconventional, it seems ignorant; because distracting, it obscures meaning; when it substitutes a word of similar spelling to the one meant, it changes meaning.

Look back at the second paragraph of this section, and mark all the misspelled words you can find. Then try to state what confusions produced the misspellings you have marked. That is, describe each mistake you marked, using the most general terms possible. If, for example, you were marking a theme I once received which began, "Honeste is the beast police," you would not leap erect in your chair with startled pleasure at this avant garde story of the brutal French fuzz named "Honeste," but would mark the misspellings *honeste, beast,* and *police,* and describe the first and third mistakes as substituting *e* for *y,* and the second as substituting *ea* (usually in fact pronounced *ee*) for *e* (pronounced *eh,* since followed by two consonants, *s* and *t*).[1] Compare your results to those on page 83.

To improve your spelling, follow these suggestions:

1. Keep a check-list on 3 × 5 cards, including all words misspelled on your themes (which your instructor will mark) and all words that you checked for yourself and found you had misspelled. Review this list frequently, having someone read you the list as you spell each word; words you spell correctly go in one pile, words misspelled in another pile for repetition after the two of you have gone through the list once.

2. Look up any words you feel hesitant about *after* writing them down. If you were wrong, of course, you put them on the card list.

3. Proofread essays just before handing them in, starting with the last sentence and working forward toward the first. That way you are less likely

---

[1] What the student meant was, "Honesty is the best policy."

to get caught up in the flow of your own ideas and can concentrate more easily on the mechanics of spelling.

4. When you misspell a word, check a list of rules (descriptive generalizations) for English spelling to see whether there is a rule governing the error you have made. If there is, memorize the rule. Example: You wrote *feind* instead of *fiend*. Rule: I before E (when rhyming with *tree*), except after C.[2]

5. Learn the correct pronunciation of the words you use. This device won't be as effective for English speakers as it would for Filipinoes who speak Tagalog, a language unwritten until the nineteenth century gave it an alphabet and completely phonetic spelling with no exceptions, but it will help. English is not completely phonetic. If you don't believe me, you didn't read Chapter Two. Read it now or take my word for it. But English spelling remains by and large a representation of spoken sounds, and you can eliminate many spelling errors by writing words the way you pronounce them.

6. Play word games. For example:

Ghost: Three or more players name letters in rotation, trying to continue a word without completing the spelling of a word. If a player thinks the accumulated spelling he has received does not begin an English word, he may challenge the player who named the last letter. A player loses a round, becoming a third of a ghost, if: 1) he completes the spelling of a word; 2) he challenges a player, and the letters so far named do in fact begin an English word; 3) he is challenged by another player and cannot name an English word beginning with the letters to which he has just added one. Example: player 1: Q. player 2: U. player 3: E. player 1: L. player 2: challenges player 1. Player 1 names the word beginning with QUEL, which is QUELL; player 2 loses the round, and is a third of a ghost. He would have lost anyway if he had said "L," completing the word. Lose three rounds and you are out. Note that just as in writing, you don't really win anything by spelling correctly; but if you make a mistake, you lose.

Letter Bingo: Two or more players. Each player marks off five rows of five boxes each on a piece of paper. In rotation, each calls out a letter, everyone writing down the letter called anywhere he chooses in his twenty-five box square. The object is to make as many four-letter and five-letter words, reading both across and down, as possible. Each letter counts one point if

---

[2]This rule has a number of exceptions, to wit: either, neither, seize, seizing, seisure, leisure, weir, weird; species, financier. Some people pronounce *either* and *neither* with a long I sound, in which case they don't break the rule. You can keep two more out of this list of exceptions by pronouncing *inveigle* in*vayg*le and by remembering that the British, who met them before we did, called *sheiks* "shayks." When E + I is *not* pronounced EE (as in weight, foreign, their, counterfeit), the spelling most often is *ei*, with *friend* the most common exception.

it is in a word reading across and one point if it is part of a word reading down. High score wins. Like all games, this seems silly unless you accept the rules and the goals; and it is less dangerous than football, although sometimes more frustrating.

The humorist H. Allen Smith described the following game in one of his books presenting his Hollywood experiences. He and a group of writers, when unoccupied by the demands of their profession, would spend hours in executive session competing for four and five letter words, working in intensive silence broken only by the howls of anguish at an unacceptable infrequent letter such as X or Q in the late stages of the game.

Here are the results of a recent game in which an English teacher defeated a Greek scholar and crossword puzzle fan. Letters called by the players, in rotation: B, R, K, O, A, L, F, O, E, U, F, N, T, E, T, M, C, I, S, U, A, E, L, L, A. The four competitors, writing down each letter as it was called, produced these results: (score 5 for a five letter word, 4 for a four letter word)

A B O U T 5	B O O K E 4	T R O O T 4	S T O R K 5
C R A F T 5	U R I N E 5	S B U N K 4	T A L E N 4
L O N E U 4	F A T E L 4	F A M E I 4	A L I C E 4
A K I E S 0	F L A C S 4*	F L V E L 0	F L O B E 4
M E L L F 0	T A U L M 0	E C I A L 0	F A M U U 0
4 5 0 4 0 __ 13	4 4 0 0 4 __ 12	0 0 0 0 4 __ 4	5 4 4 0 4 __ 17
14	17	12	17
total — 27	total — 29	total — 16**	total — 34

*The crossword puzzle expert testified that FLAC and OLIO are words, to the amazement of the other players (the player who accidentally had OLIO did not argue).

**This player, playing for the first time, didn't understand that five-letter words count, and tried only for four-letter words.

If you don't know how to spell a word (that includes just feeling uncertain), look it up in the dictionary. And, of course, add it to your spelling check-list, on cards. But looking a word up when you don't know how to spell it can involve some problems, since a dictionary is arranged by spelling. Here, therefore, is a list of some alternative spellings in case you can't find the word where you think it should be. Actually, for any one word one of the alternatives will be right, the other wrong. The dictionary will tell you which is which.

words beginning with *w*—try *w* and *wh* (*where*, *whether*)
words ending in a *tion* sound—try *sion, tion, cion, cean.*

words ending in an *ise* sound—try *ise*, *ize* (ad*vise*, civi*lize*)

words containing a *k* sound—try *c*, *ck*, *k* (practi*c*e, ba*ck*-stop, bi*ke*)

words ending with a *ch* sound—try *ch*, *tch* (mu*ch*, ma*tch*)

words containing an *f* sound—try *ph*, *f*, *ff* (gra*ph*, o*f*ten, pro*f*essor, o*ff*ensive) and in a few common words -*ugh* (la*ugh*, co*ugh*)

For some of these combinations, there are rules of pronunciation, phonetic rules, that apply in most cases. For example, a single vowel before two consonants is almost always short. (The long vowel sound says its name: long A = ay, long E = ee, long I = aye [ah-ee], long O = oh, long U = yoo [or oo].) Thus, *two* consonants *ck* are common after a *short* vowel, the *single* consonant *k* after a *long* vowel: back, bike. For another example, in the ending: vowel + consonant + E, the vowel is almost always long. Thus the single consonant *k* + *e* usually follows a long vowel, the double consonant *ck* a short vowel. Other examples: ball (short a), bale (long a); install (short a); inhale (long a).

Phonetic rule: vowel + two consonants = short vowel

vowel + one consonant + E = long vowel

Here are some more alternative spellings:

long A sound: a, ai, ei (bale, jail, veil)

long E sound: e, ee, ei, ie, ae, i (enough, reed, either, fiend, read, police)

long I sound: i, ei (imbibe, height)

long O sound: o, oa, oe, ow (no, oar, toe, bow and arrow)

long U sound: u, oo, ou, ui (unit, truth, boot, through, nuisance, suit)

any unaccented UH sound (the most common vowel sound, as in th*e* book or as in pretti*ly*): any single vowel, many vowel pairs. For example, all of the following are phonetically possible spellings:

cammaflage

cammeflage

camiflage

camoflage

camuflage

cammeiflage

camouflage

EL sound: el, al, ol, ile, le (unaccented): (enamel, the principal Metal—with a capital M, the Capitol in Washington, fragile, the principle of battle is winning) These really are more examples of the indefinite vowel or unaccented UH sound. Sometimes, adding a suffix (ending) changes the accent and makes the sound match the spelling. For example, adding *ity* to *fragile* produces *fraGILity*, in which the short I sound is very clear. And if you can remember that Monaco is a *princiPALity*, you may find it easier to remember that your high school principal was a prince of a pal and not a standard, rule, or law (princi*ple*). And metal things are *meTALlic*. And *cetera*.

ER sound: er, or, re, ur, ure (water, mayor, fire, sulfur, pressure)

R's are rahtha tricky. Many accents drop R's, absorbing them into a slight change in the vowel pronunciation. Southerners in this country and several varieties of Englishmen drop and soften their R's. A fellow student of mine from Lancaster, England, came to this country, and when he traveled in the north, he was constantly asked what part of the south he came from. (One clerk, when told he came from England, asked what language they spoke there.) In particular, R-vowel and vowel-R slip around a lot when surrounded by consonants. Therefore, beware of confusing:

consonant-vowel-R-consonant with

consonant-R-vowel-consonant.

Chaucer's word for bird was bridde. In modern times, people say and write *pres*piration when they mean *per*spiration, or *per*ty when they mean *pre*tty.

In general, any single consonant may be confused with a double consonant, and vice-versa. (Pro*f*essor is right and pro*ff*essor is wrong, but o*ff*icer is right and o*f*icer is wrong.)

TEST: Explain the difference between professor and officer as a phonetic spelling (how is the O pronounced?).

Misspellings from page 79: writen, goode, speling, iliterasy, mispeled, comunacate, corectily, speled, impresion, you're self, donot, sppel, imppresion, imppres. Confusions producing these misspellings: Some of course are different forms of the same word (mispeled, speled, imppresion, imppres). In "spe*l*ed" and "imppre*s*," a double consonant erroneously drops to a single consonant; "mi*s*peled" also reduces a double consonant to a single one, by not keeping the full prefix (*mis-spelled* is the word formation, not *mi-spelled*). "Good*e*" adds an unnecessary silent *e*, which if it had a function would probably make the word sound like "g-oh-d." "Corect*i*ly," besides reducing a double *r* to a single one, adds a non-existent syllable (*i*). "Co*m*unacate," again reducing a double consonant (*m*), replaces one vowel (*i*) with another (*a*), very easily done when the vowel is unaccented; such unaccented vowels are often pronounced the same as *uh*. "You*'re* self" fails to join a compound as one word, and confuses the contraction "you're" (= you are) with the possessive pronoun adjective "your." "Donot" mistakenly joins two words as though they were a single compound; "do not" or the contraction "don't" are OK. Im*pp*res, im*pp*resion, and *sp*pel, among their other faults, double what should be a single consonant.

EXERCISE: Divide the following list of commonly misspelled words into convenient groups (say, twenty each) and have someone read them to you on different days. Add to your card list (spelling improvement suggestion #1) all those you miss or that make your stomach hurt when you ask yourself whether what you have written is right.

Group 1

their	existence	define
there	existent	separate
they're	occur	separation
two	occurred	believe
too	occurring	belief
to	occurrence	occasion
receive	definite	lose
receiving	definitely	losing
exist	definition	

Group 2

accommodate	began	conscientious
achieve	begin	conscious
achievement	beginner	consistent
acquaint	beginning	consistency
acquaintance	belief	control
acquire	believe	controlled
affect	benefit	controlling
affective	beneficial	controversy
all right	benefited	controversial
among	busy	criticism
analyze	business	criticize
analysis	category	decision
apparent	choose	decided
appear	chose	definite
appearance	choice	definitely
argument	comparative	definition
arguing	conscience	define

describe
description
disastrous
effect
embarrass
environment
equipped
equipment
exaggerate
excellent
excellence
exist
existence
existent
experience
explanation
fascinate
forty
fourth
government
governor
grammar
grammatically
height
imagine
imaginary
imagination
immediate
immediately
incident
incidentally
intelligent
intelligence
interest
interpret
interpretation
its
it's
led
loneliness
lonely
lose

losing
marriage
necessary
unnecessary
Negro
Negroes
noticeable
noticing
occasion
occur
occurred
occurring
occurrence
origin
original
passed
past
perform
performance
personal
personnel
possess
possession
practical
precede
prefer
preferred
prejudice
prepare
prevalent
principal
principle
privilege
probably
proceed
procedure
professor
profession
prominent
psychology
psychoanalysis
psychopathic

psychosomatic
pursue
really
realize
receive
receiving
recommend
referring
repetition
rhythm
sense
separate
separation
shining
similar
studying
success
succeed
succession
surprise
than
then
their
there
they're
thorough
tries
tried
two
too
to
useful
useless
using
varies
various
weather
whether
woman
write
writing
writer

Group 3

accept
acceptance
acceptable
accepting
accident
accidentally
accidental
across
advice
advise
aggressive
approach
approaches
article
athletic
athlete
attended
attendant
attendance
author
authority
authoritative
basis
basically
before
Britain
Britannica
careless
careful
carrying
carried
carries
carrier
challenge
character
characteristic
characterized
coming
conceive
conceivable

condemn
consider
considerably
continuous(ly)
convenience
convenient
curiosity
curious
desire
desirability
dependent
difference
different
disappoint
disciple
discipline
dominant
predominant
efficient
efficiency
entertain
exercise
extremely
familiar
finally
foreign
foreigners
friend
friendliness
fulfill
fundamental
fundamentally
further
happiness
hero
heroine
heroic
heroes
hindrance
humor

humorist
humorous
hypocrisy
hypocrite
independent
independence
influential
influence
involve
knowledge
laboratory
leisure
leisurely
liveliest
livelihood
liveliness
lives
maintenance
mere
ninety
operate
opinion
opportunity
oppose
opponent
optimism
paid
parallel
particular
permanent
permit
philosophy
physical
piece
planned
pleasant
possible
propaganda
propagate
quantity

quiet
relieve
religion
response
ridicule
ridiculous
satire
sergeant
significance
speech

sponsor
subtle
summary
summed
suppose
suppress
technique
temperament
therefore
together

transferred
undoubtedly
unusual
unusually
villain
weird
where
whose
you're

8

The Efficient Arranging
of Words within <u>Sentences</u>:
How to Make a Graceful
Complement, Tuck in a
Dangling Modifier, and
Other Tidy Arts

digital Using digits, as in a digital computer—which operates with discrete entities (usu. *on* and *off*, representing 0 and 1; complex calculations use a series of on-off relationships as a binary system of digits. See ANALOG.

analog A type of computer that represents quantities by analogy to continuous physical properties such as the amount of flow or resistance to an electric current. See DIGITAL.[1]

Arranging parts within words means getting the letters in the right order, or spelling correctly. Spelling is digital: on or off; right or wrong. Arranging parts within sentences means getting words and phrases in good order, or correct and effective *syntax*. If spelling can be evaluated by a digital computer, with only two values (right and wrong), syntax, in contrast, must be evaluated by an analogue computer, with a continuous scale of increasing or decreasing value. Syntax, word order, can be bad, poor, fair, good, great, really heavy.

Review question: Syntax means

    a. meaningful word order

    b. spelling

    c. graft or payola

    d. pledge to the church's weekly offering

There are, however, some right and wrong elements in English syntax. The most universal pattern of English word order is subject-predicate. The predicate usually has two parts: verb + complement. That makes the most universal pattern of English word order subject + verb + complement. When a verb is between two nouns, the first noun is the subject and the second noun is the complement.

Complements are of two types, depending on the type of verb. The first type of complement is an object. This common pattern of English sentence is subject + verb + object. That pattern can hardly be changed.

During World War II, Ben served in the quartermaster corps in North Africa. When a riot broke out in a nearby Arab village, he was called in with

---

[1] By permission of Gene Medlin, Ph.D.

some other noncombat soldiers to quell the riot. He handled his rifle so awkwardly as they boarded the truck that the first sergeant took it away from him and carried it until they arrived at the village. They dismounted and formed two ranks; someone helped Ben fix his bayonet; at the end of the street a throng of sheeted Arabs screamed and gesticulated, dancing in the desert dust. Ben, in the first rank, advanced fearfully, step by step, clutching his bayonet-tipped rifle menacingly, when a thick Irish brogue cracked nervously behind him, "For th' love of Mayry, mither of God, Weinstein: turrn y'rr rrifle arround!"[2]

An English verb, like a rifle, is directional. The direct object is the target. The difference between "the machine made a man" and "a man made the machine" matters. Here, word order means not a difference in degree or quality, but an absolute change in meaning.

EXERCISE 1: Write two pairs of sentences in which subject and object are reversed by the second member of each pair (as in the two sentences above about a man and the machine), making a difference in meaning that you think some people would be willing to kill for or die for.

Generally, the subject goes before the verb, S-V; and even more generally, the object comes after the verb, V-O; but the feeling for subject-verb order, although very strong indeed, is not quite as powerful as the feeling for the whole pattern S-V-O, subject-verb-object.[3] Particularly, a certain kind of verb, which never has an object, accepts a following subject fairly graciously.

Verbs which have an object, like *kill it, love her, worship him,* are called *transitive* verbs—*trans* as in *trans*port, *trans*fer. They carry action across the sentence from the subject to inflict it on the object. In contrast, verbs which take no object, like *is, seem, come,* are called in-_____ verbs, *in-* meaning simple *not.*

EXERCISE 2: Which of the following sentences have intransitive verbs, which have transitive?

    a. This sentence has a transitive verb.

    b. The verb in this sentence is intransitive.

---

[2] Ancedote related by permission of Ben Weinstein, Greenville, South Carolina.

[3] Footnote for the advanced student: Many grammars distinguish between *direct* object and *indirect* objects. If you haven't heard of this difference, don't read any more of this footnote. If you have heard of this difference, then the Objects I talk about are direct objects.

    c. John loves Mary

    d. John is Mary

    e. Carry this book with you wherever you go.

    f. The spaceship fell seven million miles.

(The sentence in these exercises with two clauses is number _____; the dependent clause is introduced by "wherever".)

    You can ask two questions of any active verb: Who is it done by? Who is it done to? The one it is done *by* is the subject; the one it is done *to* is the object of the transitive verb. But if the answer to the question "Who is it done to?" is *no*body, the verb is *in*transitive.

    What kind of action do the intransitive verbs *go* and *fall* name? They are usually grouped with such similar verbs as *come, move, turn, fly.* Such verbs of motion, like *run* and *walk,* usually are intransitive. Verbs of motion have no complement; the pattern of a sentence with such a verb is simply S-V.

    Another kind of intransitive verb can be called a *linking* verb, since like a chain it ties the subject to the complement. Instead of action being *trans*ferred from the subject to the object, the two are linked in a state of being—they are made equal, so to speak. In the subject-verb-complement pattern of a sentence with a linking verb, the complement is either a noun or an adjective. This is the second type of complement. Since, whether noun or adjective, it's in the predicate—that includes the verb and its complement, remember—it will be a predicate noun or a predicate adjective.

EXERCISE 3: In each group of three verbs, identify which is *trans*itive, which is an *in*transitive verb of *motion,* and which is an *in*transitive *linking* verb.

    a. scatter, be, come

    b. stab, travel (sometimes), am

    c. seem, select, crawl (sometimes)

    d. screw, smell (sometimes), go

    e. walk (most of the time), scan, become

    Look at all those *sometimes*'s. The way the word is used makes the difference.

    "Crawl to me, baby," (intransitive crawling: Verb of motion)

    "Oh, Humphrey B., when you talk to me that awful way it makes me want to crawl the *walls!*" (transitive crawling, with the object _____)

    "Whatsamatta, kid, you don't feel so good?" (intransitive feeling: linking verb with the predicate adjective _____)

    "I feel my heart breaking!" (transitive feeling, with the object _____)

What follows what (syntax) makes a lot of difference, sometimes the difference between sanity and insanity. Freud recounts the case of an old lady who used to go around the house after her snacking grandchildren (who chewed on the run), picking up crumbs. The children's mother and father thought nothing of this habit—the old lady was just very neat—until one day she went around picking up crumbs: and the kids were eating bananas. Bananas have lots of qualities, but crumbiness isn't one. Grandmother went to the psychiatrist. And all because she stopped following cracker crumbs and started following banana crumbs.

Many verbs of motion like *crawl* and linking verbs like *feel* are intransitive when followed by an adverb or an adjective, but transitive when followed by a noun, used as an object.

In sum, the total pattern of the sentence's meaning changes the way the words within it work. Part of that total pattern is determined by word order.

	Sentence:		
	subject	+	predicate
	noun	+	(verb + complement)
Transitive:			
	noun	+	(verb + object)
Intransitive:			
	noun	+	verb (no complement; often a verb of motion)
or:			
	noun	+	(linking verb + predicate adjective-or-noun)[4]

Word order is more flexible when the verb is intransitive (*no* object) than when it is transitive. Consider the word order of the sentence, "How beautiful upon the mountains are the feet of him that bringeth good tidings." (Isaiah 52:7)

Subject: The *feet* of him that bringeth good tidings.

Verb (intransitive, linking): *are.*

Predicate[5] adjective: how *beautiful* upon the mountains.

---

[4] Note that this chart omits all modifiers: adjectives, phrases, or clauses modifying the noun or pronoun subject; the same modifying the noun-or-pronoun direct object, or predicate noun; and adverbs, phrases, and clauses modifying the verb.

[5] Footnote for the absent-minded student: The *predicate* of a sentence focuses on the verb; the complete predicate includes just about everything that isn't part of the subject. Predicate adjectives appear only in sentences with linking verbs.

The effect tends to be poetic, formal, rhetorical. Sometimes, though, that order does appear emphatically in conversation: "Gorgeous is what she is!"

Subject: what she is.

linking verb: is

adjective (part of the predicate): gorgeous

Word order matters so much in English that it can change the parts of speech around. Consider the gamma delta—which is the adjective, which the noun? Order answers: the adjective goes before the noun. If there is such a thing as a gamma delta, then the delta is the noun and the gamma is the adjective. Everyone knows without half trying the difference between a *light house* and a *house light*, between a *riot club* and a *club riot*.

With more words, the situation becomes more complex. A sign reading "Mickey Mouse watch" names a thing—for sale, perhaps—whereas a sign reading, "watch Mickey Mouse" probably calls the reader to the T.V. set.

A single adjective, or a group of single adjectives, usually comes before the noun it modifies. But a phrase serving as an adjective usually comes after the noun. (The house where I met Mama, not the where I met Mama house.) Here is a sentence from a theme I received yesterday: "I believe the most well put together setting part was the end of the story." Before reading on, try to rephrase the subject of that sentence.

The student's problem involves order. He tried to put an adjectival phrase in front of the noun it modifies. "Most well put together" works as a single unit, a single phrase, modifying the noun "setting," here used as an adjective to modify "part." One way of feeling this unity is to recognize that the words could all have been joined by hyphens: "the most-well-put-together-setting part." The writer meant not "the most part, the well part, the put part, the together part; he means the part whose setting shows the single quality of being "most-well-put-together." He should have written, "I believe the part whose setting was put together best . . . ."

When I was a teenager in Chicago, I had a chance to act as an extra in crowd scenes in operas and ballets. In the ballet Sheherazade, a Sultan comes home to find his harem partying the cooks and gardeners, and orders his soldiers to kill them all. The soldiers were all extras like me. A special assignment fell to the lot of a tall, husky-looking extra, about my age, who was to carry one of the ballerinas on-stage and kill her there. As we huddled in the wings, a ballerina rushed in among us, whispering hoarsely, "Where's the boy who's to carry me on? Where's the boy who carries me on?" Finding his way to her, he put his left hand awkwardly on her waist. Discovering that a wooden scimitar in his right hand made it useless for lifting purposes, he shifted the scimitar to his left hand, and put his right hand on her waist. Alas, now his left hand was taken up by the scimitar.

"Profane obscenity!" snarled the ballerina, "hurry or we'll miss our cue!" Blushing, the boy put his right hand around her shoulders, scooped his scimitar and left arm under her knees, and raised her from the floor. For one magnificent moment, he held her in his arms. She looked light but he looked heavy-laden. Three slow, short steps back he took, sinking lower with each step until he overbalanced backwards and sprawled with a thump in a twisted tangle of light cables, shuffling boots, and wriggling ballerina. Feminine oaths and imprecations rose from the tangle, rising above the background strains of Rimsky-Korsakov's music.

The boy struggled to his feet. Supremely determined, he flung his scimitar to one side (where it struck a passing stagehand's knee), grabbed the faintly protesting ballerina by ankle and wrist, and slung her over his back in a pretty good approximation of the fireman's carry. He lugged his victim onstage like a sack of flour, about fifteen bars late. Realism suffered, of course, because once there he had no scimitar to kill her with. But then, when he threw her down, her head bounced so hard on the planked floor that I guess the audience accepted her death as probable. And I suppose at that distance they couldn't see her quivering as she lay there. As the rest of us soldiers rushed onstage and mercifully obliterated the scene from audience view, I heard what still seems to me a strange sound. She was laughing.

Why am I telling you what happened twenty-five years ago? I started with an analogy in mind. A single adjective can precede the noun it modifies, just as a sturdy boy can carry a burden in front of him if it isn't too heavy; but a more substantial adjectival unit, a phrase, must be carried into the sentence behind the noun, just as an extra has to carry a weighty ballerina on his back.

It took me too long, I know, to make such a short comparison. Let me try to make use of the story for other purposes, as we go along.

The first sentence begins with a two-clause sentence: When I was a teenager . . . , I had a chance . . . . The order could have been reversed, and the sentence would have satisfied a digital computer checking off grammatical correctness. But the "When . . ." clause provides an immediate introduction, naming time and place, and warning you that something different is coming up. On an analog scale of effectiveness, starting with the "When . . ." clause rates higher.

EXERCISE 4:
- a. Rewrite the following sentence, making any changes necessary to improve word order:
  We huddled in the wings, crowded into a floodlight and scenery flat divided space.
- b. Find a sentence in the ballet anecdote that breaks the normal subject-verb-direct object order. Does it work or not?

The long phrase should follow the noun: the single adjective, or parallel series of single adjectives, should precede the noun. But this is one of those analog situations, not always clearly right or wrong, but better or worse according to context. Sometimes, for example, adjectives follow the noun very well. The *hot, thirsty old dog* follows his adjectives in normal order, but for the sake of emphasis, he may wear them on his tail instead of his nose—in which case he enters as an *old dog, hot and thirsty.*

That last example points up a basic principle of good writing: changing normal word order draws attention, like a woman walking into a room on her hands. Another example: Hard to please is Harry, who broke three engagements and the hopes of eleven prospective mothers-in-law before accepting as wife a neat young thing arrested two days after the wedding for treason and poisoning.

EXERCISE 5: Write two sentences using the same syntactical pattern as the following:

    a. Awkward indeed is an assignment in working backwards.
    b. Soft and tender is the love of a mother.

By far the most common sentence pattern that puts the subject after a linking verb begins with a neutral word: "There is a man in our town who lives upon a hill." *There* doesn't point to a place, doesn't tell where the man is; *in our town* is where he is. *There* is a temporary stand-in for the subject. Sometimes, the sentence pattern *There is* + subject is the best. Compare these alternatives:

There is a man in our town who lives upon a hill. (Pretty good; almost good enough to be the beginning of a nursery rhyme.)

A man in our town who lives upon a hill is. (Aargh!)

In our town, a man lives upon a hill. (Hm! "A man" without qualification, is too general; suggests that all males live on a hill, whereas women live in the valley.)

In our town, there is a man who lives upon a hill. (OK; stresses *in our town* more than the first, but maybe that's what you want, especially if you have just been discussing the plains-dwellers' towns.) Note that the pattern still is *there is* + *subject,* but with a prepositional phrase in front.

A man in our town lives upon a hill. (OK. The difference in emphasis between this sentence and the first is subtle. This one stresses the activity of living-on-the-hill; the first stresses the existence of the man-with-the-hill-home. Your choice.)

A similar pattern begins *"It is . . ."*

It is raining.

It is about time; the crops need it badly.

Yes, it's tough growing corn in Brooklyn when there's no rain.

Some parts of the sentence naturally receive more emphasis than others. The end of a sentence, like the end of a story, must be good if the reader is to be satisfied. The end naturally receives the greatest emphasis. Therefore, instead of ending your sentences with unimportant thoughts or with concessions, end with a significant bang.

EXERCISE 6: Rearrange the following sentences to put the most important idea at the end.

    a. He killed her one fine day when his patience had run out.

    b. Harry, ah, Harry, don't leave me like this or I shall kill myself, even though you don't believe I really mean to do it.

    c. We must have peace, no matter how hard it is to achieve.

    d. She finally understood, after her mother had told it to her, her father had explained it to her, her fiance had reviewed it with her, and her priest had catechized her.

The beginning, too, naturally receives some emphasis. (That leaves the middle as the least interesting location.) Even if it's not love at first sight, first impressions matter.

QUIZ: Why is it appropriate for a sentence to begin with its subject?

Modifiers must accompany the things they modify. ("I declare, he's a changed man since he married." "No wonder. She never lets him out of her sight.") Easy to do, when it's one adjective for one noun; there are only two possible places for the word "red" in the following sentence, and nobody would confuse them: "She brushed her hair back from her eyes." She's a strawberry blonde or hung-over, and where the *red* goes says which.

It's often a bit harder when the modifier is an adverb, especially if there is more than one verb form in the sentence. What does the adverb go with in each of the following:

    1. He ran the obstacle course beautifully keeping his balance in spite of the hazards.

    2. She learned quickly to brush her teeth, knowing that if she took too long he would start singing again.

    3. He urged her again to marry.

In all three cases, the adverbs (*beautifully, quickly,* and *again*) come between two things they could modify (*ran* beautifully *keeping, learned* quickly *to brush, urged* again *to marry*). Like Janus, the Roman god of doorways, they face two ways; and as with any two-faced statement, you don't know which they mean.

What does the adverb go with in each of the following?

4. She warned him against singing loudly.

5. She warned him loudly against singing.

6. She warned him against singing, loudly.

Here, location and punctuation make the difference, and there is no ambiguity.

EXERCISE 7: Complete the following with either 1) since he did not have enough cash, he could not actually do it. Or: 2) he had no intention of drinking it.

a. He wanted only to buy a beer; . . .

b. He only wanted to buy a beer; . . .

"Only" is particularly tricky, since it also can function as an adjective, and could appear two other places. Complete the following with either: 1) the others were strictly whisky drinkers. Or: 2) he wasn't in the mood for turnip greens and chitlings.

c. Only he wanted to buy a beer; . . .

d. He wanted to buy only a beer; . . .

Explain the probable mislocation of the modifier in each of the following:

e. He told her that he wanted to get married frequently, but she paid little attention.

f. Holstering his revolver, Marshall Dillon pointed out that the robber had shot first, quite properly.

Other elements belong together also. Parallel phrases—phrases that play the same role in the sentence—should be grouped. For example, modifiers of the same word should be herded and not scattered: Running the gauntlet of the impatient customers' angry stares, staggering under the heavy tray of dishes, the young and inexperienced waiter made what haste he could to fill their orders. The two participial forms, *running* and *staggering,* both modify the waiter, as also do *young* and *inexperienced;* the sentence begins to fall apart if the running and the staggering are spread too far, leaving the dishes unsupported: Running the gauntlet of the impatient customers' angry stares, the young waiter made what haste he could, inexperienced, to fill their orders, staggering under the heavy tray of dishes.

EXERCISE 8: In the following exercises, insert the phrase into the sentence at the most appropriate point.

a. Add *wanting only her forgiveness* to: Dreading her rejection, he confessed to his fiancee that he had indeed taken the buxom barmaid home.

b. Add *in the subway* to: The dashing young executive met her quite by accident on his way home one afternoon. (Note that "quite by accident," "on his way home," and "one afternoon" all modify the verb "met.")

c. Add *which he privately thought improper* to: He left the couple kissing passionately since he wished to grind his coffee beans punctually.

One last word about where adjectives go. A brown frisky puppy and an old well-dressed man have one thing in common: their adjectives are out of normal order. The puppy's color and the man's age are more a part of what they are than the puppy's present behavior (frisking) or the man's current clothing (well-dressed). The puppy and the man will get tired some time later on today, and the puppy will settle down for a nap and the man will undress to go to bed. However, the puppy will still be brown and the man will still be old. In normal order, therefore, they will be called a frisky brown puppy and a well-dressed old man. In a series of adjectives, put beside the noun the ones most closely related to it.

That rule always applies. Put modifiers beside what they modify. -Ing at the beginning of a sentence trips up many a writer. Coming at the beginning of the sentence, such present participles always should modify the subject of the sentence. If they don't, whoopee! Dangling unsupported in mid-air at the front of the sentence, you will find that such modifiers don't work at all, at all.

EXERCISE 9: Rearrange the words in the following sentences to put the participial phrases beside what they modify:

a. Reaching slowly up from the grave, the calm was shattered by a groping hand.

b. Swinging her tail from side to side to dispel flies, the girl went through the gate into the pasture with the old mare ambling behind.

    c. Clanging away, the old man watched the streetcar as it made the turn into Fremish Street.

    d, e, f: Now redo the same three sentences, changing words and structure as needed, but keeping the same participial phrase at the beginning. You will have to make whatever word the phrase modifies into the subject; an opening participial phrase always modifies the subject.

    g, h: Now write two of your own that follow this last pattern.

Even when a participial phrase comes later than the beginning, put it beside what it modifies; and be sure what it modifies is in the same sentence, not just in your mind. A bridge player sat at a bridge table, dummy for one hand. (For those who don't play bridge, that means she simply watched and waited while the other three played.) The other three players were engrossed in the tightly fought battle of the cards, when she broke in, "You know, it's wonderful to be able to sit here without worrying about drombs bopping." The others, unfortunately, had not heard the plane in the distance; Bess, unfortunately, did not tell them what she was thinking before she said "drombs bopping." If she had, they might have understood that she meant it was nice not to have to worry about bombs dropping. Similar confusion clogs a sentence when a phrase modifies something present only in the writer's mind.

EXERCISE 10: Rewrite the following sentences, making sure that all of the phrases modify a word that is in the sentence.

Example: Driving through the country, the day was beautiful. Answer: As we drove through the country, the day was beautiful. Or: Driving through the country, we found the day beautiful.

    a. Similar confusion clogs such a sentence, modifying something present only in the writer's mind. (See the sentence before the exercise.)

    b. Cleaning up after the fatal stabbing of Jean-Paul Marat was not difficult, finding him in his bathtub.

    c. The arrest was made without difficulty, having drawn their six-shooters already and pulled their hat-brims lower on their brows.

    d. Overwhelmed by the difficulty of this assignment, it will be an awfully hard one to do.

    e. Trying to forgive her for the ring around his collar, the quarrel began.

    f. When not invited, I don't approve of gatecrashing.

Review Exercise: Review the chapter, making a list of rules that apply to word order.

Too many rules—that is, too many descriptive generalizations? You can relax from here to the end of the chapter, because all that remains is rules you can break.

Grammarians used to say a sentence shouldn't end with a preposition. Thus, they claimed that you should say not "What should I put it in?" but "In what should I put it?" The great master of English prose Winston Churchill, chided for ending a sentence with a preposition, is supposed to have replied that the rule "is a piece of errant pedantry up with which I shall not put." You want to use a preposition to end your sentences with? Go ahead and put it in.

Another vanishing rule stated that an infinitive should not be split. The infinitive is the verb form that states an action not restricted as to time, person, or quality of performance; more simply, an infinitive is *to + basic verb:* to chew, to spit, to be scolded, to apologize, to clean up, to forget, to spit again, to be hollered at, to flee. Splitting such an infinitive means putting a word or phrase—it has to be adverbial—between the *to* and the verb. You want to casually divide the verb from its *to?* Do. To joyfully enrich, to delightfully divide, to happily fork, to singingly separate may not work well always, but sometimes it can be the better way, as the divorcee said.

Theme Topic: Tell how you met a work of art (ballet, opera, concert—rock or classical, painting, art movie, play—TV or movie or stage) when things went wrong—perhaps the show flubbed, perhaps you didn't react right. OR Describe how an amateur made a mess (at sports, work, etc.) In either case, draw a conclusion, some meaning, from your story.

Crumple Page

This is a crumple page. Carefully detach and crumple at will.

9

Arranging Sentences within the Paragraph, Requiring Some Attention to a Wandering EEL and Achilles' Heel

social worker once told me of a feeble-witted woman who loved cleanliness and lived in filth. It was her own fault. She started every day to clean house, but always got so involved with the first little area she started on—one corner of the room to sweep, one chair or tabletop to dust—that she never got beyond that one little part of the whole job. She spent the whole day starting, and a filthy house, often even an unfed and dirty-diapered baby, was the result.

In writing, too, you need to keep an eye on the larger task. A sentence, for all that it "states a complete idea," nevertheless remains a sub-assembly within the whole assignment. The paragraph needs just as much careful consideration. So don't spend so long on words and sentences that you ignore the paragraph and the whole composition.

As far as order is concerned, paragraphs fall into two major categories: journey paragraphs and suitcase paragraphs.

Answer: Paragraph — Journey paragraphs have a built-in, almost inevitable order. They start at one place and go to another, and in order to get there, they have to go through the places in between.

This planet has not always been alive. Indeed, as Richard Overman[1] has recently reminded us, if we conceive the five billion years of the Earth's past as though recorded in ten volumes of five hundred pages each, so that each page records a million years, cellular life appears only somewhere around the eighth volume, about a billion years ago. The story of all the plants and animals of the Cambrian period occupies only the tenth volume, and of this, the first half is taken up with how plants became terrestrial and the amphibians emerged. Around page 440 of this 500-page book the reptiles reach the height of their development, and it is not until page 465 that their dominance is superseded by that of birds and warm-blooded animals. Finally, on page 499 of this tenth volume man appears. The last two words on the last page recount his story from the rise of civilization six thousand years ago until the present.[2]

---

[1]"A Christological View of Nature," *Religious Education* LXVI, January–February 1971, p. 37. (Cobb's note)

[2]John B. Cobb, Jr., *Is It Too Late? A Theology of Ecology* (Beverly Hills, California: Benziger, Bruce & Glencoe, Inc., 1972), p. 78.

Question: How do you reproduce a chart?   The principle on which the sentences in this paragraph are ordered is _____ (from the Greek word *chronos,* time). Like the hypothetical ten-volume history of the earth, the paragraph goes through events and epochs in the order of their actual occurrence. The paragraph simply could not begin with the appearance of man, continue with the height of reptile development, go on to the rise of civilization, leap back to the first appearance of cellular life, and then conclude with the dominance of birds and warm-blooded animals. That just isn't the way you get from the creation of the earth to your reading of this page.

Other kinds of journey paragraph, with their own appropriate ordering of sentences, include all chronological paragraphs, not only histories such as the above, but all paragraphs describing steps in a process, and narratives; cause and effect sequences; and paragraphs expounding logical arguments.

Suitcase paragraphs are quite different. Suitcase paragraphs have no built-in, almost inevitable order. Instead, they contain a collection of statements all related to a central idea, the topic sentence, in somewhat the way the clothes you pack are all related to you, but have no inevitable relationship to each other. Any order in a suitcase paragraph must be selected by you, the writer. When packing clothes, you can group things in several ways: warm clothes in one side, cool clothes in the other; or all socks together, all shirts together, all underwear together, all handkerchiefs together, all trousers together; or you could group by color—blue shirts, blue ties, and blue trousers together, brown shirts, brown ties, and brown trousers together, with appropriate color accents in hankies and socks. If, on the other hand, you don't bother at all, you will have a jumbled mess indeed, and the poor person who unpacks will have a lot of sorting to do.

Suppose you wish to write a paragraph describing John. You make a list of characteristics, and come up with these:

He loved fighting. He had red hair. He had black eyes. Women admired him. He worked in high-rise construction. He walked like a cat. He was strong. Men respected him.

Those are the individual items you need to arrange neatly in the suitcase. They can be arranged several ways. For example, you could arrange them according to the things different sexes notice, the things women notice in the first pile, the things men notice in the second:

Women admired John. The contrast between his flaming red hair and dark, almost black eyes drew their attention and whispered questions wherever he went. Those who knew him liked the joy with which he entered a fight; whether they would admit it or not, he stirred certain caveman instincts. Men, for their part, respected and even feared John. A high-rise construction worker, he walked like a cat. His casually selected clothes never seemed quite loose enough to conceal the thick bulge of his shoulders and biceps, the breadth of his chest.

Alternatively, you could arrange them according to a two-fold division: physical characteristics in one pile, people's reaction in another, ending with an attitude of John's own.

John was impressive. The contrast between his flaming red hair and his dark, almost black eyes made him conspicuous. Even his soft, cat-like walk could not make him inconspicuous. His casually selected clothes, too, never seemed quite loose enough to conceal the thick bulge of his shoulders and biceps, the breadth of his chest. People noticed him wherever he went. Women admired John, whispering questions to their companions. Whether they would admit it or not, he stirred in them certain caveman instincts. Men, for the most part, respected and even feared John. A high-rise construction worker, he entered fights joyfully.

Suitcase paragraphs can be packed several ways. Here is another suitcase paragraph:

(1) Rufus died yesterday. (2) Black, short-haired, with a white triangle on his chest, he was completely nondescript. (3) Even his size was medium, about twenty pounds. (4) If dogs ever held up banks, he could have done so with no fear that the tellers could describe him to the police afterwards; "sort of normal, you know, average," they would have had to say. (5) He looked like any Sport, or Prince, or Rover—except that we could pick him out immediately from two blocks away. (6) His ears had a certain perkiness, matched in his youth by his demeanor. (7) He used to prance on his hind legs in those days, greeting us when we came home, with stiff-legged jumps. (8) Guarding our front door, he barked only at strangers, wagging his tail politely at guests. (9) One afternoon, when he was three, a car broke his hip when he dashed in front of it to chase a motorcycle in the other lane. (10) After that he didn't prance. (11) But he had dignity. (12) He was patient and forgiving. (13) He died as he lived—quietly and undemandingly. (14) Rufus was one black mutt among thousands, undistinguished, unnoticeable, unskilled—and—irreplaceable.

The paragraph reads smoothly and makes perfect sense. Sentences 1 and 13 frame the paragraph with the statements of the dog's death, which provide the occasion for the tribute; sentence 14 is the topic sentence. Successively, his appearance (sentences 2, 3, 4, and 5), his behavior and deportment (sentences 6, 7, 8, 9, 10), and his personality (sentences 11 and 12) are described.

Here is another suitcase paragraph:

Black, short-haired, with a white triangle on his chest, he was completely nondescript. His ears had a certain perkiness, matched in his youth by his demeanor. He used to prance on his hind legs in those days, greeting us, when we came home, with stiff-legged jumps. One afternoon, when he was three, a car broke his hip when he dashed in front of it to chase a motorcycle in the other lane. After that he didn't prance. He looked like any Sport, or Prince, or Rover—except that we could pick him out immediately from two blocks away. Even his size was sort of medium, about twenty pounds. If dogs ever held up banks, he could have done so with no fear that the tellers could describe him to the police afterwards: "sort of normal, you know, average," they would have had to say. But he had dignity. Guarding our front door, he barked only at strangers, wagging his tail politely at guests. He was patient and forgiving. Rufus died yesterday. He died as he lived, quietly and undemandingly. Rufus was one black mutt among thousands, undistinguished, unnoticeable, unskilled—and irreplaceable.

In this paragraph, the death notice ceases to act as a frame, and sentences 1 and 13 are both put at the end. After an introductory sentence of description (sentence 2)—there must be some identification of what is being talked about—comes the description of behavior (sentences 6, 7, 9, 10); then appearance, with some rearrangement (sentences 5, 3, 4); and finally personality (sentences 11, 8, 12). Note that the import of sentence 8 shifts somewhat with context. Surrounded as at first by sentences 7 and 9, it seems to describe behavior; surrounded as here by sentences 11 and 12, it seems to characterize his dignity and patience.

Suitcases can be arranged several different ways. Partly, this flexibility comes from a choice of order (underwear in the top pocket or the middle pocket?); partly it comes from the regrouping of sentences (is 2 introductory or descriptive? is 8 behavior or personality?)

But there must be some principle of arrangement. Consider the following:

He died as he lived—quietly and undemandingly. Rufus died yesterday. Even his size was medium, about twenty pounds. If dogs ever held up banks, he could have done so with no fear that the tellers could describe him to the police afterwards; "sort of normal, you know, average," they would have had to say. One afternoon, when he was three, a car broke his hip when he dashed in front of it to chase a motorcycle in the other lane. After that he didn't prance. Rufus was one black mutt among thousands, undistinguished, unnoticeable, unskilled—and irreplaceable. But he had dignity. He looked like any Sport, or Prince, or Rover—except that we could pick him out immediately from two blocks away. Black, short-haired, with a white triangle on his chest, he was completely nondescript. He was patient and forgiving. Guarding our front door, he barked only at strangers, wagging his tail politely at guests. His ears had a certain perkiness, matched in his youth by his demeanor. He used to prance on his hind legs in those days, greeting us, when we came home, with stiff-legged jumps.

There are many ways to arrange a suitcase, but not all are good.

EXERCISE 1: Mark the following topics J for journey or S for suitcase, according to probable paragraph type.

    a. Getting from school to your home.

    b. The domino theory: abandoning Vietnam to the communists will lead to a communist take-over in southeast Asia.

    c. My friend Cuthbert—the noblest of them all.

    d. Differences between Communism and Democracy.

    e. What it is like to be poor.

    f. How to use a can-opener (the lever-action puncturing type sometimes called "church-key").

    g. The Catholic doctrine of Papal infallibility.

    h. The night the bed fell on grandpa.

    i. Things you don't want to know.

    j. Never trust anyone over thirty (or under thirty, or under sixteen).

EXERCISE 2: Cut out the following sentences and arrange them in the best order:

This went on for weeks.

The eel was discovered later in another tank in a distant part of the Gardens.

The eel took the whole thing quite calmly.

Every time he was put back into the tank, he would escape to the other one the same evening and he would be found there the next morning.

I have never seen eels on dry land myself, but I am sure that authentic instances of eel-wandering occur.

Finally the eel was permitted to remain permanently in the tank he so obviously preferred, and business went on very much as usual.

For instance, the escape of a large eel from a tank in the London Zoological Gardens some years ago occasioned a good deal of talk.[3]

EXERCISE 3: Do the same with this paragraph:

More specifically, it is about the wrath of Achilles, a Greek warrior who as an infant was held by the heel and dipped in the Styx by his mother.

The *Iliad* is not a poem about the ill.

By dunking him in this manner, she thought to make him invulnerable (if she didn't drown him), but clumsily left an unwashed place on his heel, where she was holding onto the little squirmer.

It is about Ilium, which is another name for Troy and not the new chemical added to a toothpaste.[4]

So far, I've been talking about ordering parts within the paragraph as though they were all free and equal. They aren't. One sentence in particular lords it over the rest, and by its location affects the paragraph's style more than any other sentence. That dominant sentence is, of course, the topic sentence.

Aristotle remarked of plots that every good one has a beginning, a middle, and an end. The same can be said of paragraphs. From those three locations you must choose the best one for your topic sentence.

Usually, you will not want to put your topic sentence in the middle. Middles are very big in sandwiches, but in writing even if they are not just a lot of bologna, they are at best small potatoes. The middle naturally has less emphasis than either beginning or end. Only in those rare cases where you don't care about a sentence, therefore, will you smother it between the appetizing beginning and the taste-lingering end. For example, in the paragraphs about Mexican soccer and caravaning, on p. 66, the authors cared more about the specific details than about what the details had in common. Usually, however, you will put your topic sentence either at the beginning or at the end.

Reread the last paragraph and, having found the topic sentence, answer the following question true or false: Is a topic sentence usually put at the beginning or end? [If you found another alternative to beginning *or* end, you

---

[3]Will Cuppy, *How to Become Extinct* (Garden City, New York: Garden City Books reprint edition 1951, by special arrangement with Rinehart & Co., Inc.), pp. 57–58.
[4]Richard Armour, *The Classics Reclassified* (New York: McGraw-Hill Book Company, Inc., 1960), p. 5.

are ready for multiple choice questions offering as answers: 1. the beginning. 2. the end. 3. both of the above.]

Here is the same anecdote three times. Which location of the topic sentence is most effective?

1. "What am I? I'm an orphan!" said great aunt Heruckle. She sat on the front porch on a summer evening and rocked, surrounded by her sons, her daughters, her nieces, her nephews, her grandsons, her granddaughters, her grandnieces, her grandnephews, and a few great grandchildren. "My mother is dead. My father is dead," she explained.

2. Great aunt Heruckle sat on the front porch on a summer evening, surrounded by her sons, her daughters, her nieces, her nephews, her grandsons, her granddaughters, her grandnieces, her grandnephews, and a few great grandchildren. "My mother is dead. My father is dead," she said, rocking back and forth. "What am I? I'm an orphan."

3. Great aunt Heruckle sat on the front porch on a summer evening and rocked, surrounded by her sons, her daughters, her nieces, her nephews, her grandsons, her granddaughters, her grandnieces, her grandnephews, and a few great grandchildren. "What am I? I'm an orphan," she said. "My mother is dead. My father is dead."

Undoubtedly, the one that puts the punch line "I'm an orphan" at the end tickles more than the others. Jokes and humorous anecdotes pre-eminently need to save their punch lines for the end. A joke that occupies a single paragraph usually is a sort of journey paragraph, on its way to the laugh. That laugh is the point of the joke and comes as near as anything to being the typical joke's topic sentence. Journey paragraphs often have the topic sentence at the end for just this reason: what matters about journeys usually is where you are going, not where you are leaving.

I am amazed to realize that I am still on the pole. My body writhes slowly to the left, and my feet come up to the crossbar. My body continues turning as the bar passes under my shins, knees, and thighs, and my body stops in a half-twist as the crossbar stands directly under my waist. At this point I lock my arms in a half-bent position, the pole begins its final slight bend. My waist is approximately three feet higher than my hands and well above the crossbar. The slight bend of the pole lowers my body four to six inches. I keep my arms locked in bent position as again the pressure mounts on my tight, quivering stomach muscles. As the pole becomes a straight line, I straighten my arms out keeping my head forward and down, my body arched into a parabola around the crossbar. I stiffen my arms, and the fingertips, tired and pained, become the only things supporting my weight on the pole. I push off with my stiff fingertips, pulling my elbows up, back, and over; I throw my head back as my weak fingers barely clear the bar. I let go of all tension and let my body fall easily, down, and backward—sinking into the soft white mass, seeing only the dark blue sky. Wait! Not only the dark blue sky, but also a crossbar lying across the tops of two standards up there in the heavens, quivering a bit perhaps, but not falling, not in a thousand years. The hundred or so people who have gathered around the pit rush in to pick me up as the masses in the stands exhale a roar. I look back at the pole lying over there alone, still, and I know what a marvelous monster it is to ride.[5]

The deferred topic sentence, which makes its appearance only at journey's end, sometimes puzzles the traveler who doesn't have a ticket in hand with a clearly marked destination. For this reason, such paragraphs often follow the example of the paragraph above that I asked you to reread, and put the topic sentence at beginning and end, both. Such restatement has the further advantage of stressing the focus of your paragraph, an additional emphasis.

Unlike journey paragraphs, suitcase paragraphs usually will have the topic sentence at the beginning. The sentences in a suitcase paragraph are radially unified, like the spokes of a wheel. The hub is the clearest place to start. You can go around the rim, one spoke at a time, but usually it's not quite as easy. The journey paragraph is serially unified, as each piece connects directly to the next; once started down the track, the reader follows easily. But in the suitcase paragraph, the reader may feel disoriented if he doesn't know why you are providing him with all the pieces you toss in his lap, and he won't know why (usually) until you give him the unifying idea, the topic sentence. The following paragraph is missing its topic sentence. After you have read the excerpt, write your own version of a topic sentence. The original is on the next page.

There were no flags hanging out of the windows, as there had been in all the towns along the way from Coutances. There were no improvised signs welcoming the Americans, and two Frenchmen who saw the jeep ducked into houses when Michael called to them.[6]

For another paragraph that is confusing without its topic sentence, here is one you have seen before:

In the naval-base city of Portsmouth, the clinic is in a large general hospital tucked behind a door marked "Dental Waiting Room." In East

---

[5]David E. Dubber, "Crossing the Bar on a Fiberglas Pole," D. L. Cook, J. H. Justus, W. E. Williams, eds., *The Current Voice* (Englewood Cliffs, N.J.: Prentice-Hall, Inc., 1966), p. 119.

[6]Irwin Shaw, *The Young Lions* (New York: Random House, 1948), p. 583.

London the center is in its own building on the grounds of a mental hospital. In the Denmark Hill area it's part of the hospital's general outpatient department, and if you visit St. Giles Clinic in the Church of England Community Center you are reminded of an Alec Guinness movie. Dr. James H. Willis, a young psychiatrist, holds court, resplendent in white medical coat, in a lecture hall where he sits behind a large wooden table flanked by two pianos and a bass fiddle. He took refuge behind these church walls after neighborly people prevented him from occupying a newly constructed clinic, because they believed that his commuting addicts would infect their children.[7]

If you didn't remember the topic sentence, could you write it? The fact that the topic is the difference between the physical facilities makes seeing the unifying idea very hard; but when you are warned in advance, the problem vanishes: "Physical facilities also vary greatly."

Sometimes, a suitcase paragraph—like some journey paragraphs—will double its topic sentences, with one at each end. The reminder helps (as it does with the journey) when the paragraph contains a welter of details. This one casts its first topic sentence as a question:

Now, what is a bughouse square? A bughouse square is a public street-intersection or mall or park in a large city where gregarious, imaginative, exhibitionistic, and autocompulsive "ism" peddlers, agitators, soapboxers, folk evangelists, teachers, showmen, faddists, cultists, cranks, crackpots, dreamers, and self-proclaimed messiahs congregate to impress one another and to display their wares. These performers attract a large number of disciples, camp-followers, hecklers, "wise-guys," honest inquirers, and humble seekers. There is always present a large number of the skeptical and the disputatious. And there is invariably a sprinkling of unemployed, hobos, fey proletariat, beatniks, and the more robustious and less fastidious of the Bohemians. In short, a really first-class bughouse square is a bit of skid row, carnival, evangelistic revival, poor man's town hall, and people's university rolled into one.[8]

Sometimes, a paragraph may seem to have no topic sentence at all; or perhaps any one of several may seem equally qualified for the post of honor at the head of the paragraph. If there really is no topic sentence stated, assuming the paragraph is any good at all, then it will be clearly implied (Paragraphs describing John's physical appearance usually don't need a topic

---

[7]Edgar May, "Drugs Without Crime," p. 62.

[8]William G. Carleton, "The Passing of Bughouse Square," *The Antioch Review* (Fall, 1960).

Missing topic sentence: "There was something wrong about the town."

sentence stating, "This is John's physical appearance.") or else context will provide the necessary unifying information.

But although it sometimes may be difficult to pick out topic sentences when reading, don't omit them from your own paragraphs. Few things contribute more to clarity than the habit of stating a precise topic sentence for every paragraph. An unnecessary topic sentence may be a little obvious, but like lifeboats and motors, too many is better than too few. ("Your motor's missing!" the friend exclaimed, looking under the little car's front hood. "Oh, that's all right," said the Beetle owner, "I've got a spare in the rear.") With a topic sentence fore and aft, your paragraphs will never lack drive.

Topic: (1) Write a paragraph describing either an acquaintance, a relative, a friend, or a teacher. Then add a very short paragraph explaining why you ordered the sentences as you did.

(2) Describe some physical process (housekeeping, sports, machine operation) you are familiar with. One paragraph.

10

The Alpha and Omega of Arranging Paragraphs in the Essay: How to Start, How to Finish; How to Outline

merica appears to be the only country in the world where love is a national problem."[1]

Do you want to read on? I did. That sentence embodies one of the cardinal rules of arrangement: start off running. That principle applies to paragraphs and to whole essays. It reflects the natural emphasis of position: beginnings are important. Any essay or composition, therefore, must begin strongly to arouse the interest of the reader; for the reader assumes that the opening is typical. If you can convince the reader in your very first paragraph that your work is interesting, that first impression will tend to stay with him and keep him going through any unavoidable dry spells.

In a somewhat different vein, an essay by George Orwell begins: "As the corpse went past the flies left the restaurant table in a cloud and rushed after it, but they came back a few minutes later."[2]

Hit first, before your reader runs away.

Of course, your boffo beginning must have something to do with the rest of the essay. Neither of the opening sentences quoted would be suitable for a discussion of the relative merits of the metric system versus the British Imperial system of liquid and dry measurement. Sales' topic is in fact American attitudes towards love; Orwell's topic heavily stresses dirt, poverty, and commonplace death. But that is a matter of content, and organization concerns us here. Let us take content for granted, and look simply at the order in which the pieces are to be put.

The opening of an essay should be

1. interesting,
2. representative.

Interest is aroused by surprise: the unexpected, the startling. Orwell's flies and casual corpse arouse interest for this reason. If you find an unusual statement in your essay at any time during the process of writing it (preliminary outline, rough draft, final outline, final draft), consider putting it up front. It's what's up front that counts, as the drillmaster said, calling cadence for the straggling recruits.

---

[1]Raoul de Roussy de Sales, "Love in America," *Atlantic Monthly*, May, 1938.
[2]George Orwell, "Marrakech," in *Such, Such Were the Joys*, (New York: Harcourt Brace & World, 1953).

Unfortunately, at least as far as startling openings go, most student writing is not littered with fly-blown corpses. Interest most often must be aroused by less startling openings.

Interest can also be aroused by importance. Much of the interest of Sales' opening derives from the significance of his topic. The idea that love is a *national problem* startles, of course, because most of us tend to think of love not as a problem but as a blessing, an opportunity, a joy. The surprise here comes not from the unexpectedness of the topic as such, but from the unusual predication made about the topic. But the real interest attaches to *love* being a national problem. Why? Because, love, although not unusual, is important. Love itself just naturally arouses interest.

Some of the writing assignments you handle will deal with important topics. To arouse interest, get those topics into the beginning of your composition.

Indeed, even if your topic doesn't concern inflation, war, taxes, race relations, religion, or some other topic of national and world importance, within your paper your topic is the most important thing you are writing about. Once again, therefore, and this time in all cases, get your topic up front. Stating the topic at the beginning of the paper starts the paper off running; it fires the biggest and most important gun you have; and thereby it arouses interest.

The opening of an essay should

1. state the essay's topic, because that is interesting.

2. be representative.

Number Two follows automatically as a consequence of Number One. By announcing the topic at the beginning of his paper, the writer thereby also makes that beginning representative of the rest of the paper. Anybody reading the beginning knows what it's all about.

That matters enough to be worth stating, even if it does come automatically from beginning with the topic. The reader should not be in doubt of what it is you write about. (The advanced student of poetry will identify that sentence as an iambic tetrameter couplet.) Few experiences disconcert the reader so much as discovering halfway through an essay that the author doesn't really care about fur-bearing trout at all, and is instead analyzing bureaucratic inefficiency all the way from the fish and game warden to the supervisor of sewage and waste disposal. The reader need not know exactly what you are going to say; but he must know what you are talking about. Anyone set on eating an apple will be shocked if halfway through he finds himself eating protein, and will probably regard that protein, whatever its actual parentage, as a worm at the core. He will feel like the lady who discovered halfway through her salad a half a roach in her bowl. People like to know what they are ingesting; tell them.

The opening of an essay should

1. state the essay's topic, because that is interesting.
2. state the essay's topic, because that is representative.

Even though the title states the topic, the beginning of the essay should state it too. Some readers have a very short memory. Don't assume that just because your title names your topic your reader will remember it as he starts the essay proper. As a matter of fact, most readers don't really pay much attention to a title. (What is the title of this chapter? this section? this book?) A title, like a cover, is something you take off and set aside before getting down to it. Therefore, the title doesn't count as a statement of topic—nor, of course, should it be referred to by a pronoun such as "this" or "it."

A Review of *King Lear* by Shakespeare

He wrote it when he was feeling quite depressed, the critics say, and it certainly depressed me. As a matter of fact, I prefer a more robust play, like *King Henry IV*.

That sounds less like the beginning of a review of *King Lear* than like a review of *King Henry IV*. The same principle applies to answering test questions. If your answer is as long as a full paragraph, don't assume the question. Instead, work it into your answer. Suppose the question is:

II. Write a twenty-minute essay explaining the economic causes of the Civil War.

Bad Answer (written in a blue book, out of sight of the question itself): There are three. First, southern plantation owners feared the loss of cheap slave labor.

Good Answer (written in a similar blue book, but putting the absent question in the answer): There are three economic causes of the Civil War. First, southern plantation owners feared . . .

As an aside concerning content, we note that when you have announced a topic, whether for the whole essay or in a topic sentence for the individual paragraph, you must write on that topic and not flit like a butterfly toward every topical flower that lies along your path. Do not, for example, open with the statement, "Few people understand the nature of true love," continue with an account of how you felt about that cute girl or boy who lived in the apartment under yours in Poughkeepsie, and then spend a whole paragraph on Indian place-names as part of the American heritage.

Reread the opening sentences quoted above (they are in context complete paragraphs) by Sales and Orwell. Both are good openings. They differ, however, in one respect. Sales' sentence is very general. It announces his topic, what he is writing about; and it states his thesis, the point he intends to urge. So doing, it is the generalization which the rest of the essay supports. Orwell's sentence, however, is very particular. Not only does it not state his thesis, but it doesn't even announce his topic. What it does is to represent his topic.

As a sub-principle, therefore, we can add the possibility of beginning with a striking detail. That detail, however, ought immediately to be related to the topic of the essay as a whole. Really, what this amounts to is a re-definition of "the opening of an essay." The opening includes not simply the first sentence, and not simply the first paragraph—if that paragraph is only a small fraction of the essay's total bulk. The topic need not be stated in the very first sentences, especially if that first sentence contains interesting details, specific facts. Such specifics can serve as an introduction to the announcement of topic that itself introduces the essay as a whole.

> Jose Iberio, age six, always leaves a clean plate. His mother never has to tell him to finish his beans; with spoon or breadcrust, finger, or tongue, he scrapes and wipes his plate until it shines. The reason is simpler than neatness, or cleanliness, or obedience. Jose is hungry.
>
> Jose is one of two thousand million people. . .

An essay that begins thus, clearly has as its topic poverty and the consequent slow starvation that afflicts two thirds of the world's population. The opening paragraph introduces that topic with a representative detail. The concrete actualities of life are what sustain interest.

A topic is not the same as a thesis. A topic is what you talk about; a thesis is the most important thing you say about your topic. "What did the minister preach about this morning, Humphrey?" "Sin." (That is the topic.) "And what did he say about sin?" "He was against it." (That's the thesis.) Sometimes, like Raoul de Sales, you will state your thesis at the very beginning, as you introduce your topic. But not always.

Having begun with the beginning, let's leap to the ending.

Final paragraphs should state (or restate) the composition's thesis. The last paragraph lingers in the reader's mind like the pleasant after-taste of a sweet dessert. Since your thesis is your main idea—the point of your essay— since it is what you want to say about your topic, you want the reader to remember it. So remind him as he leaves you.

George Grella ends his essay "James Bond: Culture Hero" with this paragraph stating the thesis of the essay:

> Perhaps centuries from now, scholars will trace assiduously those references to Yardley soap, Kent brushes, Lanvin perfume, Sanitized toilet seats. Perhaps there will be a variorum Fleming, and "Fleming men" as there are "Milton men." Theses may be written on the epicene role of M, clearly a father figure (yet why unmarried? and that maternal sounding initial is rather damning). For James Bond is the Renaissance man in mid-century guise, lover, warrior, connoisseur. He fights the forces of darkness, speaks for the sanitary achievements of the age, enjoys hugely the fruits of the free enterprise economy. He lives the dreams of countless drab people, his gun ready, his honor intact, his morals loose: the hero of our anxiety-ridden, mythless age: the savior of our culture.[3]

Most probably, the thesis will appear earlier in the essay, often at the very beginning, where you announce the topic. In any event, it must be stated at the end.

If the thesis is complicated, with several parts, the end is the place to summarize it. But state it, state it, state it.

Initial and final paragraphs occupy the places that naturally get the most attention. Fill them with the things you want attended to.

The middle of an essay resembles the main course of a meal. It is the meat and potatoes of the composition. In the middle you do what you are going to do, prove what you are going to prove, say what you are going to say. Here are three outlines for the introduction, body, and conclusion of any paper:

    I. I am going to do X.
   II. X.
  III. I have done X.

or:

    I. I am going to prove that _____.
   II. Proof that _____.
  III. I have proved that _____.

---

[3]George Grella, "James Bond: Culture Hero," first printed in *The New Republic*, 1964, Harrison-Blaine, Inc. Reprinted: D. L. Cook, J. H. Justus, W. E. Williams, eds., *The Current Voice* (Englewood Cliffs, N.J.: Prentice-Hall, Inc., 1966) pp. 32–36.

or:

> I. I am going to say so-and-so.
> II. So-and-so.
> III. I have said so-and-so.

Repetition is one of the basic principles of organization. What ought to be repeated is the main idea, the thesis. It deserves emphasis, and repetition emphasizes. It needs to be understood, and restatement clarifies. Of course, repetition can be carried too far. The first year I taught, I received a theme on compulsory chapel (then in effect) which was exactly one hundred and sixteen words long—it was, indeed, a single paragraph—but contained the phrase "those hard uncomfortable benches" no less than four times. That student certainly communicated to me that his chapel experiences were far from spiritual. Excessive repetition bores or amuses, at the writer's expense in either case; but adequate repetition strengthens a paper. Indeed, illustrative details are in one sense another way of stating the point you wish to make.

With introduction and conclusion established, what is to be done with the middle? It goes in the middle, of course; but what is done within the middle? Meat first, or potatoes first? Answer: Not necessarily. That is, good organization may put meat first, or it may put potatoes first; but it does not necessarily have to do either one, for it may alternate between them.

Which is best depends on the particular circumstances of each writing. The ideal organization of the body of a paper depends on who is writing what for whom. That is the principle of relativity as it applies to organizing whole compositions. The best order depends on the writer, the specific work he is producing, and the audience he is writing for.

But there must be some organization. Meals that consist entirely of minced stew, ground and pulverized until all the ingredients are an indistinguishable mush, don't appeal for long. Every good essay, like every good meal, has parts. Clear organization makes those parts seeable as separate things.

For example: Two things, alpha and beta, are to be compared. How to organize the comparison? (The introduction will state that you are going to compare them; the conclusion will state that you have compared them, probably summarizing.) There are two basic organizations of such a comparison. You may describe each completely, or you may alternate. An outline of this part of the paper might thus be either:

> II. Comparison
>   A. alpha
>   1. xxx
>   2. yyy
>   3. zzz

　　　B. beta
　　　　1. xxx
　　　　2. yyy
　　　　3. zzz

or:

　II. Comparison
　　　A. xxx
　　　　1. alpha
　　　　2. beta
　　　B. yyy
　　　　1. alpha
　　　　2. beta
　　　C. zzz
　　　　1. alpha
　　　　2. beta

Sometimes a paper that argues a point falls neatly into two parts, the statement of a problem and the solution of that problem. One short book (Cobb's *Is It Too Late? A Theology of Ecology,* quoted earlier) follows such an order, as the table of contents—a simplified outline—shows. "Part One: The Need for a New Vision . . . Part Two: The New Vision We Need." Part One describes the ecological problem; part two offers the theological solution. Whenever an assignment can be handled as the solution to a problem, the most logical organization will almost always consist of two parts: first, present a description of that problem; second, offer the solution to the problem. Somewhere along the way you may dispose of false solutions, but where will depend on your preference, your specific statements, and your audience.

Outlining provides you, the writer, (and, at his request, the teacher who will criticize how effectively you have done what you intended) with an easily manipulated mock-up of the finished product, a scale miniature, as it were. Changes can be made in the trial model much more cheaply than they can be in the final product itself. To organize a paper well, therefore, outline. Topic outlines, which consist of phrases, serve adequately if you know what you are saying about the topics written before you; but sentence outlines, which consist of clauses, make it much easier to be sure that what you are saying belongs together.

Consider this short outline:

Title: Communication Today

I. Mass Media: Communication by Images

   A. Pictures that Move
      1. Movies
      2. Television

   B. Stationary Pictures
      1. Cartoons
      2. Photographs

II. Mass Media: Communication by Written Words

   A. Books

   B. Newspapers

   C. Magazines
      1. pulp
      2. slick

III. Interpersonal Communication

   A. With Family

   B. With Friends

If the paper actually written on this apparently reasonable outline went as follows, the instructor would have apoplexy:

Communication today is very difficult.

The mass media communicate by images. In the early fifties, average weekly attendance at movies slumped from a previous high of 47,000,000 to a low of less than 20,000,000. Television makes use of electrical energy, in on or off pulses, which is "scanned" by an electron beam in horizontal rows to produce a picture on a sensitive tube screen. Cartoons like *Terry and the Pirates* often are continued after the original creator dies or, as in the case of Milton Caniff, goes on to other work like *Steve Canyon*. A good photograph, however, should have stopping power.

Most publishing houses are sustained by one or two best-selling authors; the rest of their books make no money. Newspapers can no longer be the first with the news, since the advent of television. An interesting phenomenon among magazines is the trend toward respectability, followed first by *Life* and then by *Esquire*, which have increasingly emphasized thoughtful content and de-emphasized pin-ups. But, first consider pulp magazines. They are made of cheap paper with a low cloth content. The so-called "slick" magazines are much more expensive.

Different authorities suggest many different causes of the so-called "generation gap" with all that it implies for communication between parent and child. As for communication with friends, T.V. commercials imply that if you drink the right brand of coffee, you will chat more and make more friends.

As you can see, modern communication is very complex.

The topic outline makes sense; the individual sentences in the paper make sense, when taken separately; but the combination of sentences does not make a coherent theme. They follow the topic outline, which is reasonable. But because they say such unrelated things about those topics, chaos is come again.

Generally speaking, if you follow the seven-step process suggested in Part I of this book (1. brainstorming; 2. preliminary outline; 3. rough draft; 4. final outline; 5. final draft; 6. final copy; 7. proofreading), the rough outline can be a topic outline, but the final outline should be a sentence outline.

A few last words, about the mechanics of outlining. The usual labels for divisions, in decreasing importance, are capital roman numerals (I, II), capital letters (A, B), arabic numerals (1, 2), lower case letters (a, b), arabic numerals in parentheses ((1), (2)), and lower case letters in parentheses ((a), (b)). Any further subdivisions and your outline is too elaborate for utility; even the last two, using parentheses, will rarely be necessary. A typical outline pattern thus might go:

```
I. A.
   B.
II.
   A.
      1.
      2. a.
         b.
             (1)
             (2)
   B.
      1.
      2.
      3.
   C.
III.
```

with appropriate topics or sentences following each letter and number. Avoid too few or too many subdivisions. Too few is one. A subdivision comes from dividing, from cutting into parts. An apple cannot be cut in one; it must be cut at least in two. What constitutes too many parts can't be counted quite so easily, but at least one psychological study showed that people cannot grasp more than five items as individuals; many people have trouble with more than three. So keep the divisions down in number, either finding some way of grouping topics or treating them as a list.

In reviewing any outline, remember that your organizational goal is to put together what belongs together in an order that makes sense.

A Bestiary for Student Writers.
I. The Australian Jackrabbit

The Australian jackrabbit inhabits grassy plains, rich with tall grasses, grasses taller than the jackrabbit. A fast-moving animal, the Australian jackrabbit cannot see where he is going as he rushes through the grass. Occasionally, however, he stops and leaps straight up, looking rapidly from side to side to see where he has arrived. The plains-watcher thus sees him not at all, until suddenly a long-eared head pops up and swivels rapidly from side to side, before dropping once more from view. Those unfamiliar with his habits find that waiting for his next appearance—where will he be?—generates considerable suspense.

*MORAL:*_____

Topic: Write an essay that defines and classifies either different kinds of love *or* the major problems in America today. Add a short paragraph at the end justifying your ordering of paragraphs.

Part Four: THE WRITING—Connecting Parts

II

Prefixes–Words–
Suffixes, plus a Whole
Host of Tough Fixes:
Connecting Parts
within Words

onnections count for a lot. If your daddy's rich and your ma is good-lookin', then the song is probably right; probably you don't need to cry. This section analyzes how to get good connections into your writing, even if it was born without them.

Start with letters; the following chapters will look at connecting words into sentences and sentences into paragraphs, paragraphs into essays. Arranging letters in the right order means good spelling. In some cases, though, not arranging as such, but *connecting* affects spelling. Many words are formed by combining pre-existing units.

The German language enjoys this word-building process very freely. When Wagner decided that opera should be a blend of music, poetry, painting (scenery), and such other arts (dance, for one) as might from time to time be fitting, he coined a single word for the result: gesammtkunstwerk. Literally: together-art-work. English compound words don't stand out so clearly as compounds to an English-speaker as German compounds do for a German-speaker, because English words hide behind Latin roots, whereas German compounds just push German words together. Thus, a German unter-see-boot is an English sub-marine.

English, partly a Germanic language (its Anglo-Saxon heritage), builds compounds too, although rarely with more than two parts. For example: prizewinner, housemaid, repairman. Such compounds virtually never present a spelling problem. They come from two words which are combined so often that they come to have a single meaning and at last are written as one word; no spelling change occurs. Be a little careful, though (care + full), or you will be tearful (tear + full) and in a handful (hand + full) of cases your spelling will be awful (awe + full).

Affixes, however, often affect spelling. A unit that attaches to a word is called an affix. Few sights are more pitiable than that of a bedraggled, wretched word, creeping about the remote shadows of indifferent sentences, muttering with increasing hysteria, "I need affix!" Perhaps one sight is more pitiable: the word that finally manages to get his affix, but can't hook it in right.

A miscellany of affixes:

a-	arise, aboard, amoral
in-	inequality, incomplete, insight

ex-	export, excommunicate, ex-wife
post-	postoperative, post-mortem, postgraduate
co-	cooperate, coauthor, cohabit
contra-	contraband, contraceptive, contradiction
pre-	predigested, prepay, prewar
re-	reevaluate, rebuild, return

and a few more:

-able	workable, shirkable
-tion	prostitution, institution
-ing	running, dying, molding
-ed	wanted, battered, died
-s	books, sees, mothers
-er	killer, boaster, seeker
-ness	kindness, hardness, badness
-less	eyeless, hopeless, armless

Affixes fall into two categories—prefixes and suffixes. Prefixes are added at the beginning of a word, whereas suffixes are added at the _____ of a word. The list in the preceding paragraph began with prefixes and ended with suffixes. The *-fix* in *affix, prefix,* and *suffix* means *attach;* the *a-* in affix means *to* or *on* (with an extra *f* to hold it in place); the *pre-* in *prefix* means *in front, before;* the _____ in suffix means *underneath, at the bottom* (as in _____*-marine;* the *b* has changed to *f* in *suffix*).

Who cares? You do, if you want to spell well. (That's a pair of rhymes in one sentence.) When you attach an affix, particularly the ones that come at the end (suffixes), the spelling of the basic word sometimes changes.

Following are groups of words to which suffixes are added. In each group, the basic word behaves according to a rule. What the rule is, or how it applies, depends on the letters at the *end* of the basic word. It depends on such things as long or short vowel sound, whether a syllable is accented when pronounced, and vowel-consonant pattern. Sometimes, the way the rule applies depends simply on what the particular suffix is.

EXERCISE 1:

Group A. pity + es = pities
pity + able = pitiable
glory + ous = glorious

dry + est = driest
pretty + er = prettier
multiply + ed = multiplied

Group B. pity + ing = pitying
dry + ing = drying

Group C. coy + est = coyest
joy + ous = joyous
portray + ed = portrayed
portray + able = portrayable
survey + ed = surveyed
survey + ing = surveying
survey + or = surveyor

a. What do the basic words in A, B, and C all have in common? Make a list of more words like these.

b. How does the spelling of the root word change in A when the suffix is added?

c. Are the suffixes in A the same as those in B?

d. How do the basic words in A differ from those in C? Make a list of words like those in C. Make a separate list of words like those in A. Divide the list you made as step a, above, into C-words and A-words.

e. State the rules governing when and how the basic word changes.

A young man vacationed on the run, traveling great distances. A raise made a big new camping trailer possible, so he bought the biggest he could afford, hitched it up, and headed west. The second day he glanced casually in his rear view mirror and saw to his horror that the trailer was not three feet behind him, but four. As he watched, the distance slowly increased. One and a half tons of blind, pilotless vehicle, representing a year's raise and liability for the rest of his life's earnings, were wandering down the road behind him at sixty miles an hour.

Now see if you can figure out how to hook up these suffixes better than he hooked up his trailer:

EXERCISE 2

Group D. occur + ing = occurring
admit + ed = admitting
rid + ing = ridding
bid + able = biddable
hot + er = hotter
red + est = reddest
prefer + ed = preferred

Group E. fail + ing = failing
heal + ed = healed
peel + ed = peeled
fool + ish = foolish

Group F. hot + ly = hotly
red + ness = redness
hat + less = hatless

Group G. offer + ed = offered
bluster + ing = blustering
madden + ing = maddening
prefer + ence = preference

a. What do all of the basic words in D, E, F, and G have in common? (If you have the right answer, you will know why these words don't appear: fall, bundle, request.) Make a list of similar words.

b. What change in the spelling of the basic words in D do the suffixes require? Do the basic words change in E, F, or G?

c. How do the words in E differ in pronunciation from the words in D? How do they differ in spelling? Make a list of similar words, pulling from your list in *a* all words that belong here.

d. How do the suffixes in Group F differ from the suffixes in D, E, and G?

e. How does the pronunciation of the words in Group G differ from the pronunciation of the words in Group D? What syllable is accented? Make a short list of similar words, pulling from your list in *a* all words that belong here.

f. State the rules governing when and how the root word changes.

Did you make it? So did the young man; he slowed down gradually, staying just in front of the trailer, which miraculously enough ran the same straight line you followed in these exercises before coming to a safe halt and a new understanding of how things hook.

A Bestiary for Student Writers
II. The Remora

The remora, or sharksucker, comes modestly sized, like a trout. A saltwater fish, the remora's distinguishing physical feature is his head. Flat and slanted slightly downward toward the nose, the upper surface of the remora's head is a suction cup. It looks like a small rubber washboard or the ridged heel of a shoe. Attaching itself firmly to the

*underside of a shark's chin, the remora lives on the food
driblets from the shark's jaws. It cannot survive when un-
attached.*

MORAL:_____

EXERCISE 3: Here's another group of words and the suffixes that sometimes
change their spelling, sometimes don't:

Group H.   wade + ed = waded
            pile + ing = piling
            ride + er = rider
            brace + ing = bracing
            replace + ing = replacing
            outrage + ed = outraged
            invite + ing = inviting
            desire + ous = desirous
            love + able = lovable
            note + ably = notably
            brave + est = bravest

Group J.   replace + ment = replacement
            care + less = careless
            peace + ful = peaceful
            love + ly = lovely

     a. What do all of the basic words in H and J have in common? Make
a short list of such words.

     b. What is the effect on spelling when the suffixes are added in H?

     c. How are the suffixes in Group J different from those in Group H?
(Hint: What letters do they start with?)

     d. How is the effect of adding the suffixes in Group J different from
the effect in Group H?

Group K.   courage + ous = courageous
            replace + able = replaceable
            bridge + able = bridgeable
            outrage + ous = outrageous
            trace + able = traceable
            police + able = policeable

Group L.   encourage + ing = encouraging
            replace + ing = replacing
            police + ed = policed

police + ing = policing
race + er = racer
nice + est = nicest

e. What do the basic words in K and L have in common beside their very last letter?

f. How is the effect of adding the suffixes in K different from the effect in L?

g. Which group seems not to follow the rule for Group H?

h. How are the suffixes in K different from the suffixes in L?

j. The pronunciations of the letters g and c are affected by the letters that follow. Pronounce these words: *game, ago, got, gun*—but *age, giant;* pronounce *car, core, cunning*—but *ace, icing*. Pronounce these words: raga, rage, raging, Mr. Rago, raygun. What two ways do you pronounce the g's? Now suppose they were spelled differently; how would you pronounce the g's if the words were spelled this way: ragea or ragia, ragae or ragoe or rague, ragaing or ragoing or raguing, Rageo, or Ragio, raygeun or raygiun. Now give a reason based on pronunciation for what happens when you add the suffixes in group J to the basic words in that group.

All of these exercises deal with suffixes, because suffixes change spelling in the most regular way found in English. You are entitled to find that depressing if you noticed that *pay-paid, say-said,* and *lay-laid* are all exceptions to the rule governing group C. But take heart. Those are the only three. And if stated accurately, the rule for group D has *no*—count them: zero— exceptions.

Prefixes involve spelling changes too, but usually it is the prefix that changes, not the basic word. A very common one that changes spelling as a chameleon changes color to make itself blend with the ground it sits on is the prefix *in-. In-* means *no* in some way or other (not, without, or just about the same as two other prefixes, *un-* and *non-*): independence, invisible, infinite. But *in* adapts to the first letter of the word it hangs on:

in + balance = imbalance
in + legible = illegible
in + moral = immoral
in + potent = impotent
in + relevant = irrelevant

Prefixes get even more complicated. Not only do they change forms,

they also change meanings. At least, some of them mean more than one thing.
QUIZ: If incredible means not credible, what does each of these mean:

1. inflammable
2. ingrown

The prefix *in-* means not only "not," but also *in* as the opposite of *out* (as
in *ingrown*) and also at times just about nothing (as in *inflammable*, which
means the same as *flammable*.)

And not only do prefixes change forms and meanings, but there are
many different prefixes which mean the same thing. For example, *in-* as a
negative means the same as *un-* and *non-*.
QUIZ: If *not sane* means *insane*, what does each of the following mean:

1. not sure
2. not sense

There are also prefixes quite different from the remora (sharksucker).
Remora-like prefixes cannot survive alone; they are bound to the words they
precede. But other prefixes are free, and also serve as words.
Under is one such.

EXERCISE 4: Add the free prefix *under* to as many of the following words
as you can:

Don't estimate or value ground newspapers, which, I stand, take to
cut and mine the wearing of clothes, garments, shirts, and shorts.

The most common ending[1] of all in English is the -s (or -es) which makes
nouns plural (one hat, two hats) and makes verbs—guess what?—singular (in
the third person; all of them run, he alone runs).

Verbs that inflect irregularly have already been discussed (in Chapter
4); nouns that inflect irregularly, specifically that form irregular plurals,
deserve a little space, since all mans, womans and childs will meet an irregular
plural sooner or later. A team of oxen, a flock of sheep, or a gaggle of geese
may cross your path if you wander as far as the farm. Those come to us from
Anglo-Saxon. A host of others come to us from Latin and Greek, as all alumni
and alumnae know, whatever the radii of their travels and however many
phenomena they encounter or data they collect. Too long a list to memorize
as such, they are learned by following the techniques of Chapter 6.

---

[1]Not really a suffix, but an inflection; see the next chapter, under "Case."

For the rest, add *-s* or *-es* depending on how the word's plural is pronounced (if you don't know, ask a friend or go back to Chapter 6). If all you do at the end of the word is hiss like that gaggle of geese or snore like a cartoon character's zzz, add -s. Since most plurals are formed this way, a roomful of plurals seems a sibilant set.

EXERCISE 5: Make every noun plural (with any necessary adjustments):
When the band left, the boy left his shoe under the piano in the room by the stair.

If, in contrast, at the end of a word, you buzz without a *b*, making the syllable *-uz* or *-iz*, the plural is spelled *-es*. (If the *e* is already there, you don't need to add one.)

EXERCISE 6: Make every noun plural (adjusting other words as needed:
After running in a daze the maze of seeking a raise, the lush in a bush took an ax and broke a latch of a church, struck a match in a batch, and put a hex on sex.

Some other words are fancier; a number of *-o* words add *-es;* some *-fe* carry the hum of the plural "-z" sounds (voiced *s*) back to the *f* and make it a *v* (*v* is a voiced *f, f* is an unvoiced *v*); and, of course, the *consonant-y* words follow the rule you have already defined for group A.

EXERCISE 7: Make every noun plural (adjusting other words as needed):
"If a housefly lands on that tomato," said the wife, "I'll take his life with a knife," but our hero zoomed from the sky to a potato, and the lady of the family let the little hobo go, to end our story happily.

If you liked the gaggle of geese, how about a pride of lions? The book *An Exaltation of Larks*[2] explores such terms, no longer as common as they were in the middle ages. Such special names for groups of particular kinds of animals may be extended indefinitely. Try some yourself.
QUIZ: If the plural of *louse* is *lice,* and the plural of *mouse* is *mice,* what is the plural of *spouse?*

---

[2] James Lipton, *An Exaltation of Larks, or The Venereal Game* (New York: Grossman Publishers, Inc., 1968).

Crumple Page

This is a crumple page. Carefully detach and crumple at will.

12
Connecting Words within Sentences: Being a Manual on How to Attach Words to Phrases, Phrases to Clauses, And Clauses to Each Other by Means of Such Handy Devices As Conjunctions, Apposition, Relative Pronouns, Parallelism...

140

onnections matter, as the toe-bone said to the foot-bone, who passed
it on. Those dry bones just won't walk around if they're not connected. In the previous section, we looked at arrangements; this
section concerns connections.

Sometimes order doesn't matter. The red and blue hat can hardly be
distinguished from the blue and red hat. One plus two equals two plus one.
Even when there is a verb involved order does not always matter greatly,
if it's a linking verb. "John is Mary" and "Mary is John" are compatible and
overlapping statements, even if somewhat different. But the connectors always
count. One plus two is not the same as one minus two; a red *or* blue hat is
not a red *and* blue hat. "Is it a boy or a girl?" gasped the expectant father.
"No," said the nurse, and the poor man fainted before she could tell him he
had twins.

Words can be combined into phrases, clauses, and sentences.

A phrase is any group of words that belongs together and is not a clause.
Examples: The old purple hat of my grandfather . . . to have loved and lost
. . . the fear of the Lord . . . would never have believed . . . brandishing a
blood-dripping two-headed axe of the Minoan sort . . . beyond the last abyss
of despair.

A clause is a group of words containing the basic subject-verb pattern,
stating an action.

Some clauses are complete sentences. "You see the whites of their eyes."

Clauses that begin with some connectors (such as subordinating conjunctions) are not complete sentences and must be joined to other clauses.
"Until you see the whites of their eyes." (The connector in this case is the
subordinating conjunction _____.) If such a clause cannot stand by itself,
it is called a dependent clause. Like an insecure husband, it needs a sturdily
independent wife to support it. "Don't shoot until you see the whites of their
eyes."

Every normal sentence contains at least one independent clause. "Don't
shoot." (As with most orders, most imperatives, the subject "you" is understood.)

EXERCISE 1: Complete each of the following with the most appropriate
comparisons. Make each a comparison of a grammatical term to human beings
as if you were a writer trying to make definitions come alive.

Grammatical terms:

  A. An independent clause is like . . .

  B. A dependent clause is like . . .

  C. A phrase is like . . .

Human beings:

  a. . . . a wispy wife who does the housework as long as she has her husband's broad shoulders to cling to.

  b. . . . a single person moving purposefully through life.

  c. . . . three brothers, a sister, and their two nieces sitting in the back bedroom waiting for grandmother to tell them what to do.

PHRASES

Glance rapidly at the following table:

Advance Summary

Noun phrases:	The ever popular noun style
	The cat in the hat
	The giant ape on the skyscraper
	a lot of nonsense
Verb phrases:	can be expected to consist
	will never be able to kidnap the girl
	had often wondered
-Ing phrases:	slamming the cup of chowder to the floor
	mounting the skyscraper
	crushing one bi-plane in his hairy paw
-Ed phrases:	battered by night sticks
	roused once too often
	brought on by passions
	struck by the wonder of it all
To + (verb) phrases:	to err
	to forgive

to free the helpless girl in the monster's grasp

Prepositional phrases:

in prepositional phrases

upon a white horse

in King Kong's power

Now read rapidly:

Foreword, stressing practical uses of phrases:

Suppose you want to write about a hat, and to say that the hat is purple.
How many ways can you put that information about the hat?

Two sentences: *This is a hat. It is purple.*

Two independent clauses: *This is a hat, and it is purple.*

One independent clause, plus one dependent clause: *This is a hat which
is purple.*

Or—which is what we are talking about now—you could construct
any of a number of phrases:

A noun phrase: *The purple hat . . .*

An -ing adjective phrase (that is, a participial phrase):
Radiating purple, the hat . . .

An -ing noun phrase[1]: *Being a purple hat.*

An -ed phrase: *Colored purple, the hat . . .*

A to + (verb) phrase (that is, an infinitive phrase):
To be a purple hat . . . or *To empurple a hat . . .*

A prepositional phrase: The hat *with purple hue . . .* or The hat *of
purple . . .* or The hat *in purple . . .* or He wanted to be hatted *in purple.*

Now read carefully:

Body of section on phrases, including exercises

Phrases come in several styles.

The ever popular noun style illustrates itself; that is, "the ever popular
noun style" is a **noun phrase**—basic noun (style) with adjectives (ever popular
noun) often preceded by a, an, the, or a number (one, three, seventeen and
four fifty-thirds), or words such as some, many, etc.

EXERCISE 2A: Write a number of noun phrases by inserting adjectives before
these nouns;

    a. The . . . street lamp

    b. The . . . co-ed

---

[1]That is, a gerund phrase

c. The . . . student

d. The . . . rioter

e. The . . . policeman

2B: Write a number of noun phrases by adding a noun after these adjectives:

a. The ancient, withered . . .

b. The brightly flashing, eye-searing . . .

c. The black and blue . . .

d. The most noble and celebrated . . .

e. Many once safe . . .

Verb phrases usually can be expected to consist of verbs and verb helpers.

EXERCISE 3: Write a number of verb phrases by adding verbs to these incomplete sentences:

a. The boy . . .

b. The boy . . . to . . . the girl.

c. He . . . the work by the time you arrived.

d. Peace . . . in our lifetimes.

e. Studying . . . me.

-Ing phrases, which use the present participle of a verb (*slamming, mounting, crushing, missing* are present participles of *slam, mount, crush, miss*) come in two styles: the fashionable adjectival use (called a *participial phrase*), which modifies a noun, and can add so much to the quality of a particular sentence if worn with taste: *Slamming the cup of chowder to the floor,* Rory refused. Alternatively, there is the more solid noun use[2], which—like all nouns—appears as subject or object of a verb, or after a preposition: "*Slamming the cup of chowder to the floor* was a damned silly deed," said his father. "I forbid *slamming any more cups of chowder to the floor,*" said his mother. But how was he to be punished for *slamming a cup of chowder to the floor?*

EXERCISE 4A: Write a number of participial phrases to introduce these clauses:

a. . . . , she screamed. (example: Seeing the mouse, she screamed. Or: Fearing for his life, she screamed.)

---

[2]Most people forget that such uses are called *gerunds.*

b. . . . , he failed his examination.

c. . . . , Renée thought the period would never end.

d. . . . , the construction worker tumbled through space.

e. . . . , the rocket landed safely.

EXERCISE 4B: Provide an -ing noun phrase (a gerund) for each of the following:

a. . . . is believing.

b. . . . is hard work. (example: Doing these exercises is hard work.)

c. . . . really blows my mind.

d. She had warned him to avoid . . .

e. . . . is better than . . .

-Ed phrases come from the past participle of the verb (*battered, bruised,* are past participles of *batter, bruise*). Their equivalents (such as -en, -t phrases) come from verbs which are irregular (such as *beat, beaten; bring, brought;* and *strike, struck*). They also function like adjectives: <u>Battered by night sticks,</u> <u>bruised by flying rocks,</u> the innocent bystander fled the riot <u>brought on by</u> [1] <u>passions</u> [2] <u>roused once too often.</u> #1 and #2 modify the bystander, [3] who is a battered and bruised noun; #3 modifies the riot, which was brought on [4] as described; #4 modifies passions, which were roused.

EXERCISE 5A: Add an -ed verb to each of the following, completing the phrase:

a. . . . by the police, he didn't have a chance.

b. The young priest, . . . for so many years, made the right choice.

c. . . . for the fourth time, the mayor could only be grateful.

EXERCISE 5B: Now add an entire -ed phrase (or -en, -t, etc.), a phrase built on the past participle:

a. The student, . . . , ran down the hall. (example: The student, chased by his angry teacher, ran down the hall.)

b. The teacher, . . . , opened the door with trembling fingers.

c. They watched the telephone pole, . . . , topple over.

d. "If you've never seen a man . . . , look out your window now!"

To + (verb) **phrases,** using the infinitive form of the verb (*to blame, to cherish, to graduate,* are the infinitives of *blame, cherish, graduate*), most often appear as nouns: *To err* is human, *to forgive* [is] divine. Occasionally they appear as modifiers (adjectives, adverbs): 'Atta way *to go,* baby!—as an adjective, modifying the noun *way.* We must bomb, burn, and kill *to have peace*—as an adverb, modifying the verb phrase *must bomb, burn, and kill.*

EXERCISE 6A: Complete the infinitive phrases by adding a to + verb—that is, an infinitive:

    a. . . . or not . . . , that is the question.
    b. I want . . . .
    c. Don't you tell me . . .
    d. The most conscientious student often finds it difficult . . . his assignment.

EXERCISE 6B: Now add an entire infinitive phrase, including an adverb and/or a noun:

    a. . . . requires skill, practice, and some ingenuity. (example: To peel a rotten grape [noun] neatly [adverb] requires skill, practice, and some ingenuity.)
    b. If you really want . . . , if your only desire is . . . , then you are doomed to a lifetime of disappointment.
    c. . . . , I will.
    d. Why? Why? Why, do it . . .

The most common adornment of sentences will be found *in prepositional phrases.* A prepositional phrase consists of a noun (often plus adjectives) introduced by a preposition: I'd ride a black horse *to Banbury Cross* to see a fine lady *upon a white horse; with rings* ON HER FINGERS *and bells* ON HER TOES she shall have music wherever she goes.

QUIZ POP QUIZ POP QUIZ POP QUIZ POP QUIZ POP QUIZ POP QUIZ POP QUIZ

Why isn't *to see* a prepositional phrase? Why isn't *to sea* an infinitive?

END OF POP QUIZ

Prepositional phrases function as modifiers, either adverbial (*to Banbury Cross* modifies the verb *ride*), or adjectival (*upon a white horse* modifies *a fine lady; with rings . . . and bells* modifies *she; on her fingers* modifies the noun *rings,* and *on her toes* modifies *bells*).

EXERCISE 7: Add prepositional phrases to these sentences, by inserting a preposition and one of the following nouns, wherever appropriate: the house, the station, the subway, his job, his motives, his wife, his beliefs, the afternoon, the evening.

a. He drove quickly. (Example: In the evening, he drove from the station to his house quickly.)
b. He telephoned.
c. He saw him.
d. He told him.
e. She didn't believe him when he said it had happened, but she did believe it had happened. (Keep this sentence from contradicting itself by adding different phrases to the independent clauses before "but" and to the independent clause after "but.")

How are words connected into sentences?

Phrases, we have said, combine with the rest of a sentence through tack-on connectors (such as *and, under*); in some charming cases, they may simply be plunked into the sentence.

Particularly, noun phrases can often be added to a sentence as *appositives*. A noun phrase in *apposition* acts as a mirror. It sits beside another noun, showing another view of that noun, identifying another side of it. For example: My dog, that stupid beast, that shaggy mat of tri-colored hair, that short-legged deep-chested fringe-faced cross between a poodle and a bassett hound, Falstaff, has just come wagging into the study where I write this sentence, from the out-of-doors where he belongs. The subject is dog; the following noun phrases are appositives:

that stupid beast
that shaggy mat of tri-colored hair
that short-legged deep-chested fringe-faced cross between a poodle and a bassett hound
Falstaff

Dog-beast-mat-cross-Falstaff. (While we're at it, notice how the rhythm of those appositives accelerates, reaching a climax in the one-word appositive of his name; two-word subject, three-word appositive, six-word appositive, twelve-word appositive, *name*.) Writing sentences is fun.

EXERCISE 8: Make up a noun phrase to put in apposition with the subject of each of the following sentences:

a. That great ugly eyesore of a building, . . . , brings back many happy days. (example: 123 North Fullware; or, my childhood school, P.S. 237; or, the one on the left)

b. Tell that man, . . . , to stop that outrageous behavior this second.

c. Jane, . . . , dazzled us all.

d. The difficulties you face, . . . , will some day be overcome.

e. A noun phrase acting as a sort of alter ego, . . . , can be inserted without connecting word after the noun it identifies.

Somewhat like appositives made of noun phrases are phrases acting like adjectives that follow the noun they modify. They too can be inserted without connecting words. My grandfather's old purple hat is the same as my grandfather's hat, purple and old; the mink coat, beautiful and new, is the same as the beautiful new mink coat. Emphasis differs, of course; *the heavy but impartial hand of fate* seems neither quite as heavy nor quite as impartial as the more rarely encountered arrangement of *the hand of fate, heavy but impartial.*

CLAUSES

A phrase is any closely related group of words which does not have both a verb and its subject. A clause is a group of words including a verb and its subject. Phrases depend on clauses; some clauses—the dependent ones—depend on other clauses; sentences contain phrases and consist of at least one clause.

So what?

So:

Rule 1. Don't write a phrase as though it were a complete sentence (unless you have very good reason for breaking the law, as the starving bank-robber explained apologetically).

Rule 2. Don't write a dependent clause as though it were a complete sentence.

Rule 3. Use the right connectors.

Rules 1 and 2 outlaw sentence fragments. They concern writing correctly; Rule 3 concerns writing well.

Conjunctions make juncture of one thing *with* (con) another. Conjunctions are connectors. Some conjunctions imply equality between the clauses joined; they are co-ordinating conjunctions. Which one you use depends on what you mean. Few people have trouble here. Differences in meaning among the following need no explanation:

I love you and you detest Quincy.

I love you but you detest Quincy.

I love you for you detest Quincy.

I love you or you detest Quincy.

Some conjunctions imply that what follows is dependent; they are called subordinating conjunctions. Why? Because sophisticated language-users (whom you want to imitate) will not allow a clause which begins with one of them to stand by itself.

I love you because you love Quincy.

I love you since you love Quincy.

I love you if you love Quincy.

I love you while you love Quincy.

I love you although you love Quincy.

I love you whether or not you love Quincy.

I love you when you love Quincy.

I love you as much as you love Quincy.

Etc.

Actually, Quincy himself isn't that interesting a person. But your writing will improve if you attend to connectors. Each subordinating conjunction carries two meanings: First, it says that what follows is less important than the independent clause it hangs from. Second, it names a particular relationship, defined by the particular word.

Therefore, two bits of advice. First, co-ordinate equal ideas, subordinate unequal ones. Take you, me, and Quincy. You love Quincy, who is doing his best to get my job, the bum. I love you. These two facts conflict. Two conjunctions clearly express conflict: *but* and *although*. With tears of anguished indignation in my eyes, then, I can say to you either "I love you but you love Quincy," or, "I love you although you love Quincy." What's the difference? The first co-ordinates your love and mine; the second subordinates your love to mine. Do I see an equal conflict between two facts each as important as the other? Then I say the first, using the coordinating conjunction *but*. Alternatively, do I want to stress my love for you in spite of your perversity in favoring Quincy? Then I say the second, using the subordinating conjunction *although*.

Note that the order affects emphasis. Putting "although you love Quincy" at the end emphasizes it, and makes it seem a little less subordinate in importance. To make its subordination clearer, put it in the place of lesser emphasis, at the beginning (since the sentence consists of only two parts, there is no middle available to de-emphasize it further). "Although you love Quincy, I love you." A protestation of enduring fidelity in the face of cruel endurance. Contrast that to: "I love you but you love Quincy." A protest, an objection, a charge levelled against the beloved with her laughing eyes and fickle ways. Reversing the order of this one reduces the emphasis, but leaves it still a protest: "You love Quincy but I love you." Independent clauses; equal status; equal weight; balanced conflict.

EXERCISE 9: Which of the following pair would be followed by the sentence, "There is no justice in firemen," and which by the sentence, "Angela can carry her beauty proudly as her rightful possession"?

> a. Hermione was named Miss Firehouse #273, but Angela is more beautiful.
>
> b. Although Hermione was named Miss Firehouse #273, Angela is more beautiful.

By careful use of subordination, you tilt the scales of meaning to weight the sentence as you wish. That is the first bit of advice that comes from what a subordinating conjunction means.

The second bit of advice is to use the right word. When ideas are opposed, use conjunctions conveying the idea of opposition. Don't write, "He is the handsomest, the best-looking man in the world, and above his left nostril he has a purple wart with three red hairs." These ideas conflict; *and* does not imply conflict. *And* is probably the most overworked conjunction at the sentence-fitters' union. Use a conjunction that implies conflict; "*Although* he has a purple wart with three red hairs above his left nostril, he is the handsomest, the best-looking man in the world."

That difference between implied conflict and implied cooperation seems to be one of the hardest to learn.

EXERCISE 10: For each of the following, fill in the blank with the most probable conjunction (several may be possible.)

> a. Jane: Hurry up _____ we'll be late.
> b. Harry: We'll arrive on time _____ the others will all be late.
> c. Jane: Do what I say _____ you want me to get hysterical.
> d. Harry: I'll be ready to go _____ you're still combing your hair.
> e. Jane: We'll never make it on time for supper _____ we have a flat tire.

f. Harry: Leaving now, we would be on time _____ we had one flat tire or four.

g. Jane: Harry, I'm telling you for the last time to hurry up _____ I don't want any more backtalk.

h. Harry (muttering): What's the use; she'll go on like that _____ I'm ready.

Go back to page 148 and find the sentence which I began with a subordinate conjunction.

Did you find it? That sentence breaks its own rule. Why? *Because* it occurs in a particular context. Specifically, it occurs as the answer to a question. That's one of the times when it is good to break the law, as Peter Sellers said in *Dr. Strangelove,* shooting open the coke dispensing machine to get a dime to call the president and tell him the secret codeword that would recall the atomic bombers about to destroy the world.[3] If you are reading carefully, you should have noticed that inconsistency. And if you are using your textbook properly, you should have written a question in the margin when you read that sentence fragment. Even I am not infallible.

A subordinate clause cannot stand as a complete sentence. (An independent clause can.) Connectors mark subordinate clauses, connectors like subordinating conjunctions, which are one of the two basic categories of subordinating connectors. The other basic category is relative pronouns.

Like people, all pronouns are related to something, since standing for something is what makes a pronoun a pronoun. (Warning: a list is coming up.) Those good old pros: I, you, he, she, it—we, you, they; me, you, him her it—us, you, them; myself, yourself, himself herself itself—ourselves, yourselves, themselves; who, which, what; whoever, whichever, whatever; whom, whomever; this—these, that—those; any, few, some, several, much, many, all; anything, something, nothing; one, someone, anyone, everyone, no one; somebody, anybody, everybody, nobody; either neither, both; each, other, another; all have antecedents, things that come before, for which they stand. These pronouns are personal, intensive-reflexive, interrogative or relative, demonstrative, or indefinite. (See the glossary if your teacher wants you to know which is which.) The interrogative (questioning) pronouns don't exactly have antecedents—the word coming before the pronoun, which the pronoun represents—but they are desperately in search of antecedents. Answering the question they ask means naming the thing they stand for.

---

[3]But you still have to answer to the Coca-cola Company (read "teacher"), as Keenan Wynn told Sellers; you have to be able to justify every sentence fragment, every use of a dependent clause as an independent clause.

EXERCISE 11: Write as short an essay as you can, using as many different pronouns as possible. Assume that earlier paragraphs than the ones you write set the scene and explain the antecedents. After you have finished, compare your results to the following, which uses each of the pronouns once, at a density of slightly over 42% pronouns.

"Hand that over!"

"What, this?"

"He can't have it!"

"Who said that?"

"She spoke."

"As for myself, not me; they spoke—ask them."

"Ask whom—us? We ourselves didn't tell you 'no.' Ask him or her."

"Someone spoke—will anyone confess? Speak, some of you, or something worse than you imagine will happen to whomever I choose; all will suffer because of a few, because of several who don't care whatever happens to many, whoever must suffer."

"You can't have the last of these to yourself; which of those will do instead?"

"Either will do, everybody; somebody, anybody, just hand over one or both . . . . No one will? Nobody? Is whichever goes worth so much to any? Surely neither in itself is . . . Nothing to say? Ha! Ask yourselves why."

(Eyeing themselves, each the other, everyone fears betrayal of himself or herself by another.)

Some of these pronouns can be used as subordinating connectors. In particular, the interrogative pronouns—*who, what, which, whom,* and their combinations with *-ever*—can be used as subordinating connectors. (So can *that* when used like *who* or *which.*) Then they are called relative pronouns.

I'm really sorry, but they are just called different things when they are doing different functions. Your teacher is Professor Washington while teaching, Daddy while helping junior with the homework, Herbie while helping clean up the kitchen after supper, Herbert while refusing to help clean up the kitchen after supper, Herb at the poker table, buddy while dodging a car, sir while tipping a wino wiping his windshield, Herbert R. Washington while writing a check, and H. R. Washington while getting a traffic ticket. When things that look identical do different jobs they have different names.

Who, which, what: pronouns (sometimes adjectives). *That:* often a pronoun (sometimes a conjunction, sometimes an adjective). *Who, which, what, that:* often relative pronouns, that is, pronoun connectors that subordinate the clause that follows. Examples:

1. I want the man who got away. (*Who got away?* can stand by itself as a question. In the question, *who* is an interrogative pronoun. Who got away,

period, cannot stand by itself as a statement. In the statement, *who* is a subordinating connector, and the clause *who got away* is dependent.)

2. Here are pictures of the Colosseum and Madison Square Garden, two gladiator rinks. Which is in New York? Madison Square Garden, which is in New York, is the right answer. (Again: *Which is in New York?* can stand as a separate question, but cannot stand as a declarative sentence, as this fragment shows: *Which is in New York.*)

3. I want the man that got away. (. . . *that got away* is a dependent clause, hanging on to the man; the whole clause describes the man, thus acting like an adjective.)

4. Say what you want. (. . . *what you want* is the direct object of the verb *say* and thus acts like a noun; it is a dependent clause.)

EXERCISE 12: Here is a famous speech reduced to a series of one-clause sentences. Rewrite with longer sentences. Make some clauses dependent, and combine them with clauses that you leave independent.

> Four score and seven years ago our fathers brought forth on this continent a new nation. It was conceived in Liberty. All men are created equal. It was dedicated to that proposition.
>
> Now we are engaged in a great civil war. It tests that nation. Can that nation, or any nation so conceived and so dedicated, long endure? We are met on a great battlefield of that war. Some gave their lives here that that nation might live. We have come to dedicate a portion of that field as a final resting place for them. Our action is altogether fitting and proper.
>
> But in a larger sense, we can not dedicate this ground. We can not consecrate this ground. We can not hallow this ground. Brave men, living and dead, struggled here. They have consecrated it. Our poor power to add or detract is much less. The world will little note our speech. It will not long remember it. But it can never forget their deeds here. People fought here. They have thus far nobly advanced an unfinished work. It is for us the living, rather, to be dedicated here to that work. It is rather for us to be here dedicated to the great task remaining before us. That task includes a number of items. These honored dead gave the last full measure of devotion to a cause. We should take increased devotion to that cause from them. These dead shall not have died in vain. We here highly resolve that. This nation, under God, shall have a new birth of freedom. We highly resolve that too. Government of the people, by the people, for the people, shall not perish from the earth. We highly resolve that, too.

EXERCISE 13: In this paragraph, draw a line through all of the subordinate clauses introduced by who (or whom), which, and that.

Who has not known the ecstasy of eating corn on the cob? The man who has not known the ecstasy of eating corn on the cob has not begun to live. Who among us has not thrilled to that succulent crunch which starts us down the golden rows? There is no pleasure, there is no joy that can compare in relish to the juicy bite that packs in fibers between the teeth, fibers which no tongue can fully remove, fibers which will yield finally only to the probing finger (hidden, of course, behind a proper napkin). But ah! the salt delight of buttered hotness belongs to him who peels back husk and silk from steaming cob. Which is the man whom you would most prefer to become—the corn-eater or the jaded jet-setter? There can be no doubt; it is the former that all would wish to be—peeling, buttering, salting, down one row, rotate, up the next—in that golden heaven of God's good grain.

PARALLELISM

Earlier in this chapter you worked with appositives, nouns that name the same thing standing beside each other. Appositives are a special case of lining up equivalent things side by side. The general term for such alignment is parallelism (which includes appositives, parallel phrases, and parallel clauses). Parallel phrases attach to the same spot in the sentences, play the same role; the same is also true of parallel clauses.

To live a decent life you need the insight to perceive the truth, the courage to speak your convictions, and the ability to run like greased lightning.

That is, you need: 1) the insight to perceive, 2) the courage to speak, and 3) the ability to run. Any time you can count off items like that, they are parallel. These parallel phrases all hook onto the sentence at the word "need"—they are all the direct objects of that verb. Moreover, they have the same pattern—in this case, noun and infinitive.

Racing up the stairs, panting heavily, dropping books as she ran, she heard the tardy bell ring.

That is: She—1) racing, 2) panting, 3) dropping—heard. These parallel phrases (their pattern is participles acting as adjectives) modify "she."

One of the shortest instances of parallel clauses came from the mouth of the conquering Caesar, who boasted "veni, vidi, vici." Not quite as terse in English, it comes out, "I came, I saw, I conquered."

Some truly great preachers have a strong feeling for the rhythm of repeated parallel constructions, as in Dr. Martin Luther King's famous speech repeating the clause, "I have a dream . . . ." Here is another complex use of parallel construction, combining parallel subordinate clauses within a single sentence.

I guess it is easy for those who have never felt the stinging darts of segregation to say wait. But when you have seen vicious mobs lynch your mothers and fathers at will and drown your sisters and brothers at whim; when you have seen hate-filled policemen curse, kick, brutalize, and even kill your black brothers and sisters with impunity; when you see the vast majority of your twenty million Negro brothers smothering in an airtight cage of poverty in the midst of an affluent society; when you suddenly find your tongue twisted and your speech stammering as you seek to explain to your six-year-old daughter why she can't go to the public amusement park that has just been advertised on television, and see tears welling up in her little eyes when she is told that Funtown is closed to colored children, and see the depressing clouds of inferiority begin to form in her little mental sky, and see her begin to distort her little personality by unconsciously developing a bitterness toward white people; when you have to concoct an answer for a five-year-old son asking in agonizing pathos: "Daddy, why do white people treat colored people so mean?"; when you take a cross country drive and find it necessary to sleep night after night in the uncomfortable corners of your automobile because no motel will accept you; when you are humiliated day in and day out by nagging signs reading "white" men and "colored"; when your first name becomes "nigger" and your middle name becomes "boy" (however old you are) and your last becomes "John," and when your wife and mother are never given the respected title "Mrs."; when you are harried by day and haunted by night by the fact that you are a Negro, living constantly at tip-toe stance never quite knowing what to expect next, and plagued with inner fears and outer resentments; when you are forever fighting a degenerating sense of "nobodiness";—then you will understand why we find it difficult to wait. There comes a time when the cup of endurance runs over, and men are no longer willing to be plunged into an abyss of injustice where they experience the bleakness of corroding despair. I hope, sirs, you can understand our legitimate and unavoidable impatience.[4]

The long list of wrongs dominates the paragraph in a single mammoth sentence, leading finally to the topic sentence, "There comes a time . . . ." But although the sentence equals many paragraphs in length, the reader doesn't lose his way. Parallel constructions introduce each charge that Dr. King makes: "But when you have seen . . . when you have seen . . . ; when you see . . . ;

---

[4] Martin Luther King, "Letter from Birmingham Jail" from *Why We Can't Wait* (N.Y.: Harper and Rowe, 1963).

when you suddenly find . . . and see . . . and see . . . ; when you have to
concoct . . . ; when you take . . . and find . . . ; when you are humiliated
. . . ; when your first name becomes . . . and your middle name becomes . . .
and your last name becomes . . . and when your wife and mother are never
given . . . ; when you are harried . . . ; when you are forever fighting . . . ."
"You" are the subject of every clause, with the exception only of the two
clauses (unseparated by semicolons) dealing with your names and your wife's
and mother's titles. Even the verbs are the same at the beginning—"When
you have seen . . . when you have seen . . ." and shift gradually, first with
a change to the present tense "when you see . . ."—and then with a complex
sentence starting with a new verb—"when you suddenly find"—but continuing
with the same one—" and see . . . and see . . . and see . . . ." Dr. King thus
varies his clauses, even while keeping the repetitive form of parallelism.
Moreover, he builds towards a climax. The last parallel verb in his long
sentence, "are fighting," introduces the ultimate resistance that comes as a
consequence of the wrongs he has listed. Note, too, that the sentence comes
between much shorter ones; a reader can't ride that kind of swelling syntactical
wave more than once without a little rest, a time to pant in shorter sentences.

For clarity in parallel clauses, begin them with the same kind of phrase
(in Dr. King's letter, "when you" + verb).

EXERCISE 14: Rewrite this paragraph, keeping all of the sentences in the
order in which they occur, but using as much parallelism as possible: parallel
words, parallel phrases, parallel clauses, parallel sentences. (You may want
to change word order within some sentences and change others from active
to passive or vice-versa.)

Example: I like to eat good food. Fine wines are something I like
drinking. Singing a brisk song has always pleased me. I like it when I find
a new friend. Answer below.

He has disgraced me, and I have been hindered by him; my losses have
made him laugh. He has mocked at my gains. He scorns my nation. As for
my bargains, them he has thwarted. Besides cooling my friends, he has heated
my enemies. And what's his reason? I am a Jew. Has not a Jew eyes? Doesn't
a Jew have hands? Organs and dimensions a Jew has too, hasn't he? I would
say he has senses and affections. Wouldn't you say he has passions and is fed
with the same food as a Christian? The same weapons hurt him. He is subject
to the same diseases as Christians. The same means heal a Jew as a Christian,
and the same summer warms him. He is cooled by the same winter as a

I like eating good food, drinking fine wines, singing a brisk song, and finding a new
friend.

Christian is. If you prick us, do we not bleed? Don't we laugh if you tickle us? If we are poisoned by you, our deaths will result. We shall, if you wrong us, take revenge.

CHANGES IN WORD FORM (INFLECTION)

While travelling in Europe with his family in a small camping van, my eldest son Christopher lurked in the van, hiding from foreigners, until we were well into the south of France. His first foray out among the natives was so embarrassing that he withdrew again for four more days of seclusion. The encounter was accidental, as he sought a flush toilet in what he thought to be an empty campground. Alas, he met a Frenchman, who tried to return to Chris the purse, with all our passports and identification, which my wife had casually dropped on the ground the night before. Chris refused it, saying, as explanation, "Vous ne parlez pas Francais." "Oh, no, monsieur," replied the Frenchman in his own language, "*I* speak French, *YOU* are the one who doesn't speak French."

Christopher's error was inflection. The difference between *I* and *you* is one of the ways pronouns inflect, one of the ways they change. Pronouns change to show their relationship to the speaker. This kind of pronoun change shows *person:*

1st person	the pronoun is the speaker	I
2nd person	the pronoun is the audience	you
3rd person	the pronoun is anyone else	he, she, it

If there is more than one of each person, the pronouns may change again. This kind of change shows *number:*

	1st person	2nd person	3rd person
singular	I	you	he, she, it
plural	we	you	they

When words connect to make sentences, the words may change. In a sense, that is what happens when a verb moves into a sentence. Verbs, like pronouns, change in several ways. All of the different ways verbs can change—mood, voice, tense, number—are adjustments to fit them into particular sentences with particular meanings. Similarly, nouns and pronouns may change as they are used different ways; they may change even if person and number remain the same. These different forms of nouns and pronouns are called *cases.* Some languages (highly inflected languages) have so many different cases, change nouns and pronouns so much, that you don't need order to make clear what goes with what. In English, noun-verb-noun is subject-verb-direct object. Dog bites man is too bad, but man bites dog is news. But in a language such as Latin, the word order could be anything, because changes in the nouns themselves would make clear which was the subject, which was the direct object. Each noun carries a sign (a change in its ending) which tells its role in the sentence. To match Latin, we would have to tack, say, *subj* on the ends of all subjects and *obj* on the end of all objects. Dog bites man would become *Dogsubj bites manobj* and could be written in any order, including *Manobj bites dogsubj* without changing the meaning.

English has a few inflections. Nouns don't vary much: they can become plural or possessive, and that's about it. But pronouns change a lot. Not only are they plural or singular, but they change to show person (three forms) and to show case.

Mother used to send Mary, Jane, Betty, and I to the saloon. Would Mother send I to the saloon? Thousands of people would say she would. Why?

To begin with, they ought to say Mother would send *me* to the saloon. Me is the objective case (used for objects) of the pronoun whose subjective (used for subjects) case is I. I do the verb action, but the verb action is done to me. If we expand the table of pronouns above to include case, we will have to add objective to the subjective forms listed above; while we are at it, I add the possessive case as well (singular and plural are paired side by side to save space, since the printer refused to produce a three-dimensional page—across for person, down for case, and out for number):

	1st person	2nd person	3rd person
subjective	we	you[5]	he, she, it; they
objective	me; us	you	him, her, it; them
possessive	my, mine; our, ours	your, yours	his, her-hers, its; their, theirs

Remember, what I'm working toward is why thousands of people say Mother would send I to the saloon.

In the long run, it all comes down to me. Yes, it's me. The first English grammarians used Latin grammar as their model. They thought: A predicate noun (It is *John*) is the same as the subject, and should be in the subjective case. Therefore, these reasonable people thought, when a pronoun is used in

---

[5]The plurals of the second person are the same as the singular.

place of a predicate noun (it's *John*, remember), it should be in the subjective case (it is *he*). Therefore, the objective case is wrong after *is*, and you should say not "it is him," but "it is he"; not "it is me" but "it is I."

In fact, nobody has ever talked or written that way except someone who was told to do so by a Latin-loving grammarian. The normal English expression is, "it's me." Having been taught to say "it's I," contrary to all their lusty and wholesome linguistic lusts, many English speakers now struggle to put *I* in other places where I don't—oops, where *I* doesn't belong. So while just about nobody would say "send I," many, once that *I* gets far enough from the verb to seem to be standing alone, would say "send Mary, Jane, Betty, and I to the saloon." Back in the olden times, before TV, a radio comedy featured a boy—Henry Aldrich—always in trouble, who always responded to his mother's angry summons with the quavering question, "Are you calling I, Mother?"

EXERCISE 15: Each of the italicized pronouns is in the wrong case; correct it.

    a. Between you and *I*, this assignment stinks.

    b. Some of them, particularly Harry and *her*, may have trouble with it.

    c. Yes, but most teachers—for example, Dr. Thinque and *me*—believe students shouldn't find an assignment too easy.

    d. You just want *they* to fail.

    e. No, I know *them* will succeed.

    f. *Whomever* hasn't noticed may ask *whoever* he wants, "*Whom* has a book *who's* index tells *who* to write about **who, whom, whose, whoever, and whomever?**

EXERCISE 16: Two forms are given for many of the possessive pronouns in the pronoun table (for example, both *my* and *mine; our* and *ours*). Read the following grammatically correct sentences, and state the rule for when to use which of the possessive forms. (For example, when to use *their* and when to use *theirs*—note that no apostrophes are used.)

    A. Who is our mother? Our mother is ours,
       Whistling and skipping through sunshine and showers;
       Where is their doggie? Their doggie is theirs,
       Scratching and barking and chewing up chairs;
       What is your carpet? Your carpet is yours,
       For beating and cleaning and covering up floors;

Why is her tailor? Her tailor is hers,
For sewing up muffs of incredible furs;
When is my bedtime? My bedtime is mine,
For I'll be asleep by the end of this line.

B. What does *his, its* form? *His, its* forms *his, its.*
And all of this grammar is giving me fits.

Topic: Write a paragraph on some aspect of race relations. Include at least one instance of parallel clauses and at least one instance of parallel phrases; label each in the margin.

13

...and Punctuation.

e think in words. If we say "I know what I want to say, but I don't know how to say it," we really don't know what we're thinking and, therefore, we don't know "what we want to say." Assume you do have the words—a sentence—full of precise words that clearly express your meaning. And you write them down and expect the meaning to be as clear to the reader as it is to you. After all, we're using a common language with all the words arranged in a logical, commonly understood sequence. So, what's the problem? Why does so much that is written have to be read and reread? Why do so many themes come back to the student splattered with obscene red marks and with marginal notes like "awkward," "not clear," "run-on sentence"?

The answer is simply that an uninterrupted flow of words is not enough: some words fit tightly together and some do not. To make our meaning clear, we sometimes must use "non-words" as well as words. These "non-words" are, of course, punctuation symbols—punctuation marks—that *puncture* the sentence to separate words or phrases that don't belong together. When the lack of them clouds your meaning or distorts it, your reader has to do part of your job for you; he has to provide, as he plods along through the unmarked sentence, the signposts—the commas, the semi-colons, the apostrophes that are not there. It's like writing his own road signs as he drives along the superhighway. And he may miss your meaning to the extent that your whole effort—and his—is pointless.

Writing what you really want to say is tough. It's tough even if you know the words to think with and the words to write with and even if you have a sense of the non-words that so often make sense out of nonsense. How much easier it is to talk to someone. You say something. He says, "say that again." So, you tell him again. He gets the message. In addition to being able to repeat or re-define what you're saying, you can use all sorts of body motions to explain your meaning: the up-raised eyebrow, the lowered eyelid, the pointed finger, the sweeping arm, the shrugging shoulder. This is the "silent language." We dramatize our heard words with un-heard gestures to make our meaning clearer. We make our meaning clearer, also, by what we *don't* articulate and by what we *don't* gesticulate. What we don't say or do helps to make the said words better understood; pauses speak.

How can *not* saying something help make it clearer? It's simple, as the teacher said, beating his head against the blackboard, chalk dust sifting onto his twitching shoulders and powdering his agonized eyebrows with the frost of premature age. When we speak, we punctuate. We punctuate by intonations of the voice and we punctuate by pauses. We can speak a paragraph or a page and—without thinking a thing about grammar rules or knowing any of them—punctuate that paragraph or page perfectly. There's the raised-tone question mark (Did I score?); there's the explosive-toned exclamation point (Did I score!). And there are the silences—the pauses in our speech which properly partition every sentence we utter. The comma pause is a short one because the meaning of the words or phrases, while different, is closely related—blood brothers. The semi-colon pause is longer: the relationship between the connecting phrases or clauses is less close, but certainly they belong to the same family. A colon pause is longer than a semi-colon one and a period pause longer than a semi-colon one—because each represents more distance from the words that preceded it. (What pause most refreshes a class period?) How to do as well in writing punctuation marks as you do in talking them? That's the question and part of the answer is to *hear* what you write and to *listen* to what you hear. If you do this—you can if you try—then all you need to know are the simple little signs that translate the pauses, the silence of your speech. Lend an ear to language as you do to music. This is the sensual approach to punctuation. There is a rhythm to words and part of that rhythm is—as it is to music—involved not only with sound; it is also involved with what isn't heard: the silences which as symbols of punctuation can make your sentences more clearly understood.

All of this is prelude. To those of you who happen to have a sensitive ear or two, it can be helpful, maybe. But some of us can't carry a tune and some of us can't completely hear the language. So, let's supplement the sensual approach to punctuation (Heavens!) with the mechanical approach. There are some "rules" that can be an aid to literate writing and, besides, there are several punctuation marks that can't be transmitted by sound or lack of it: the apostrophe, quotation marks. There are a few things to learn and remember and use—but not many. But do remember this: nearly every compound or complex sentence needs some kind of punctuation if it's to be immediately clear to the reader, even a short one: "Me, Tarzan; you, Jane." Comma (point at breast), semi-colon (nod and drop voice); comma (point at breast), period (leer seductively). That punctuation represents tone of voice, gesture: hear and visualize the scene, and you will punctuate it correctly. Punctuation that doesn't correspond to vocal presentation can get a little complicated.

"Say 'boots' without 'shoes,' " my wife's sadistic father told her. "Boots without shoes," she piped in a childish treble. "No, 'boots' *without* 'shoes,' " he corrected her. "Boots *without* shoes," the little girl tried again. And so it went for hours on end: " 'boots' without '*shoes*' " produced "boots without *shoes*," and as far as she can recall this childhood trauma, she never thought of saying simply "boots."

Here this teaser disappears on the printed page, where silent punctuation comes into its own.

Of the various punctuation symbols (thirteen of them there are) three of them are most often used in writing and they are, therefore, the ones most often misused or not used where they should be. They represent our chief sins of commission and of omission: the comma, the semicolon, and the apostrophe.[1]

In Part I of this chapter on punctuation, the examples of the uses of the comma and the semicolon have a certain continuity to them: that is, by adding all the examples together, you'll find the core of a story. The examples of the uses of the apostrophe are more random. With the apostrophe you'll meet some characters (Mr. and Mrs. Clay and their pigs, for instance), familiar from their work with commas and semicolons, but there will be all sorts of other things thrown in to illustrate the apostrophe's uses.

At the end of Part I, you will find the selection from which many of the specific examples came—but without the commas, semi-colons, and apostrophes. You put them in.

This book is concerned with the USAGE of the English language: its words and the symbols that hook its parts together. Using these symbols correctly makes the language clear. I'm leaving that part to you.

GROUP 1

, a comma is a comma, a comma, a comma. Inside most sentences, it is probably the punctuation mark which is used most frequently and is, also, the one that can get so out of control that a sentence becomes a mass of marks without meaning. Its purpose is to help make your thought clear to the reader—that's all. Its purpose is to separate words that logically don't belong tightly together; its purpose is also to enclose words that do belong logically together. Again, hear what you write: note where, for a second, there's a silence—and put a comma there. But, again, if your language ear is sometimes—or usually—tuned out, fix sharply in your memory the following uses of this symbol so vital to clear sentences. Even professional singers follow the sheet music until they know the score by heart. You'll be glad if you do. So, here goes.

First of all, I must tell you that there are a dozen or more "rules" about commas, but I'm going to describe in detail only about eight of them.

---

[1]The period would make this group a foursome but that it is rarely misused in its basic role—as terminal punctuation. See, however, the remarks on sentence fragments in chapter 4.

The rest I'll pitch into one pithy paragraph when we say farewell to commas. The lucky eight uses are:

1. in a series
2. after introductory words
3. between independent clauses
4. to enclose parenthetical expressions
5. between adjectives of equal weight
6. with quotations
7. to separate dates, places, and numbers
8. to avoid confusion

1. *the comma in a series:*

   When we moved, only our clothes and a bust of Longfellow with a battered nose were brought along—*the house, the furniture, the china, the pots, and the pans* were all there waiting; and waiting, too, were the ladies of the church—as bright and clean and warm as the house itself.

   (The last list, the list of adjectives—bright, clean, warm—needs no commas because all words are separated by *and*.)

2. *the comma after introductory words*
   word or short phrase:

   However, he knew the heifer didn't know what hit him.

   After all, Mr. Clay said it wouldn't know what hit it.

   Nevertheless, I wasn't sure.

   (Note that these words and short phrases mark a transition, a change or contradiction in thought.)

   phrase

   From his scrawny farm, he supplied the grocery with meat.

   Picking up the ax, Mr. Clay turned the blunt end toward the heifer.
   clause

   While Mr. Clay was mighty interesting and did a lot of things that were fun for a boy, I guess I liked Mrs. Clay better.

   The key word in this rule is *introductory.*

3. *the comma between independent clauses*

   He was happy only when he was outside the house, and she was never happy when he was inside.

   I turned around and started walking for the gate, and then there was a dull thud and a kind of grunting sound. (In these two sentences, the comma plus the coordinating conjunction *and* separates what could have been two sentences. Other coordinating conjunctions are *but, yet, or, for, nor.*)

4. *a comma is used to enclose parenthetical and non-restrictive words, phrases, or clauses*

word

The next morning it was still there, *however,* and with a stubborn set to it as if it were determined that, whatever the odds, it would stay right there.

phrase

The next morning, however, it was still there and with a stubborn set to it as if it were determined, *whatever the odds,* that it would stay right there.

clause

She mentioned time after time that Newton D. Baker, *who was one of her relatives,* had written her about the progress of the war.

If the parenthetical word, phrase, or clause comes at the end of the sentence, one comma can enclose it, trapping it against the period at the end.

word

The next morning it was still there, *however.*

(Notice that a sentence like this is a reverse image of a sentence that begins with an introductory word, as in Rule 2.)

phrase

The next morning it was still there, *with a stubborn set to it.*

clause

Mr. Clay was mighty interesting and did a lot of things that were interesting for a boy, *although I guess I liked Mrs. Clay better.*

Note that a phrase or clause which gets a comma when it comes first won't get a comma when it comes last *if* the phrase or clause is restrictive. Thus: *first, (introductory and restrictive):*

After picking up the ax, Mr. Clay turned toward the heifer.

last, restrictive:

Mr. Clay turned toward the heifer *after picking up the ax.*

last, non-restrictive:

Mr. Clay turned toward the heifer when he was ready, *after picking up the ax.*

(In the third example, the added clause—when he was ready—spells out the time restrictively and turns the last phrase into a non-restrictive detail.)

Parenthetical and nonrestrictive words and groups like those used above are not essential to the sense of the sentence: the sentence is a complete thought without them; they simply add something extra—extra information, extra flavor.

Take the Kiosk Sphinx, which is (or at least used to be) in Chicago. The Kiosk Sphinx, visible from the I. C. suburban trains around 36th Street, is a forty-foot tower—twenty-five feet of laced steel with a small square platform at top, mounted on a fifteen-foot four-legged concrete base with "Kiosk Sphinx" in raised two-foot letters. Nobody I know, including the Answer Man, has any idea what it is. But whatever it is, one thing is sure: there is only one.

Therefore, when you refer to the Kiosk Sphinx, which is (or at least used to be) in Chicago, all description after *Kiosk Sphinx* is pure decoration—it does not restrict the meaning of *Kiosk Sphinx* by distinguishing this *Kiosk Sphinx* from all the other Kiosk Sphinxes, because there aren't any others. *Which is (or at least used to be) in Chicago* is therefore a *non-restrictive* clause. Use the comma.

5. *Use a comma between adjectives of equal weight.*

Mrs. Clay was a *nice, sweet, kind,* aged lady.

These are called coordinate adjectives and modify (describe) the noun, *lady.* But notice that there is no comma between *aged* and *lady,* even though aged is an adjective. The commas keep the adjectives apart from each other, not apart from the noun: no comma between the last adjective and the noun.

Coordinate adjectives work as a team, on equal footing. If two adjectives are equal, you can put *and* between them.

Take those *yelling, waving* boys trying to get your attention. If you can say "the yelling and waving boys" without awkwardness (and you can) then *yelling* and *waving* are coordinate. But even though the boys are the Clays' two slack-mouthed young sons yelling and waving because a pig is about to eat your foot, you cannot say "the Clay's two and slack-mouthed and young sons" without awkwardness. *Two, slack-mouthed,* and *young* are not co-ordinate: no commas.

6. *Use a comma with quotations*

Mr. Clay *said, "I think* this is a good day for some chicken killin'."

"Come on, *pardner," he would say, "we've* got some chicken killin' to do, as the man says."

7. *Use a comma to separate dates, places, numbers*

Even after writing so many pages about punctuation, my memory is still not so dulled that I can't recall the exact date when we moved to our new town.

It was December 6, 1915, that we moved in. Of course, I remember the name of the town: Old Mill, Virginia.

I even remember how many people lived there the day before we arrived. There were precisely 2,101. The next day, there were at least 2,107 in the town, because we were six: a father, a mother, two daughters, and two sons.

I know, too, that the gross income was increased by $2,400 on the day of our arrival. That was my father's salary.

8. *Use commas to avoid confusion*

Of course the only reason for using commas—or for using any other punctuation mark—is to avoid confusion in a sentence: to make it as clear as you can. But there are times when you can't bring to mind the rules; there are times when no rule you remember seems right, but the sentence seems wrong. Like these?

Soon after Mr. Clay felt slightly sick.

When they were alive and kicking the pigs really enjoyed them more.

To her Clay got his just desserts.

Without the commas, these look like *after Mr. Clay, kicking the pigs,* and *her Clay.* The commas keep the confused parts separate. Do they make sense this way?

Soon after, Mr. Clay felt slightly sick.

When they were alive and kicking, the pigs enjoyed them more.

To her, Clay got his just desserts.

I will end this section about commas by listing a few other examples that occur to me:

He is G. F. Brown, M.D.

He is, also, G. F. Brown, Jr.

This is the place, isn't it?

Dear Harum, [informal letter] Sincerely yours, Scarum

Students who have just been confronted with the many comma rules tend to confront the instructor with too many commas. Commas can cloud as well as clear. If after listening hard and thinking hard, you still don't know whether to stick one here or there—don't. Comma-sense is really common-sense.

And now we'll approach the *semicolon*—the second of our symbolic triumvirate of the most often used punctuation symbols. It isn't used as often as it should be, and when it is, it usually shouldn't be. When that exactly right moment suddenly appears on your paper, you will probably use a comma, use a period, or use nothing. But once you try it, you'll like it. You'll like it because your sentences will show more variety in their structure, you will be able to make the content of your sentences more interesting and coherent, and you will love to see more frequently one of the first two letters of the alphabet marked in emphatic red at the top of your paper instead of the third, fourth, or sixth. Believe me, a semi-colon in its right place is a thing of beauty and of at least temporary joy to your instructor, who may forget or forgive some other grammatical mishaps—dazzled by the sheer wonder of your sensitive rendering of this noble mark.

1. *Use a semicolon between clauses*
   1a. *Use a semi-colon to separate independent clauses that are usually joined together by a comma and a conjunction.*
That is, a semi-colon equals a comma plus a conjunction.

> She was a very smart woman, and her whole family was just as smart. (comma plus the conjunction *and*)

> She was a very smart woman; her whole family was just as smart.

> I would carry the chicken to the wooden block near the henhouse, and the chicken would be quiet and sorrowful as if somehow it knew what was about to happen. (comma plus the conjunction *and*)

> I would carry the chicken to the wooden block near the henhouse; it would be quiet and sorrowful as if somehow it knew what was about to happen. (semi-colon)

   1b. *Use a semicolon to separate independent clauses that are not separated by a conjunction.*
> Mr. Clay's name seemed to be always in our house; he was like another person living there.

> Our town had thirteen churches; five of them were actually above ground.

   1c. *Use a semicolon when conjunctive adverbs or transitional expressions separate independent clauses.* Are you more bewildered than usual? Don't worry, or—rather—do. It is at this point that semicolon errors are most frequently made; this is where we separate the illiterate boy from the literate man. At any rate, it's one of the crowbars. What in Funk and Wagnalls are conjunctive adverbs and transitional expressions? They list conjunctive adverbs as follows: *hence, nevertheless, furthermore, besides, accordingly, also, however, moreover, then, therefore, thus*—and there are more of them. But you have the idea. Transitional expressions are more obvious: *for example, on the other hand, in fact, by the way*—and there are more of them of similar ilk.

I would carry the chicken to the wooden block; *however,* I wasn't man enough to cut off its head.

Mr. Clay would fling the body away; *nevertheless,* it would thrash around headless in the snow for a while.

Soon, the poor future dinner would be quiet; *then,* Mr. Clay would drip it into the kitchen for Mrs. Clay to cook.

I didn't like the way Mrs. Clay cooked chicken; *in fact,* I didn't like the way she cooked anything.

But, I give her credit, she insisted that before she cooked it the chicken be dead; *on the other hand,* the pigs really enjoyed them more when they were alive and kicking.

Look at these sentences again, mentally substituting commas in the places where the semicolons are. Which way do the adverbs and transitions face? Which clause do they go with? You can't tell without the semicolons. You could use periods instead of semicolons and be quite correct. But you'd have a series of short, jerky, declarative sentences in a kindergarten row: I saw a cat. The cat was fat. The cat had kittens.

2. *Use a semicolon between items in a series when there is punctuation within the series.*

Along the sleeping body of Main Street, there are at the center, the Hotel Jefferson, the drugstore, and the general store; at left, more exotic emporiums—Miss Prescott's Apparel Shoppe, Miss Amy's Millinery Salon, and Miss Emily's Tea Shoppe; and on the right, the Uncompromising National Bank and Trust Company, and the County Court House that housed a judge who was jolly and gentle with his erring and solvent friends but adamant in his application of the law to those criminals who were financially anemic.

3. *Use a semicolon to prevent confusion in a sentence.* Remember, all punctuation marks are not created equal—especially the comma and the semicolon.

The Old Mill *BLAST* reported that Miss Prescott had been elected President; Miss Amy, Vice-President; and Judge Larceny, Treasurer.

It further reported that the Old Mill stream had a number of bathers last Saturday: Old Wes, the village drunk; the Methodist preacher, who had been trying to sober him up; even the Baptist preacher, who believes in total immersion—especially on baptismal Sunday—all immersed themselves on this hot Saturday.

' The apostrophe has three general functions:

1. to show possession
2. to form plurals of numbers, letters, and symbols
3. to indicate contractions

1. *Use an apostrophe to show the possessive form of singular nouns and singular indefinite pronouns*

Mr. Clay's pigs are exceptionally dirty pigs, and it would be to everyone's advantage if, by happy chance, they disappeared some wild and windy night.

Mr. Clay's pigs (noun)   everyone's advantage (pronoun)

However, if these filthy pigs belonged to Jesse James, you could write the sentence this way:

Jesse James' pigs are exceptionally dirty pigs because Jesse's last name ends in *s* and one syllable names ending with an *s* or *z* sound sometimes add 's, sometimes just the apostrophe. It depends whose rules you read.

Mr. Clay's pigs   Jesse James' pigs

At this point, let me make a NOTE to you:

Never use an apostrophe to show possession with personal, relative, or interrogative pronouns. For example, if mother's sow ate one of *its* personal pronoun pigs—no apostrophe. Or if you are writing about Mrs. Clay's favorite dirty pig and you say "the pig is *hers*"—no apostrophe. Or if you're referring to both Clays, you would say the pig is *theirs*—no apostrophe. Or, attracted by the lush perfume of the Clays' dirty pigs, you asked "*whose* pigs are those"—no apostrophe.

And let me make this note even longer. Don't get mixed up between *contractions* and *possessive personal pronouns.*

You should say, "it's time to feed the pigs" because it's means "it is." But please don't say "the pig was taking it's time." In that sentence what meaning does "*it is* time" have? And if one pig grunts to his brother, "guess *who's* coming to dinner," even a dirty dumb pig would have sense enough to put in the apostrophe and not snort "guess whose coming to dinner."

TEST: Make up a sentence in which the phrase "guess whose coming to dinner" is spelled *correctly.* (Answer next page)

End of note. To get back to the apostrophe with singular nouns and pronouns, remember this, please: words of two or more syllables ending in *s* usually need only an apostrophe, but if you want the added *s* or *z* sound pronounced—making two (sounding ziz or sis or siz)—'s should be used. Like:

Angus's kilt was a real killer. (Angus is Clay's first name. *Angus's* is pronounced Angussiz.)

The Clay's pigs have Achilles' heels but so do anyone's and everybody's pigs.

Words of one syllable take the 's, even if the word ends in an -*s* or -*z* sound (but not everybody agrees, especially about names):

Here comes old Hoss, he

Leads the posse;

"Honeste" is not

The fuzz's name—

'Tis Hoss's shot

Will bag the game.

This has been fun. More of the same ahead with **plural nouns and plural indefinite pronouns.**

And this is what you should remember: if the plural ends in *s*, only an apostrophe is required; but if it ends in any other letter, add 's. (Are you fascinated as I am by the Clays and their pigs? We'll greet them again soon.)

Ballplayers' bats are bigger and better, but single ladies' bars are banned in Boston.

In that silly sentence, you notice that "ballplayers" and "ladies" end in *s*—so the apostrophe trails after. But in this sentence something happens that's different.

Men's ways are wild and weird, but women's ways are wilder.

The apostrophe comes before the *s*. Think of other words whose plural does not end in *s*. Datum? Goose? Others?

And speaking of "others," how about this sentence to show where the apostrophe goes with plural indefinite pronouns:

Others' rights are very good rights but my rights are righter.

We need to take a minute with

compound nouns and compound indefinite pronouns

(Answer to test on page 171: Guess whose coming to dinner surprised me?)

Whether hyphenated or not, only the last word takes an apostrophe. (We're going to mix singular and plural here.)

Angus's *son-in-law's books* were as dirty as the Clay's pigs. (singular)

But their *daughters-in-law's books* were clean, clean, clean. (plural)

Anyone else's pigs would turn up their snouts at the Clays' diet.

And the *attorney general's pigs* told them this.

Something else. Will this never end! When you write about joint possession (not about owning a joint) use the apostrophe in the last word only. As

Angus and Archie's mother—poor thing—had been eaten by the pigs. (I told you they'd eat anything!) (two brothers, one and the same mother)

Angus often used Sears and Roebuck's catalogue. (two partners, one catalogue)

BUT: However, Bill's and Bob's mothers avoided the desperately hungry pigs. (two boys, different mothers; no joint relationship)

Of course, you can dodge the whole issue:

The decision of the sheriff and the judge to kill the pigs was sincerely appreciated by everyone except the Clays.

Now that the uses of the apostrophe as *possessive* are clear, it's time to review a second function of this wormy little symbol:

2. *Use the apostrophe to form the plurals of numbers and letters, of words used as words, and of abbreviations.*

And here are some examples arranged in that order:

If you add four 5's to two 3's, you will probably come up with the number 26.

You will, that is, if you mind your p's and q's.

It was a long sentence; there were five *and's* in it.

He was writing about the six YMCA's in New York, and instead of using commas in the series he used *and's*.

There are more YMCA's there now, but he was writing in the early 1900's.

Could you write one sentence containing all of the uses of the apostrophe in rule 2? I can't.

3. Finally, the apostrophe is used to form contractions: *that is, the omission of a letter or letters in a word or a number or numbers in a figure.*

> I can't write a sentence containing all the uses of the apostrophe listed in rule 2. I really cannot do this, and I won't.
>
> I know one unfortunate chap who tried to, and his wife has alerted the men in white. They're coming for him, I hear, at two o'clock this afternoon.
>
> But he's getting on in years and hasn't the cope he had as a brilliant grammarian in the famous class of '23 (1823).

We're about to say farewell to the apostrophe, but before the tender parting, let's take one last, brief look. He has his little—but essential—place in phrases more abstract than those we have mentioned. And these phrases are often concerned with idiomatic expressions[2] and with things like time, distance, cost.

> After this book is finished, I'm going to take a week's vacation or maybe a two weeks' vacation. (a week's—singular—or two weeks'—plural—vacation)

Here are a few more commonly used expressions requiring apostrophes: a day's work, two cents' worth, a stone's throw, and—to finish forcibly— the bum's rush.
Postscript: Look up the meaning of the word *gerund*. Gerunds need apostrophes, too—the possessive form:

> I hate Mr. Clay's kicking the pigs. (I love Mr. Clay, but I do hate *his kicking* the pigs, even if they are old and dirty.)

If you want to say you hate Mr. Clay, who just happens to be booting porkers, say: I hate Mr. Clay, kicking the pigs.

> I hate Mrs. Clay's cooking. (I love Mrs. Clay, but I hate her cooking, and even the pigs approach the leavings reluctantly.)

---

[2]An idiomatic expression is something in language that has no rhyme or reason; people just do it that way. The French word for idiom is "idiotisme."

Thus concludes our sharing together the why's and wherefore's of the comma, the semicolon and the apostrophe. I hope—with acute qualms of doubt—that all the talk about the town, the Clays, the pigs, the chickens has not bored you out of your skulls. I must admit, with you, that rules and examples of punctuation marks do not make highly amusing reading; there was an absence, I am sure, of loud laughter, of soft chuckles, of—even—a sliding grin. So be it. At any rate, we have now come to that part of this chapter where I put down the whole thing from which so many examples were extracted. I have omitted, as I said I would, the commas, semicolons, and apostrophes. The selection contains many of the examples exactly as quoted; some, it does not contain. But as you work through it, it would be instructive to refer to them to help you put 'em where they belong. Warning: don't commit Helter-Skelter—blithely tossing them here and there in the sheer joy of their use. There are only so many needed, and I list them below in the order of their appearance on stage.

, , , , , , , , , , ;   '   , , , , , ;

, , , , , ,   ,   ,   ;   , , ,   , , , ,

,   ,   '   ;   '
, , , , , , ; , ; , ;   ; ,   ; ; , ;

,   ,   ,   ,   '
, , , , , ,   ,   ,   '   , , ; , , , ;

,
, , ,   , ,   :   ;   , ,

When we moved only our clothes and a bust of Longfellow with a battered nose were brought along—the house the furniture the china the pots and the pans were all there waiting and waiting too were the ladies of the church—as bright and clean and warm as the house itself. For many days they had been making ready for the new minister. The house was cleaner than it would ever be again—until the next minister came. Crisp white pique doilies graced the ravaged backs of the chairs. There were little vases with flowers in them stuck in the niches in the living room. When the evening was over the flowers lay abandoned in their niches the little vases were to go away with their owners.

The Clays house was directly across the street from the Parsonage and it looked as if it might fall down at any minute. During the day you forgot about it but as darkness came it looked more and more helpless and in the night you felt sure it would kneel down in the wind and snow. But the next morning it was still there and with a stubborn set to it as if it were determined that whatever the odds it would stay right there. Its roof and its porches had sagged with the burden of many winters Mr. Clay was constantly walking

around the house with some nails in his mouth and a hammer in his hand
and as things gave way he nailed them where they stopped moving. By now
the house looked like a small child sitting hunched over and cross-legged on
the large lawn. Mr. Clay was like the outside of the house—stooped and
awkward and indestructible. Mrs. Clay was like the inside—neat and dainty
and clean and her skin was like the light that shines through a pink lampshade.

Mr. and Mrs. Clay must have been just right for each other. He was
happy only when he was outside the house and she was never happy when
he was inside. There was a hard-packed fenced-in back yard behind the house
where the chickens and the pigs pecked and rooted in amiable confusion.
Among them Mr. Clay could spit without aiming. But in the house Mr. Clay
sat on the edge of his chair with his mouth working and his eyes focused on
the nearest door—like a dog pointing—while Mrs. Clay watched him with
a cold and speculative eye.

I was very fond of Mr. Clay and looked up to him. From his scrawny
farm he supplied the grocery store with meat. He sold milk to a few customers—most of the people of the town said Mr. Clays milk had a "high percent-
age of water content" but Mr. Clay and I knew that its greenish color was
due to the fine grass the cows found in the stony pastures of the farm. When
John would make unkind remarks about Mr. Clays milk I would get mad and
chase him around the dining room table with a butcher knife. Mr. Clays name
seemed to be always in our house he was like another person living there.
He called me his "pardner."

"Come on pardner" he would say "weve got to kill some chickens as
the man says." He never made a remark that was his own. Everything he
said it was "the man" who said it. "Its a cold day as the man says" or "Thats
a mighty fat hog as the man says"—this is the way he talked and Father said
it was because he lacked confidence in himself. But when he said "Lets kill
a chicken" I would get his ax for him and he would dive among the squalling
feet-hopping wing-flapping chickens and grab one. I would carry the chicken
to the wooden block near the henhouse it would be quiet and sorrowful as
if somehow it knew what was about to happen. There would be the sudden
sharp click of the ax and Mr. Clay would fling the body away headless
nevertheless it would thrash around in the snow for awhile. Soon the poor
future dinner would be quiet then Mr. Clay would drip it into the kitchen
for Mrs. Clay to cook. I didnt like the way Mrs. Clay cooked chicken in fact
I didn't like the way she cooked anything. But I give her credit she insisted
that the chicken be dead before she cooked it on the other hand the pigs
really enjoyed them more when they were alive and kicking. And sometimes
I wondered whether Mr. Clay cared one way or another he ate fast and had
some queer notions.

We killed a heifer once. Mr. Clay asked John if I could help him and

John looked at me for a long minute thinking about it before he said it would be all right. Although it was early in the morning it was not very cold in the buggy but I shivered all the way to the farm. I wanted to get there and I hated to get there because I felt sorry about the heifer. Mr. Clay said "It wont know what hit it as the man says. It doesnt even know its a heifer as the man says." "How do you know it doesnt know?" I asked him and it was because Mr. Clay didnt answer me that I felt sorry about the heifer.

The snow had melted around the stable and the ground was steaming as if it were warm. I waited outside while Mr. Clay went in for the heifer. In a second I heard the sharp tap of its hoofs on the stable floor and then Mr. Clay led it through the door and the fog gathered around its body as he tied it to a stake. Picking up an ax he turned the blunt end toward the heifer. I turned around and started walking for the gate and then there was a dull thud and a kind of grunting sound. I looked back to see the heifer kneeling in the snow. Then Mr. Clay twisted down and cut its throat with a long knife the purple blood spurted out and made a big black blot in the snow and then ran in little streams toward the ground around the barn. Mr. Clay put his ax on his shoulder and headed back for the barn and the heifer just kneeled there for a second and then turned over and fell on its side with its head at an angle looking up at the sun.

While Mr. Clay was mighty interesting and did a lot of things that were fun for a boy I guess I liked Mrs. Clay better. She was a very smart woman her whole family was just as smart. She mentioned time after time that Newton D. Baker was one of her relatives and she would tell me things that Newton had written her about the War the policy in Washington the talks with Englands Prime Minister the cities taken the battles won important things like that. She was also a descendant of Patrick Henry some of her relatives were in high places in the French government. "I am really able" she said "to keep in close touch with the 'situation.'" The Clays had two sons who wandered around with their mouths open.[3]

How did you do? Your instructor knows. You'll find out. Blessings.

I mentioned that there are thirteen punctuation marks that will be dwelt on in this chapter. Ten more, then, lie ahead—like patients "etherized upon a table" (see T. S. Eliot's "Prufrock") to be dissected. We have done this to the three most important "patients." Now, in Group II, let us examine the four next most important: the colon, the dash, quotation marks, and the hyphen.

---

[3]James Knox, *Sunday's Children* (Boston; Houghton Mifflin Company, 1955), p. 8, pp. 56–59.

GROUP 2

: the **colon** usually comes *before* something:

1. before a list of things
2. before a direct quotation
3. before a summary
4. before something emphatic

But sometimes it follows *after* something:

5. after such expressions as "the following" or "as follows"
6. after a formal salutation.

And sometimes, it nudges *between* something:

7. between chapter and verse
8. between hours and minutes

1. ***The colon before a list***
Our house has many attributes: a rheumatic pump, a seepy roof, a musty smell, and a cat with twenty-three toes.

What should we do? The solution is: plug our ears, buy many buckets, hold our noses, and exhibit our cat.

2. ***The colon before a long or formal quotation***
The mayor's face flamed with anger: "There is a house in this town with a rheumatic pump, a leaky roof, a musty smell, and a weird cat."

My wife's response did little to pale the Mayor's face: "We all know about the deplorable condition of your house, Mr. Mayor, but we didn't know it included a weird cat."

3. ***The colon before an emphatic word or phrase or clause***
The Mayor's wife screamed one word: bitch!
I restrained the rage in my voice: "Takes one to know one!"

The Mayor hurled the supreme insult: He said my cat has twenty-three toes!

4. ***The colon before a summary***
There were other frothy exchanges: the air was whipped with verbal wind.

Our neighbors looked at one another: all quite interesting.

5. **The colon between chapter and verse** and **between hours and minutes**

In the midst of all this, the minister was thinking of Luke 6: 37–41.

My wife and I glanced at our watches—it was 5:10; we had lost ten minutes of the happy hour.

6. **The colon after formal salutations**

Gentlemen:

I am calling on you, the members of the Town Council, to condemn the house belonging to our esteemed Mayor. It is an eye-sore on the facade of our fair city.

Dear Mr. Mayor:

I enclose a copy of my letter to the Town Council. If you demand satisfaction for my action, demand it from someone else: I am an abject coward.

7. **The colon after "as follows" or "the following"**

Our Happy Hour consists of the following: two thirsty people, two thin-stemmed glasses, two amber liquids, two rosy glows.

8. **The colon after the title of a book if there's a subtitle**

Roger Longhouse has written a book about our town.

It's called *Captain Endon Paige: His Period.*

(The colon should always be used outside quotation marks, and it is never used with a comma, a period, or a dash. Sentences in parentheses should never end with a colon. The major mistake in using this mark is placing it after a linking verb [are, were, shall, should be] when a series follows. This separates the verb from the complement that follows. The clue to follow is to make sure that what precedes the colon is a complete sentence by itself—otherwise, don't use it.)

—the **dash** is a very handy device; if you're at a loss about what to do, it often solves the problem. Students tend, however, to use it either too often or never. There's nothing quite like it but use it in sensible moderation—don't exhaust it.

There are four main uses for the dash:

1. to mark an abrupt break in the thought of a sentence
2. as an informal parenthesis
3. to introduce a rephrasing or summary of a preceding statement
4. to show that a sentence is unfinished

1. *The dash between two very different thoughts*
   Old Mill is a nice, quiet, friendly town—it bores the hell out of us.

   There are many interesting things to do here—if you're a moron.

2. *Dashes around an informal parenthesis*
   John Glass—a transparently honest fellow—must watch himself carefully.

   Use a dash with an iinfiormial—sorry, got a finger stuck in my i—parenthesis.

   The dogs in our town—we are proud to say—prefer our garbage cans to all the others in Old Mill.

3. *The dash before a rephrasing or summary*
   We often talk with our neighbors—saves money on tranquilizers.

   We asked the Coffins in for cocktails—it was a lively time for all of them.

4. *The dash after an unfinished sentence*
   As for my wife and me—

   Consider the dash something like a horizontal exclamation point without the point. Think of it as more emphatic than the comma or the colon. But beware the lure of emphasis; you may use a dash too often when one of the other symbols is preferable: review the other two marks—note the subtle differences, differences in emphasis, between all three. And don't overwork the dash—because if you do—

   Something else: a dash should never be combined with a period, a comma, semicolon, or colon. In typing, a dash is two hyphens with no spaces before, between, or behind. It can go either inside or outside quotation marks, depending on the context of the sentence.

   ". . ." use *quotation marks*

   1. around direct quotations—the exact words of a writer or speaker in the exact order in which he spoke or wrote them.
   2. around titles of short stories, songs, poems, chapters from books, essays, articles from newspapers and magazines (do not underline; see *italics*)
   3. around words or expressions to show that they are being used in some special way
   4. around words being written as words, and around letters being written as letters
   5. around definitions

If a quotation is long, you should indent it; if the quotation covers several paragraphs, put quotation marks at the beginning of each paragraph but *not* at the end of each paragraph. The one and only "end" quotation marks, you place at the end of the total quoted material.

I've been talking about *direct quotations;* there is such a thing as an *indirect quotation*—a paraphrase of what has been said or written:

Direct: I asked, "You do love me sincerely, don't you?"
"Not sincerely," she said.
Indirect: I asked her whether she loved me sincerely.
She said *that* she didn't love me sincerely.

1. *Use quotation marks around the exact words of a speaker*
   I knew she wasn't sincere when she said that; her faintly negative reply was, I knew, intended only to maintain that sense of doubt and mystery so essential to a deeply sincere relationship. I said, "How do you feel about Twinkletoes?" "Oh," she said, "I do sincerely love Twinkletoes."

   a writer
   Rancid McCumber, the editor of The Old Mill BLAST (who is usually pretty well bottled up inside), writes a weekly editorial, under the caption "Mill Dew." Usually there's little substance to them: the substance is in poor Rancid. But yesterday's Mill Dew column had something really sober to say: "Something is happening in Old Mill," he wrote, "that disturbs me and the other old-timers. The quiet, friendly days are gone. Strangers from the city are coming in—throwing fancy cocktail parties, quarreling in the streets, and what other devilment, I don't know." I think he's right, for once.

2. *Use quotation marks around titles of short stories, songs, short poems, chapters from books, essays, newspaper or magazine articles*
   "The Bath Not Taken" is my wife's favorite poem.
   I go more for short stories—especially murder mysteries. Have you read Nickey Spitoon's "Kill Me Once and Kill Me Twice"?
   We recommended to the mayor that he read an article in the current issue of *Fume* called "Is It Right to be Wrong?"

3. *Use quotation marks around words or expressions to show they're being used in some special way.*
   In our town "a jug of wine" means a bucket of moonshine. And when you fall in love, you "melt."

4. *Use quotation marks around words used as words or letters used as letters*
   The good word is that the word "word" is a good word.
   I asked Rusty Coffin what the word "ethic" meant.

He wanted to know if there was a "k" in it. Conversation is hard in Old Mill.

5. *Use quotation marks around definitions*

Rancid McCumber found that it meant, "It's something that gets in the way of what you really want to do."

When quotation marks are used, other marks are also used. Where do these marks go? Inside or outside the quotation marks? The quotation marks always come

1. after commas and periods.
2. before semicolons, colons, and dashes.
3. after question marks and exclamation points if these marks are part of what is quoted.
4. before the question mark and exclamation point if these marks are not part of what is quoted.

- The use of the **hyphen** is myriad and complicated. When do you, when don't you, why, wherefore, and if! One is well known: Use a hyphen when the last word of a line is too long for the space, dividing words of two or more pronounced syllables between the syllables; BUT words of one syllable, of course, should never be divided, *although* double consonants should be divided, *except* in a one syllable word with a suffix, *whereas* prefixes are hyphenated in some words when the root word begins with the same vowel the prefix ends with, *or* when the root word begins with a capital letter, *and also* to form certain compounds such as compound adjectives before a noun (*although* you shouldn't hyphenate compound adjectives *if* one of the words is an adverb ending in -ly) *and* compound numbers from twenty-one to ninety-nine *and* to distinguish between two meanings of a word (*nevertheless* you have to watch not to confuse certain words that seem as if they could just as easily have one or not have one such as recreation or reformation which you might think ought to be written re-creation or re-formation). . .

(pant pant) Bewildered? (pant pant) The point of that endless stream-of-consciousness sentence is how confusing the use of the hyphen can be. Can be? Is! But we can get order out of chaos by naming our hyphen-blessings one by one.

1. *Use a hyphen when the last word of a line is too long for the space*

Something new happened at the kitchen stove after Nellie came. Before her happy arrival, the food was *nour-
ishing* but . . . She would stand
at the foot of the steps for a few
moments gathering her lungs: *"BREAK-
FAST* in ten minutes!"

Divide **words of two or more pronounced syllables** between the syllables:
> Awed, the cowpunchers watched the tall, lean man *walk-*
> *ing* across the saloon's sawdust floor.

Words of one syllable, of course, shound never be divided; you would *not* write:
> Awed, the cowpunchers watched as the tall, lean man *walk-*
> *ed* across the saloon's sawdust floor.

Divide **double consonants:**
> Startled women and children ran and hid as the *quar-*
> *rel* was settled by a shoot-out in the dusty street.

> By the time the two arch-enemies faced each other, the *com-*
> *mittee* had met and voted to execute any surviving duellist.

> By the next morning, the committee had made the *neces-*
> *sary* arrangements for the execution of the survivor.

Except in a **word with a suffix:**
> After a long search, the zealous committee found the *miss-*
> *ing* killer hiding on the roof of the calaboose. That afternoon,
> my father, always ready, gave his *bless-*
> *ing* to those assembled to watch the execution;
> but since I left town before any died and haven't been either
> place myself, I have no idea whether his effort was *success-*
> *ful.* I hope it was.

(It's preferable to place more letters after the hyphen than before it; there must be at least two letters before the hyphen and at least three letters after it.)

2. *Use a hyphen with some words with prefixes* when the **root word begins with the same vowel the prefix ends with:**
> The *co-owner re-entered* the store to *re-employ* the *anti-intellectual* he had just fired for saying "Between you and I."

when the **root word begins with a capital letter:**
> It is *un-American* to be sad during the *pre-Christmas* season. If you're not *pro-Hoover,* you're *anti-Motherhood.*

3. *Use a hyphen to form certain compounds*
compound adjectives before a noun:
> His *devil-may-care* attitude about seeing a *second-rate* show in a *tumble-down* shack only *one-third* full annoyed me. It really did, fellows.

and **compound numbers from twenty-one to ninety-nine**
> My first reaction was: *thirty-five* men on a dead man's chest—strange! Thirty, yes; even forty—but *thirty-five?*

(There are really no rules to determine whether certain words are solid—*baseball, starlight*—or compound—*star-spangled, fair-minded*—or separate—*fair ball, compound interest.* When in doubt, as you often will be, use the dictionary. (See ch. 6)

4. **Use a hyphen to distinguish between two meanings of a word**

I *remarked* to the courteous manager of the supermarket that the price on a can of beans seemed high. He said, "Hell's bells, I've *re-marked* that can of beans three times already this morning." "Up or down? I distinctly *recollect* that I *re-collected* the remnants of your contact lenses."

GROUP 3

If you will turn this page and just a few more, you will see with a sigh that the . . . punctuation chapter is nearly over! (done [with], fini [?]) through. The uses of the bracket, the ellipsis, the exclamation point, the parenthesis, the question mark; and the period ends the whole thing—as it should.

[   ]**Use brackets to set off parenthetical matter within parentheses**

When Milton wrote "When I consider how my light is spent" (the sonnet on his blindness [1652]), he had been blind for several years.

Use brackets to include editorial comment in quoted material

"There are many reasons given for his [Shakespeare's] departure from Stratford."

"Brackits [sic] are very seldom used except in formal writing."

The "sic" (from the Latin word meaning "thus") in brackets tells the reader that a word is being copied exactly as it was originally written—usually indicating misspelling.

. . . **Use an ellipsis (. . .) to indicate omitted words**

Its main use is in quoted matter when only a part of a quotation is used. If the ellipsis occurs at the end of the sentence, add a fourth dot—to serve as the period.

Complete	With ellipsis
"He decided the time had come to pick up his cane, kiss the maid, and leave."	"He decided the time had come to pick up his cane, . . . and leave."

EMERGENCY PUNCTUATION KIT

Instructions: In the event of a punctuation emergency, use the contents according to the instructions contained in the kit.

FOR EMERGENCY USE ONLY

Emergency Punctuation Kit

—
—
—

;

;

( )

List of contents
1. Three (3) dashes
2. Two (2) semi-colons
3. One (1) matched pair parentheses

Instructions for use:

     1. WHEN YOU HAVE NO IDEA AT ALL WHAT PUNCTUATION TO USE—use one of the dashes.

     2. WHEN YOU CANNOT DECIDE BETWEEN A COMMA AND A PERIOD—use a semicolon. There is a good chance the semicolon will be wrong, but if the alternatives are a period and a comma, it will be less offensive than the wrong mark would be.

     3. WHEN YOU WANT TO ADD AN IDEA TO A SENTENCE AND CANNOT MAKE IT FIT—use the pair of parentheses.

WARNING: These marks, used as instructed above, are intended for emergency use, and must not be applied indiscriminately. Indiscriminate use may be offensive to the reader and result in a lowered grade.

*Use a whole line of ellipsis marks to indicate the omission of a paragraph
or a line of poetry*

Jack and Jill went up the hill,
To fetch a pail of water.

. . . .

And now they have a daughter.

! *Exclamation points are used to denote very strong or intense emotion.*

Strong and intense emotions do not, with sane people, occur in rapid-
fire succession—rata-tat-rata-tat-Bam! So spare the exclamation points; otherwise you will give an impression of gushing insincerity. And don't use an
exclamation point and a question mark together to indicate shocked surprise.
With literate people this is as much of a no-no as too many!!! If you wonder
whether you should use an exclamation point—don't! But you might try an
occasional interrobang. ("Interrobang?" "Yes, interrobang—if your teacher or
publisher. . ." "My teacher or publisher?" "Don't interrupt. If your teacher
or publisher will let you." "Let me? Coo!")
Use the exclamation point

1. after strong commands
2. after emphatic words, phrases, or clauses
3. within quotations to call special attention to a certain word
4. after interjections.

1. *Use the exclamation point after strong commands*
   "Go to, you wretch!"
   "Get out of here!"

2. *Use the exclamation point after emphatic words, phrases, clauses*
   Word: Ouch!
   Phrase: How painful!
   Clause: It hurts like hell!

3. *Use the exclamation point within sentences to call attention to a certain
   word*
   She had fifteen (!) bras and nothing to show for them.

4. *Use an exclamation point after interjections*
   Echhh! How can you eat that?
   Wow! Look at that walk.

Many exclamation points naturally find themselves involved with quotations. When one belongs with what is quoted, put it inside the quotation marks; when it does not, put it outside.

> The audience screamed, "Stop the music!"
>
> With his mouth in mid-air, the leader looked like a "tar-gum chewing nit"!

And also use an exclamation point as if it ends a sentence, even when it doesn't. Begin the next word with a capital letter.[4]

> Alas! We shall never hear his like again.

Don't use a comma or a period with an exclamation point:

> She yelled, "Ouch!, That hurts." (That's wrong.)

Instead write:

> "Release my fingers!" the dentist shrieked.

( ) *Use parentheses*

1. to set off elements (phrases and clauses) which seriously interrupt the main thought of the sentence or are of minor importance
2. to set off numbers, dates, and references
3. to insert illustrations, definitions, or other information not a main part of the main structure of the sentence, but which are useful for a clear understanding
4. to set off numbers or letters in a list

Note: Use parentheses only for insertions in a writer's own sentence. In quoted material, put insertions in brackets.

1. **Use Parentheses to set off elements which seriously interrupt the main thought of the sentence or are of minor importance**

   The one-eyed sheriff (*how stupid can you be*) decided to shoot it out with Dead-Eye Dick.

   His wife (*one wonders why*) urged him on.

   The sheriff (*poor chap*) is now totally blind.

---

[4]Unless a quotation mark comes between: "Alas!" he cried.

2. *Use parentheses to set off numbers, dates, and references*

The sheriff's wife was young (only 22) and was considered quite friendly by both the rangers and the rustlers.

On the other hand, the sheriff, getting up in years (born in 1865), now only vaguely remembered those delicate arts of congeniality. The melancholy outcome of this fated union is referred to (see pp. 44–52) in Longhouse's classic, *Captain Endon Paige: His Period.*

3. *Use parentheses to insert illustrations, definitions, or other information not a main part of the main structure of the sentence:*

In two states (Texas and Arizona), this whole tragic story aroused intense interest.

It formed the basis of a popular play, *Never Trust a One-Eyed Sheriff's Wife,* starring Maude Muller (her first appearance on any stage) as the rampant wife, Cecelia.

Maybe, we shouldn't call it a play: it was really a melodrama (a play in which the emotions displayed are violent or extravagantly sentimental), but it did touch the hearts of its audience.

4. *Use parentheses to set off numbers or letters in a list*

Certain things can be learned from this sad story: (1) one-eyed sheriffs should never fight two-eyed gunmen; (2) one-eyed and aging sheriffs should never marry bright-eyed and younger women; (3) however old a man gets he should never forget the delicate arts of congeniality and their essential uses.

A parenthetical expression does not affect the other punctuation of a sentence in which it is placed. Any mark required at the point of insertion should be placed after the last parenthesis. No punctuation is used inside the parentheses unless the material in parentheses begins with a capital letter and makes a complete, separate statement. In that case, the appropriate punctuation mark, whatever it might be (period, question mark or exclamation point), would be used. And if the complete statement in parentheses is a quotation ("Quotation marks are the flyspecks of a tiny, imitative mind, buzzing about the remains of original thought."—J.-P. Mouche) quotation marks would be used.

¿ Do you think that it would be a good idea to follow the Spanish practice and give advance warning that a question is coming by putting an upside-down question mark in front of the sentence?

1. Use the question mark when you ask a direct question
2. when a question is phrased as a statement
3. when there is uncertainty about what has just been said

1. *Use the question mark when asking a direct question*
   Did you feed the cat his din-din?

   Do you have to call it his din-din?

   No, but you did promise to give him his din-din, didn't you?

2. *Use the question mark when a question is phrased as a statement*
   Daddykins doesn't want to feed kitty-poo before din-din?

3. *Use the question mark when there is uncertainty about what has just been said*
   Our courageous (?) constable takes his mother with him on patrol.

   Paul Lawrence Dunbar, who died in 1905 (?), wrote "He Wears the Mask."

   If the question is part of a quotation, put the question mark within the quotation marks:

   "Was he really so young when he died?" the student asked.

   If the whole sentence is a question, however, put the question mark after the quotation mark:

   Did I hear you say, "He was really so young when he died"?

Use periods

1. to end declarative and imperative sentences and indirect questions
2. after abbreviations
3. after certain non-sentences
4. to indicate decimal fractions and to set off dollars from cents.

1. *Use a period to end most sentences* **declarative sentence (statement)**
   The cat has twenty-three toes.

   imperative sentence (command)
   Polish every one of them.

   indirect question
   My wife asked if she couldn't skip a few of them.

2. *Use a period after abbreviations*
   Mr. Longhouse

   Mrs. Clay

   Va. N.Y.

   Ms. but not after Miss

3. *Use a period after certain non-sentences*
   salutations
   > Good evening.

   fragments answering questions
   > What did you wear this morning? A shirt and tie and a pair of high-button shoes.

4. *Use a period to indicate decimal fractions and to set off dollars and cents*
   > What π (*pi*) is I don't know; what it's supposed to mean I don't know. All I do remember are the numbers: 3.14159. . . .
   > Sterno, which is used for heating outside things outside and, unfortunately, for heating inside things inside has an alcoholic content of 8.6 (?).
   > It's known as the "poor man's poison" because it costs only about $1.60 a quart.

Except after abbreviations, never use a period with other punctuation marks that stand for a silence (comma, colon, semicolon, dash, question mark, exclamation point). If an abbreviation is pronounced as it is spelled (Prof, exam) it is considered informal usage and is not followed by a period. Also, do not use periods with acronyms or abbreviations consisting entirely of capital letters: HEW, PTA. Periods are always placed inside quotation marks (as is the comma), just for consistency—"the hobgoblin of petty minds." Unless a parenthetical expression is complete in itself (It may begin with a capital and make a complete sentence.), a period is not used inside parentheses.

Topics: (1) The advantages (or disadvantages) of living like Tarzan.

(2) Man's relationships with animals, from pigs and parakeets to elephants and eagles.

(3) Justify and praise your favorite reading material (murder mystery, science fiction, western novel, historical novel, contemporary novel, sports page, newspaper column—Dear Abbie, Art Buchwald—editorial page, history, religious meditation, movie review, etc.). Flex your punctuating muscles by using as great a variety of marks as you can, putting in the margin beside each mark the page number and rule number that call for that punctuation.

14

How to Grow a Unified Paragraph and a Reasonable Essay

any texts blend types of paragraph development with types of order; this book does not. "Order" means what goes where, particularly where the topic sentence goes, but also how details are organized. I have discussed *order* **within** the paragraph in Chapter 9. The problem of *making sense* within the paragraph includes more than order: it includes thinking of ideas and keeping them hooked together. Since ideas that grow as a person grows hang together better than separate ideas that are hooked mechanically, like the parts of a robot, since a live President has more unity than all of the robots in Disneyworld's Hall of Presidents, I will emphasize the *development* of content as one growing process, rather than hooking pieces together. Here I am concerned with how sentences grow out of a topic into a connected whole.

PARAGRAPH DEVELOPMENT

Paragraph development matters. How can a paragraph be developed? You have a topic sentence, but no paragraph. The bones of your essay are all connected toe-bone to foot-bone and so forth, but you had better add a little flesh if they are going to walk around without sending the audience running screaming from the armchair. Or worse, perhaps, some audiences will pulverize unfleshed bones, grind those bones to make their meat—especially if the audience is an English teacher who has assigned 800 words and receives only 192.

The basic technique of paragraph growing: feed it details.

Both journey and suitcase paragraphs expand when filled with details. With a journey paragraph, whose point of departure and destination are already known, adding details means filling in the middle. With suitcase paragraphs, however, adding details means surrounding the central idea, the topic sentence, by filling it out all around. Or, if you think of it as a process of expansion, journey paragraphs are stretched lengthwise and made longer, suitcase paragraphs are stretched out in all directions and made fatter. But in both cases, you add details. The question now isn't "where do the details go?" See Chapters 8 and 9 for that. The question now is, "How do you think of details that belong? How do you grow a unified paragraph from a topic sentence?"

Take for example an assignment to write about your first encounter with someone. Probably, you will write either narration (journey) or description (suitcase). If I were given such an assignment, I might take my first sight of my oldest son, Christopher.

Topic sentence: When I first saw my son Christopher, he looked hideous. A descriptive paragraph will result, including his misshapen head, his puffy eyes, the bloodstains, the wrinkles, and the umbilical remnant. Having jotted those down right away, all of which specify *how* he was hideous, I am ready to write a suitcase paragraph describing him.

But then I reflect that the whole point of this description, the reason it occurred to me as a topic, is the effect it had on me. I therefore revise the topic sentence: When I first saw my son Christopher, he looked much worse than I expected. Checking this topic sentence, I see that I should give my expectations first, then the description. Apparently, a little narrative introduction will be necessary for this journey from expectation to actual encounter. I therefore jot down the events preceding my sight of him: I left my wife at the hospital, woke up and read the clock wrong before going back to sleep (implies I was casual, but shows I wasn't awake)—woke up again, excited this time, dashed to the hospital arriving just after Chris was born, imagined what he would look like as a boy, and then saw the (ugh) baby. Having done all this, I would be ready to write the finished product.

It's harder, of course, when you are not selecting from memories. Suppose your topic sentence (from your outline) is: Rudeness produces chaos. The paragraph could be either suitcase or journey. If you think of a number of results, each of which is chaotic and is caused directly by rudeness, you will have built a suitcase paragraph.

Rudeness produces chaos. A shopper tells a counter clerk to hurry up, hurry up; the clerk impales a cardboard shirtbox top and two sheets of tissue paper on the shopper's head. A commuter tells a bus driver he will move along to the rear of the bus when he damn well feels like it; the bus driver throws up his hands in despair, and the bus swerves off the street into the front window of a wig store, knocking over two garbage cans and a passing garment worker's clothes rack on the way. A little boy says a dirty word to his mother; she spills the stew, shrieks at her husband, spanks the boy, and bursts into tears.

Even though each sentence is a little journey from cause to effect, the whole paragraph is a suitcase. Sentences two through four exemplify the opening topic, and they could be arranged in any order.

If on the other hand you trace a sequence of events, showing how one consequence becomes the cause of another, you are creating a journey paragraph.

Rudeness produces chaos. A teenager insults his mother. Startled, she whirls toward him, emptying a pan of gravy across the kitchen floor. "My gravy," she sobs. "What's all the ruckus aboOW" says her husband, quickly lying down in the gravy. The doctor puts his leg in traction for six weeks. During his absence from work, 4,672 cars get through his plant's assembly line without his checking their left front door. During the next half year, 187 car owners pull off their lockbuttons, 58 cannot close their windows (31 of those in a driving rainstorm which gives 8 of them bad colds and 2 pneumonia), 19 cannot open their windows during a heat wave which prostrates 5 with heat-stroke and drives 3 to bitter quarrels with their wives, and 3,018 pull the door completely off the car hinges, breaking one or more bones in 1,758 cases. 2,310 sue the manufacturer, prompting a federal regulatory agency to order recall of all cars for inspection. Production stops during the inspection period, laying off 15,000 workers who riot in the third week of the shutdown. The influx of government troops arouses popular sympathy; demonstrators in Detroit start 17 fires and demonstrators in Toledo are fired upon; the national guard is mobilized; a national emergency is declared; unions arm themselves; troops are recalled from stations overseas; Russia and China both try to take over our weakened overseas installations; World War III begins. [A little extreme, but. . . .]

In a sense, this second rudeness-chaos paragraph provides one great big hypothetical example to illustrate the main point. If you are having difficulty providing a number of single details, you may have more success thinking of one big detail, one big illustration such as how World War III was started by a teenager being rude to his mother (and let that be a lesson to you all).

Several avenues lead a struggling writer to ways of making a paragraph grow, whether large or small. You can seek a number of effects, as in the first rudeness-chaos paragraph; or you can trace a chain in which one effect becomes the cause of another effect, as the second does. Sometimes, you will want to list causes, although very rarely will you ever want to follow the cause and effect chain backwards—that's a journey in the wrong direction.

The topic sentence "Rudeness produces chaos" could be developed either of two ways: 1) you could try to think of *cause-effect* relationships; 2) you could try to think of *examples*—whether several small examples or one big one. Either approach could have produced both of the paragraphs above. The important thing is not whether the paragraphs are cause-effect paragraphs or example paragraphs (actually, they are both); the important point is how you can think of the details. Search either path—examples or cause-effect—and you may come to the same goal.

Practically any topic sentence can be developed by examples. Here is a paragraph that develops a definition by two examples:

Irony involves a tension or conflict between what is said and what is meant; this tension is not a slight difference but a real contrast. When a man's best friend, whom he has not seen for a month, slaps him on the back and says, "Hey, you old s.o.b., how've you been?" no offense is taken. The man knows his friend is not really imputing to him canine ancestry on the distaff side. Usually, the tone of voice in irony is more biting. The grumpy child who says "oh, goody. Spinach again," is bitterly ironic: he means not "Oh, goody" but "Oh, baddy."[1]

Or ask yourself whether you need to *define* something—certainly technical terms should be defined. Often, you may be using simple terms in a somewhat special way that you need to explain to your reader. Value judgments (beautiful, good, fair) often need such explanation, and relative terms (big, small, fast, promptly) can use some help too. Suppose you were expressing your views on the candidates for the House of Representatives in 1898. You might write that John McCandid would make a bad representative. (Then you brood. How can you explain why you would not have voted for McCandid, had you been on the nominating committee? One way to approach your explanation is to *define* what you mean by "bad.") We've already had twelve years of bad Congressmen. (Implicitly, you mean by "bad" "like our last Congressman.) McCandid wouldn't get us out of Cuba after we got back from the Maine quickly; he wouldn't stop inflation soon enough. (Stuck again. Surely that's clear enough. Woops! How fast is "quickly"? How soon is "soon enough"? Define your terms.) Supporting President McKinley's policy as he does, the best he offers is withdrawal in four months. Even that isn't good enough with the war costing what it does in money and trade, and that four months is the earliest withdrawal, the best that could be hoped for. The worst seems to be permanent occupation. (Although the cigars are great.) And as for inflation—partly caused by the war—it must stop immediately. Gradual decline over a year or more isn't soon enough. A good policy would halt inflation within one month.

Or see if you have introduced things that should be *listed*. For example, describing how you spend your day, you write that during the latter part of the morning you help your husband with odd jobs around the house. Clearly, a little list will add some meat to this topic, and you promptly list as many of the chores you have helped with as you can think of, all the way from getting the great Dane's foot unstuck from the toilet bowl to charting the flying times of your husband's latest model-airplane design modifications.

Cause and effect, example, definition, listing, all are ways to make a paragraph grow. Another way, probably next after example in usefulness, is comparison and/or contrast. Suppose that you meant during the 1896

---

[1] C. Carter Colwell, *A Student's Guide to Literature* (New York: Washington Square Press, 1968), p. 38.

presidential campaign, that McKinley would make a bad president because he ran before and was defeated. You would have said: "McKinley would make a bad president because he ran before and was defeated." But make it more concrete by adding a comparison to something similar: . . . like a bride left standing at the church once too often, who carries her grudges against men into her marriage bed when at last she is not jilted. Or: . . . like a mountain climber on his second attempt, whose bruises and broken bones from the previous fall make it impossible for him to stand erect even if he should reach the top this time. Or suppose you want to say that classifying art is hard, because artists do so many different things. You might write this paragraph, in which the comparisons have been italicized:

The classification to follow, although systematic, does not produce a tidy bin of completely separated literary types. A certain blurring of the classification is inevitable when what is being classified is art, *for art is more like living nature than like the grocer's sorted and labeled vegetable remains. Like living nature,* art does not stand still; it develops and changes. Artists, *like any force that produces mutation and evolutionary change,* are constantly seeking novelty and variety. Thus, no sooner has a critic defined a difference between two kinds of literature (or any other art, for that matter), separating them neatly from each other, than an upstart artist hurries to see what he can create that falls between the kinds, defying classification, or, at least, making classification much harder and less tidy. *Just as nature seems constantly to expand, filling every available niche with some kind of life, varying in order to take every possible opportunity for living the environment offers,* so all artists as a group seem constantly to expand their efforts, apparently trying to develop every possible kind of art work. *Some children, when they go down a sidewalk, play the game of never stepping on a crack.* The artist tries to step on them all. The classification that follows, although in broad outline almost universally accepted, suffers all the consequences of the inconsiderate artist's concern for the individuality and uniqueness of his own work.[2]

Especially when what you write about is abstract, making concrete comparisons gives impact and flavor to your words. How much real gut impact is there in the words, "You get out of an education what you put into it"? But make a concrete comparison, and how much more vividly the words appeal to our everyday experiences: "Education is like a sewer. You get out of it what you put into it."

Finally, to develop a paragraph effectively, repeat yourself. Pretend you are talking to a deaf mute, who keeps cupping his hand inquisitively around his ear, and say it again. Of course, if he didn't catch the words you

---

[2]Colwell, A *Student's Guide to Literature,* pp. 85–86.

used at first, use slightly different ones when repeating. If you say exactly the same thing, you will annoy your audience as the old hard-sell television commercials annoyed. If you say exactly the same thing, you will annoy your audience as the old hard-sell television commercials annoyed. If you say exactly the same thing, you will annoy your audience as the old hard-sell television commercials annoyed. But if you vary your wording somewhat, you may succeed where others, more terse, brief, and tight-lipped, have failed. Varied wording of the same idea, like a person you have seen in varied wardrobe, gives new insights into the real nature of what is clothed.

Reread the paragraph on classifying literary types quoted from *A Student's Guide to Literature,* and see how many of the paragraph's sentences restate all or part of the central idea, the idea that artists always make new types that won't fit any system. Repetition in the form of *restatement* is a very important means of developing a coherent and effective paragraph.

Suppose you are working on a topic sentence, watering it with the sweat of your brow as you try to think of ways to grow a paragraph. Suppose, too, that you have thought of a few details—whether by listing, or by defining, or by comparing or contrasting, or by working out causes and effects or examples. But suppose (beat your forehead with your fist) that you just can't think of any more. What then? Probably you have been concentrating on single details. Stand back from the paragraph, look at what you have done already and see if your details so far are part of a larger pattern.

Topic: The night was beautiful. Details: The air smelled sweet. The city lights twinkled softly. Even the stars were visible, for once. It was quiet, too.

You want to say more about the beauty of the night, but all you can think of is the way it looked, the way it smelled, and the way it sounded. As soon as you have said "looked, smelled, and sounded," you remember the other senses, touch and taste, and you add:

The softly moving air was cool on the face. The beauty of the night was so intense it seemed you could taste it.

Here, you have thought of more details by recognizing a pattern in the details you started with. Remember the paragraph on big John, back on page 105? Trying to describe him, you might have thought first of the way women regarded him. What often goes with women? Answer: men. So you added some details on how men regarded him.

EXERCISE 1: Suppose you have added details to a topic sentence, but not enough; and suppose that when you review the details you have already added, you find they fall into the categories listed below; what other categories of additional details might you think of? Example: children. answer: adults. (Not as part of an answer to this exercise, but just to see how these ideas might work in a writing situation, suppose your topic were: Severe marijuana laws are bad for society. First details thought of: Children who smoke it [as most do at one time or another] are breaking the law, and come to develop a contempt for the law, the officers who enforce it, and citizens who endorse and support it. As a result of noting that your detail concerns children, but that adults are a great untapped source of enrichment for this paragraph, you add: Parents suffer financially and morally. They must pay the court costs of their errant children's explorations, sometimes a substantial fee; and, more serious, they are tempted into well-meant lies, as they try to make marijuana seem so unattractive that no one—particularly their child—could possibly want to smoke it.)

    a. Males of all ages—

    b. Country—

    c. Air, land—

    d. Up, around—

    e. Inside—

    f. Top—

    g. Cause—

    h. Mothers—

    i. Good citizens—

    j. White men, black men, red men—

    k. Employers—

    l. Good effects—

    m. The past, the present—

    n. At home, on the way to work—

    o. Insects, plants—

    p. Attempt—

From the seeds of ideas you have already grown, you may raise a whole new crop. Use the ideas you have already thought of, in order to think of more. As I have just said, by reviewing the details you have already thought of, you may notice that they are of certain types: those types may naturally suggest another type, that you associate with the first; and you may then think of details to write about the topic sentence in connection with this last type.

Alternatively, as you try to expand a half-completed paragraph, try shifting gears. If you have been concentrating on single details, see if you can think of details to expand the details. Go back to our night of nights. Instead of following out the pattern of the five senses, you might add to the details already there:

The night was beautiful. The air, newly washed by a light shower of rain, smelled sweet as a baby fresh from his bath. The city lights twinkled softly. Lamps behind translucent shades spread a soft glow that muted the glare of the flickering movie marquee, and beyond the rooftops of the houses across the street the valley shopping center blended blue-green expressway lights with yellow parking lot lights. The movement of white headlights and red taillights animated the web of light, with more exotic storefront hues radiating from slender tubes of neon, krypton, and a host of exotic gases whose names she had never heard. Even the stars were visible, for once. They seemed close to her in the silence, which was intensified rather than broken by the distant ring of a trolley bell at the foot of Meander Hill.

All that from: The night was beautiful. The air smelled sweet. The city lights twinkled softly. Even the stars were visible, for once. It was quiet, too.

Notice that in expanding these details, you could have thought of the additional details by using the methods suggested earlier. Thus, the sweet smell of the air is expanded by giving its *cause* (a light shower of rain) and by *comparing* it to something else (a baby fresh from his bath). The city lights are expanded by *listing* (lights in windows, movie house lights, expressway lights, parking lot lights, headlights, taillights, storefront lights) and by *description* of appearance (the colors). And the quiet is expanded by *contrast* (to the sound of the bell) which also states a cause (the bell intensified the silence).

In sum, when developing paragraphs, ask yourself the following questions:

1. What details can I add? (The most general question.)

2. Have I omitted steps between the first and last sentences of the paragraph? (Most appropriate to journey paragraphs such as narrations.)

3. Are there details I can group around the main idea to make it clearer and more vivid? (Most appropriate to a suitcase paragraph such as description.)

4. Can I add one large detail, probably an example?

5. Would stating either causes or effects of the topic sentence help?

6. Are there examples I have overlooked?

7. Do any terms need definition? (Look particularly for technical terms, ordinary terms used in a special sense, value terms, and relative terms.)

8. Are there details that need to be listed?

9. To what could I make a comparison or contrast? (Seek vivid and concrete comparisons that clarify your meaning.)

10. Can I restate the main idea?

11. Are the details added thus far only part of the whole scene? Does what they have in common suggest what I have omitted? (To be asked when you feel stuck with an incompletely developed paragraph.)

12. Can I expand the details with sub-details? (Also for a half-grown paragraph in need of more branches.)

CONNECTIONS WITHIN AND BETWEEN PARAGRAPHS

A well-written paragraph grows organically. Sometimes, though, things that are really part of each other may look unrelated. In such cases, adding some links may help make the real unity obvious.

Pre-Test: Read the following two paragraphs. They follow the paragraph quoted earlier (on p. 104) which compares the history of the planet to a ten-volume work, man appearing on the next-to-last page of the last volume. Then re-read and mark every word or phrase that serves as a link between sentences.

Throughout the last two volumes life proliferated, creating an environment in which more complex forms of life could emerge and prosper. Both life and the capacity to support life increased millennia after millennia. Man entered the scene on a planet that was biologically very rich indeed. To that organic richness he contributed little. In fact, in certain localities over limited periods of time his treatment of his environment was quite destructive. But only when we reach the last letter of the last word on the last page does he turn the tide against life. Only then does man begin the process of killing the planet. What is astonishing is that all that has been produced over the course of a billion years is so vulnerable to destruction by this late-comer to the scene.

Yet it should not surprise us that what takes so long to create can be so easily destroyed. It took only a moment for an assassin's bullet to destroy the complex richness of the life of a John F. Kennedy or a Martin Luther King. That richness of thought, will, and feeling had been many years in the making, but it depended on an organic base that could be destroyed almost instantaneously. The life of the planet similarly depends on a physical base which, now that its secrets have been mastered by man, is vulnerable to his destruction. For at least a hundred years, and with ever-quickening acceleration, we have been destroying it. The eleventh volume may recount the much poorer story of a lifeless planet.[3]

You should find 16.

That paragraph by Cobb is a model of coherence. To *cohere* is to hang together; coherence is connectedness. Not everything published coheres. The

---

[3]John B. Cobb, Jr., *Is It Too Late? A Theology of Ecology* (Beverly Hills, California. Bruce, 1972), p. 78.

script of the movie *The Hellstrom Chronicle* showed a remarkable incoherence in basic attitude. An exquisitely photographed movie about bugs, this film argued that bugs would inherit the earth, and soon, too. But the writers either didn't know or couldn't agree whether that replacement of man by insect as dominant life-form was fitting, proper, and just, or whether it was a horror and an abomination. In one line they would praise the insects' ability to survive; in the next line, the very same characteristic would disgust them. In one line the writers were glad, in the next they were sorry; in one line the insects were beautiful, in the next they were repulsive.

If you write like that, not all of the connectors and links in the world will make your writing cohere. Maybe, though, if (heaven forbid) you have written like that, the effort to put in appropriate links and connectors may reveal what doesn't fit. Make those connections before you hand your paper in, or, like the man who married a homosexual, you may not discover your mis-match until it is too late. Trying to add links such as *Therefore,* and *On the other hand,* requires you to think about how one idea relates to another.

The words and phrases that help hold this next passage together have been italicized. The passage, by Isaac Asimov, suggests a possible source of fuel: deuterium, a form of hydrogen, which releases atomic energy by fusion.

Earth's vast oceans are made up almost entirely of water molecules, and each water molecule contains two hydrogen atoms. Even if only one in 6,000 of *those* hydrogen atoms is deuterium, that still means there are about 35 thousand billion tons of deuterium in the oceans.

What's more, it isn't necessary to dig for *that* deuterium or to drill for it. If ocean water is allowed to run through separation plants, *the* deuterium can be extracted without very much trouble. *In fact,* for the energy you could get out of it, deuterium from the oceans would be only one hundredth as expensive as coal.

The deuterium in the world's oceans, if allowed to undergo fusion little by little, would supply mankind with enough energy to keep going, at the present rate, for 500 billion years. Since the sun won't last nearly *that* long, we might just as well say that if we are careful, hydrogen fusion will supply mankind with energy for as long as we will exist on earth.

Then, too, there is no danger of hydrogen fusion plants running out of control. *They* would be simpler than fission plants and if anything at all went wrong, the deuterium supply could be automatically cut off and the fusion process then would stop instantly. *Nor* is there any pollution problem, for in the fusion process all that is formed is ordinary helium, which is the least dangerous substance known.

Well, then, when can we expect to have controlled hydrogen fusion plants supplying mankind with energy?

There is a catch. A big catch. To start *the fusion* going we need a temperature of a hundred million degrees. At *that* temperature, all substances become thin vapors that spread out beyond our control at once. Is there a solution?[4]

Mr. Asimov concludes that there is a solution, even though we don't have it yet; perhaps by 1980. But although he may not have the solution to super-heating deuterium, Mr. Asimov clearly has the solution to how to write coherently. Look at all the links he uses:

1) Pronouns and pronoun adjectives (*those* hydrogen atoms; *that* still means; *that* deuterium; *that* long; *They* would be; *that* temperature). They make it clear that he is talking about the same thing he was just talking about a sentence ago. Note how often he uses the pronoun adjective, and repeats the noun. If in the second sentence he had said "Even if only one in 6,000 of *them*. . ." you might have been a little unsure whether he meant oceans, water molecules, or hydrogen atoms. For a pronoun to be an effective link, the antecedent must be certain. If there is room for doubt, use a pronoun adjective and repeat the noun, as Asimov does.

2) Transitional clause (*What's more.*)

3) Transitional sentence (the next to last paragraph). Asking a question links forward rather than back, as the reader gets ready for an answer.

4) Adverbs and adverbial phrases (*In fact; Then, too; Well, then*). They are very useful for showing logical relationship.

5) Conjunctions (*Nor.* . .) Most often used between clauses within one sentence, conjunctions can begin a sentence to relate it to the one before.

6) Definite article (*the* deuterium, *the* fusion). *Articles*, you remember, are *a, an,* and *the. A* and *an* are indefinite; *the* is definite. It is definite because when you say the something—the tree, the hat, the deuterium, the fusion—you mean a particular, specific, definite something—not just any old tree, or hat, or deuterium, or fusion, but this precise tree, hat, deuterium, or fusion that you are in the process of talking about. If the noun has no adjectives—if it isn't the tree of life, or the orange hat, or the deuterium we find in oceans, or the hydrogen fusion—if, that is, you don't describe the noun at all, but just say *the something,* then the only way it can be specific is because of what you have already said. If you have been talking about a tree of life, or an orange hat, or deuterium found in oceans or hydrogen fusion—then when you say *the* tree, *the* hat, *the* deuterium, *the* fusion, you are reminding the reader of what you said before, of the identification or descriptive details you have already given. (Note, as an aside, that if you mean any old tree or hat, etc., you would say trees or a tree, hats or a hat, deuterium or some deuterium, fusion or a fusion. Note, too, that you should not use the definite article with

---

[4] Isaac Asimov, "The Power Crisis That Threatens the World." Reprinted by permission of the author and Boy's Life, 23 Nov. 1971, pp. 33–35, published by the Boy Scouts of America.

an unmodified noun [a noun with no adjectives] if you have not described or identified it earlier; don't refer to the tree, the hat, etc. the very first time you mention trees and hats.)

EXERCISE 2:

    a. List all of the single *words* you can think of that could go at the beginning of a sentence to serve as a link with the sentence preceding.

    b. List all of the *phrases* you can think of that could serve a similar linking function.

    c. Write a transitional *sentence* to go between the paragraphs described in each of the following:

        1. The first paragraph describes a beautiful North Carolina wooded mountain scene; the second paragraph describes the stench coming from the nearby textile mills.

        2. The first paragraph argues that the government must do more tasks than it used to; the second paragraph argues that the government must spend less money.

        3. The first paragraph says that more schools are needed because of rising population; the second paragraph says that more schools are needed because a higher percentage of school-age children are going to school.

        4. The first paragraph says that more schools are needed because a higher percentage of school-age children are going to school; the second paragraph says that less money is available for education.

That last exercise required you to know what direction a paragraph was headed. Sometimes, consecutive paragraphs (as in some of these exercises) change direction. Indeed, sometimes a paragraph will change direction in the middle. Such a paragraph might be called a hinge paragraph, since it swings in the middle and heads a different way.

For an example of a hinge paragraph, look at this paragraph about Christmas quoted earlier.

There's nothing like an old-fashioned Christmas—goodies on the groaning board, halls decked with holly berry, gaily wrapped presents piling up on the window sills, loved ones chiming carols. It can put you flat on your back for a month. For years I spent the whole of January in bed with what was diagnosed as "my bronchitis" but was clearly battle fatigue brought on from my days in Macy's and my nights in Bloomingdale's.[5]

[5] Jean Kerr, "I saw Mommy kicking Santa Claus," *Penny Candy* (Garden City, New York: Doubleday & Co., Inc.) 1970, p. 73.

The first sentence seems to be praising Christmas; but the middle sentence swings around and criticizes Christmas. The last sentence then develops that reversed approach. The paragraph thus has two hinge-plates: Christmas is good; Christmas is bad. The hinge-pin is the middle sentence, in which the apparent good turns into an actual bad. Since the point of such a paragraph is the contrast between the first half and the last half, the middle hinge-pin sentence really is the topic sentence. In such a case, the transition, or link, or connection is the main idea.

Topic: Write a paragraph on each of the following, underlining all of the connections that link sentences: (a) The Christmas season. (b) Human life is fragile. (c) The universe may be big, but most of it doesn't matter. (d) The history of _____ (a movement, a nation, a state, a religion, a family, an idea, etc.)

LOGICAL ARGUMENT

The first half of this chapter has dealt with how to connect sentences and paragraphs from two approaches: paragraph development, or how to get unified details from a topic sentence; and connections within and between paragraphs, or how to use linking words and phrases. The rest of the chapter deals with a different sort of connection: logical argument, or how to think straight without stalling or getting lost. If your ideas don't hang together properly, not all the details nor all the links in the world will do more than show up your incoherence.

"There is only one argument for doing something; the rest are arguments for doing nothing." Writing with a critical eye for human comedy, F. M. Cornford thus begins his advice on arguing with professors in *Microcosmographia Academica, Being a Guide for the Young Academic Politician.*[6] Mr. Cornford exaggerates, fortunately; he tells us not about the nature of argument, but about the nature of professors—indeed, the nature of all men who would just as soon keep things the way they are. "If it's all the same to you, Mrs. Lerming," the first grader said to his teacher the second day of study on the multiplication tables when she asked him what two times two equals, "I think I'd just as soon stay on the one-timeses. I know them pretty well."

Change is difficult. It tires people, and even frightens them a bit. And that—alas for the writer who would rather convince casually—is the whole

---

[6] F. M. Cornford, *Microcosmographia Academica, Being a Guide for the Young Academic Politician* (Bowes and Bowes, London, 1922, n.e. 1970), p. 19.

purpose of argument. You argue in order to make someone change. If he already agrees with you, you don't need to argue; you simply remind him. If he doesn't agree, you want him to change his mind. And that will require some doing.

Any writing that tries to prove a point is arguing for its thesis. Unlike narrative writing, whether fictional or factual, and unlike expository writing, which simply recounts facts, offers information, argumentative writing tries to change something that by the nature of human nature doesn't want to change—the reader's very human mind.

The consequence? Any writing that argues has to be good. To be good, it must—like all writing—be clear. It must—like all writing—be interesting. But most of all, it must make a coherent and valid case. It must prove its point.

When Mr. Clay's dairy customers sued him, the Old Mill jury agreed that some circumstantial evidence is highly inferential—as the plaintiffs' lawyer triumphantly displayed trout found in the milk.[7]

Evidence convinces. The strength of any argument depends on the strength of the evidence. How then do you present evidence? What is it? Where do you find it?

The Rule of Evidence:

Opinion is not evidence.

Recently I read a student theme about good use of detail in setting a short story's scene. The essay consisted of six sentences. Four of them stated the author's opinion that the last two paragraphs of the story use detail effectively in setting the scene. That statement (or parts of it) came four times in a row. No evidence was offered. The author simply stated his opinion over and over.

> "Just the place for a Snark!" The Bellman cried,
>   As he landed his crew with care,
> Supporting each man on the top of the tide
>   By a finger entwined in his hair.
>
> "Just the place for a Snark! I have said it twice:
>   That alone should encourage the crew.
> Just the place for a Snark! I have said it thrice:
>   What I tell you three times is true."[8]

My student went the Bellman one better.

---

[7] For further information on Mr. Clay, see Chapter 13, Group 1 (pp. 164–177), especially p. 176.

[8] Lewis Carroll, *The Hunting of the Snark.*

Now, I have suggested earlier that you repeat, and it was good advice. But the purpose of repeating your thesis, of repeating the point you want to make, what you wish to get across, the purpose of repeating is clarity. Say what you mean often enough for the reader to get it. The issue now is *proof*. And that student's opinion, the thesis he believed and wanted me to believe too, was just not its own proof. People have argued that the idea of God is self-validating, that it proves itself; but as far as I know, that and a few basic premises of logic (whatever is, is; a thing is equal to itself) are about the only self-evident propositions still around.

Arguments build up or work down. *Induction* builds up, moving from particulars to a generalization. *Deduction* works down, starting with a generalization and applying it to a particular. Induction says, "It's true of this and this and this and this and this; therefore it must be true of everything." Deduction says, "It's true of everything; therefore it must be true of this." Usually, of course, the everything isn't quite everything, just everything of a certain type.

EXERCISE 3: What *inductive* conclusions might you argue for by citing this evidence? That is, how might you make a general statement from these facts?

  a. Every member of the opposite sex I have known has been a no-good two-timer.
  b. On five occasions I have tried to kill a wasp. When I swung at them, the first and third stung me on the back of the neck, the second stung me on the wrist, the fourth stung me on the ear, and the fifth got his stinger stuck in my hip pocket handkerchief.
  c. Sewage, before being pumped into lakes, rivers, and oceans, may go through three stages of purification. A small fraction of the American population's sewage now receives third-stage treatment, which removes up to 90% of the dirt, poisons, unwanted fertilizers, and what have-you. Sewage from about two-fifths of the population gets only second-stage treatment, which generally cleans out about 75% of the unwanted items. Sewage from about one-fourth of the population gets only first-stage treatment, which removes about 33% of *some* of the unwanted items. Sewage from about one twentieth of the population gets no treatment. About one third of the population has no sewers. (1972)

EXERCISE 4: What *deductive* conclusions might you argue for by citing these premises? That is, what single fact might these generalizations—the first sentence in each pair—prove, once linked to a particular by the second sentence in each pair?

a. All men are mortal. Socrates is a man.

b. When an electrical appliance doesn't work, either the appliance is defective, or it is not getting electricity. This brand new toaster, which I tested in the shop just before bringing it home, is not defective.

c. When an electrical appliance is not getting electricity, it is either turned off, not plugged in, or plugged in to a circuit whose fuse has blown. This toaster is not getting electricity.

Note that arguments of this deductive type (called syllogisms) can be misused. First, in a deductive argument, the premises have to be true, or no conclusion follows. For example, if the power transformer at the end of the block or the generator at the end of the city is not working, something besides switch, plug, and fuse may cut off the electricity to a toaster. A deductive argument is only as good as the generalizations or premises it works from. Second, since deductive arguments work from A to C by going through B, B has to be the same in both premises. In *c* above, the first premise dealt with "an electrical appliance," and the second dealt with "This toaster." But a conclusion still followed (if the statements were true), because the difference between "toaster" and "an electrical appliance" is a difference in word only; a toaster *is* an electrical appliance. But if you try to apply the same argument to a water heater, you had better make sure first that it doesn't run on gas. Third, each deductive argument has to go downhill all the way. If all men are mortal, and Spot is mortal, it doesn't follow that Spot is a man. The general type *mortal* includes the lesser type *men*. If men contains *Spot* (if, that is, Spot is a man) then it follows that Spot, like Socrates, is mortal. But if the second premise says that *mortal* contains *Spot*, the downhill movement toward smaller and smaller types until a conclusion is reached is broken. Spot goes back beyond the type *men* to the bigger type *mortal*, and you cannot conclude anything about old Spot.

The basic patterns of syllogistic argument have been known for more than two thousand years. In most non-scientific argument, they are taken for granted. A lot can be said about both bad and good argument without going farther than this short step into classical logic. Consider some of the errors of argument, in the paragraphs that follow.

Many techniques make writing clearer without making the argument any stronger. One such device comes mislabeled, as *argument by analogy*. Argument by analogy affirms that the topic is like something else; since the thesis is true of the something else, it must be true of the topic too. "He's just like all those other blankety-blank so-and-sos," goes one popular form of argument by analogy, and you know what the speaker thinks ought to be done with all of *them*.

As a device for clarity, analogy often can make your meaning much clearer. But as proof, it fails. If you want to prove that your thesis is true of your topic, you can't prove it by saying that your thesis is true of something else that is like your topic. John and Jim can be identical twins, alike in every respect—but if one of them is alive and the other has just this moment died, all their similarities won't prove that the corpse still lives.

For example, the Lutheran documentary movie *A Time for Burning* includes an example of tempting misuse of argument by analogy. The point a church official wants to prove, his thesis, is that a preacher isn't lying if he doesn't tell a racist congregation that their race prejudice is sinful. (That is not, however, the point the movie wants to prove.) His analogy: not telling an ugly woman that she is ugly, isn't lying. Why isn't the argument valid? True, there are similarities. Prejudice, a form of spiritual ugliness, resembles physical ugliness in many ways—it is unattractive, it drives people away, nobody who doesn't have it wants it, it is psychologically damaging to the person who has it. Unfortunately for the argument, in this case none of that matters. The ugly woman can't change her ugliness; it isn't her doing. The prejudiced congregation can change their prejudice; it is their doing. They differ precisely in the issue that matters—can they change if they want to? The woman can't, the congregation can. Therefore, the man who should not try to make the woman want to be beautiful still should try to make his congregation want to be moral.

Repeating your opinion and argument by analogy both increase clarity, even though they fail as arguments. Other types of bad argument don't have that virtue. They include arguing in a circle, the straw man, *argumentum ad hominem*, the red herring, begging the question, *post hoc*, the overhasty generalization, and the false dilemma.

The straw man substitutes for your real opponent. You attack him instead of your real opponent because a straw man doesn't fight back and can easily be beaten, cut into ribbons, or what you will. When intentionally done, by unscrupulous writers, the technique involves supposing that your opponent means something which he doesn't mean at all, and then destroying that something (the straw man). For example, if your opponent urges raising welfare payments, you say, "He wants incompetent, lazy ne-er-do-wells to have more money than God-fearing, hard-working, loyal citizens," and then you demolish that supposed wish on moral and financial grounds both: they don't deserve it, and the nation can't afford it. Actually, most people on welfare take all the work they can get; but job scarcity, inability (including lack of training and education as well as physical disability), and low pay for hard, unpleasant work reduce their income below minimum wage levels. Nobody who proposes raising welfare is proposing paying more in welfare than most people earn. To suggest that he is puts up a straw man as an easy target.

A Bestiary for Student Writers
III. The North American Rubber Boa

The North American rubber boa is one of many snakes that have developed deceptive defensive techniques. Like some other snakes, the rubber boa, when attacked, rolls itself up in a compact ball. To distract attackers from its head and other vital organs, the boa offers for attack a less critical part, waving its tail invitingly in the air.

MORAL: _____

Sometimes people set up a straw man without really meaning to be unfair. The best way to avoid this kind of unthinking dishonesty is to approach every position you intend to attack from this unusual angle. Try to state the position you disagree with in the strongest possible terms; make what seems to you the best case for it that can be made; put it in the best light possible, taking it to mean the truest things it can mean. Then, as you argue against it, you will be coming to grips with the real issues, not skirting them; then you will have some chance of arriving at truth rationally rather than by lucky prejudice. (Most prejudices are unlucky.)

Note that the straw man comes into being when you attack a position, not when you support one.

Another bad attack is called *argumentum ad hominem,* a Latin phrase which means an argument directed against the person who speaks rather than against what he says. This argument works on a form of guilt by association (which, you may recall, is unconstitutional). So-and-so says this; so-and-so is a rotter; conclusion: this is no good. In one of its most painfully ironic forms, *argumentum ad hominem* appears when a loyal American attacks peace because some Communist (Russian, Chinese, Viet Cong, or what have you) has said something publicly in favor of peace. The irony is that people who argue that way often don't even realize that on the same basis they should give up eating and sleeping, because the worst people in the world think very highly of both.

My attack on *argumentum ad hominem* doesn't mean that you should believe that everyone who praises a good thing means it. A man may praise racial equality and not mean a word of it. But the fact that a racist praises racial equality doesn't mean racial equality is a bad thing. The same thing applies whether a capitalist, communist, white, black, or red praises it. And when you write, you shouldn't claim that a statement is bad because someone bad makes it. That would be *argumentum ad hominem.*

The red herring resembles the straw man. When dragged across the trail, the red herring deludes the bloodhound sniffing eagerly after his quarry, truth, into turning off the path and following the herring instead. As its name implies, it stinks. The only difference between the red herring and the straw man is that the straw man is designed to be a patsy, a set-up, an easy victim; the red herring is designed simply as a diversion, to distract the reader. The only thing a red herring has to be is interesting, whereas the straw man has to be obviously wrong.

A Bestiary for the Student Writer
IV. The Sidewinder

The sidewinder, found in southwestern America, travels by lifting successive coils to the side. His presence in the vicinity can be recognized immediately by the tell-tale dragging marks his diagonal progress leaves in the sand. His motion once seen is never forgotten, for he does not travel in the direction he seems to be pointed, but off to one side at an acute angle. A venomous creature, his name has become a synonym for deception.

MORAL: _____

You won't be tempted to use the red herring deliberately in writing, because all it does is to keep the reader from getting at the main point, and whenever you write, you decide what the main point is. If you don't want the reader to think about it, for heaven's sake don't write about it, and you won't need any fish. But accidentally you may drop a red herring in your own trail, and, caught by its fragrance, pursue it through brambles and briars, far afield from what you meant to say. I'm sure you believe I mean that, as you think back over the times in this book when I have been lured a little far from the topic of grammar and rhetoric by the delicious aroma of an anecdotal red herring. So let's all watch it, and try to stick to the point.

Another faulty argument is begging the question. Begging the question is a broad category that includes arguing in a circle. In general, you beg the question when you try to prove your point by arguing from another statement that itself needs proof. When the second point depends on the first, you are arguing in a circle, as we have seen. A non-circular question-begging might go as follows:

"Angels have tiny feet." "What makes you say that?" "If they didn't, they couldn't spend all that time dancing on the head of a pin." Pin-head dancing, of course, has never been proved to be an angelic activity. Or, if you don't care for the terpsichorean proclivities of angels, how about this one: "Men are stupid," the feminist said contemptuously. "Now, don't say that," protested her harrassed lawyer, "you know that's not true." "Oh no?"

Her lip curled more tightly. "Then why can't they keep more than two out of three marriages out of the divorce courts?" The question she begged is, Is the stupidity of men responsible for sending one out of three marriages to the divorce courts? Since that point is unproved, the argument has no base to stand on.

Many arguments concern cause and effect, concluding that such-and-such is the cause of so-and-so. One fallacy with a Latin name, *post hoc, ergo propter hoc,* mistakenly says such-and-such causes so-and-so just because so-and-so comes after such-and-such. Translated, *post hoc ergo propter hoc* means "after this, therefore because of this." Don't think that because it is in Latin it doesn't matter. Why did you miss the bus? Why did you fail math but get an A in mechanics? If you want to catch the bus tomorrow, if you want to make straight A's next semester, then you need to identify real causes, not imaginary ones. Indeed, why did human reason develop, if not to enable man to assess the true causes of events and the true consequences of his actions?

A true cause doesn't just come first: it is both necessary and sufficient. "I had such a bad cold that the old so-and-so fired me." Did the bad cold cause the firing? 1) Is a bad cold necessary to firing? For example, did the old so-and-so fire anyone else, who didn't have a bad cold? And was the self-pitying speaker fired from any earlier jobs when he didn't have a cold? 2) Is a bad cold sufficient to produce firing? For example, was Miss Sniffle, who wheezed all day, fired? And when the speaker had that really messy laryngitis-*cum*-catarrhal-discharge last month, was he fired then?

In some ways, the *post hoc* fallacy resembles an over-hasty generalization, the next fallacy on the list. The *post hoc* says: A came before B this time. Therefore, I conclude that *whenever* you have A you *always* have B (A is sufficient to cause B), and I conclude that *whenever* you have B you *always* had A first (A is necessary to cause B). That is, A is a cause of B.

The next-to-last faulty argument on my list is hasty generalization. The impulse to generalize too fast runs hot and strong in human blood. We need to generalize to survive, since we learn by carrying over from past experience an idea that may apply to a future experience. That process is generalization, called by logicians *induction*. Experiments have shown that puppies have to learn such simple things as not to bang their heads. They have to bang their heads (not fatally, one hopes) many times to get the idea that banging your head hurts. Their reponse may be conditioned reflex, but a human can think about it, and operate much faster. The human head-banger says (as one of my sons did at the age of three), "I have banged my head angrily against this plastered wall three times. It hurt the first time; it hurt the second time; it hurt the third time. [In fact, his eyes crossed slightly after the third time.] I conclude, by an act of induction, this generalization: banging your head against a plastered wall hurts. (And besides, it just made my parents, who were the ones I really wanted to hurt, laugh.)" You see how useful such ability to generalize can be. Since that day, he has never once banged his head against a wall.

The usefulness of generalizing perhaps explains why so often we do it too fast. Consider the case of Little Orvie, hero of a book with the same name by Booth Tarkington. Little Orvie one afternoon, while waiting on the sidewalk for his aunt, noticed for the first time a bush in her yard. It was laden with small green berries. Little Orvie plucked one, put it in his mouth, and chewed it experimentally. It tasted horrible. Little Orvie spat it out. Picking another berry with some care, he put it too in his mouth, and chewed thoroughly. It too was bitter and rancid, and with a mutter of disgust, Little Orvie spat it out also. At this point, many would have abandoned the investigation. But not Little Orvie. He reached out, grabbed a whole handful of berries and popped them into his mouth, chomping on a dozen at once. Their acrid flavor puckered his mouth so, that he had trouble spitting them out, and only with repeated spittings could he finally rid himself of the bitter green mess.

The ironic thing about this anecdote is Orvie's scientific reasonableness. To throw away a whole barrel of apples because you found one rotten apple would be an overhasty generalization. Why is it funny when Little Orvie doesn't make that mistake? Largely, I think, because it is a mistake so many of us make so often. Little Orvie's actions may have been reasonable, but they weren't typical of human caution, human fear of bitter green taste, and human willingness to generalize fast.

Finally, the last fallacious argument: the false dilemma. A dilemma, of course, is an unpleasant choice between unattractive alternatives, frequently called horns. (Cliche users are often caught on them.) The false dilemma, thus, says you must do A or B when you actually could do C or D or . . . N instead. A typical false dilemma might go: We have to punish marijuana users harshly. After all, we don't want to legalize an industry that panders to escapism and drop-outs the way legalized marijuana would, now do we? Analyze that one, and what do you find is implied? The argument assumes that if we are not harsh with marijuana users, we must legalize the marijuana industry—production, distribution, and all. That is the false dilemma: you must be hard on users, or you must legalize the whole industry. As a matter of fact, the presidential commission did find another alternative: abandoning harsh reprisals against private users, but continuing to punish production and sale.

The false dilemma, in fact, seems to appeal particularly to the western mind, which likes two-valued systems. A two-valued system cuts the number of possibilities to two: good or bad; yes or no; true or false. It is digital rather than analogue. It ignores pretty good, O.K., fair, and rather poor; if you like, well just for you, maybe, I'd rather not, and you're going to have trouble talking me into that one; probable, possible, improbable, unknowable, and presently unknown; and a host of others. Many very important practical arguments sometimes fall into the trap of false dilemmas. If we think of our foreign affairs as a game which we must win by defeating others, or lose when they win, we are working with false alternatives. Game theory calls this approach a "zero-sum" game: what one wins, the other loses. A better game model, however, probably is a "non-zero-sum" game, in which all may win (surviving prosperously) or all may lose (in nuclear catastrophe). And there is a long string of possibilities between (including survival with living conditions severe by American standards, if we finally manage to control pollution and over-population, on through survival with moderate comfort, if we manage to reverse present trends rather than simply checking them). "I defeat you or you defeat me" is thus a false dilemma, and one that could get us into serious trouble. Track has non-zero-sum aspects—although one man usually comes in first (there may be a tie), there is also a second, not to mention third and fourth; more appropriately, every runner can better his own time—and in that sense, all can win. Phone-booth and Volkswagen crowding are non-zero-sum games, in which a group cooperates to make the maximum score possible. And in spin-the-bottle and post-office you could argue that everybody wins. The next time someone says to you, "Don't enter a war you don't plan to win," suggest that in place of the false dilemma of winning or losing, we base our foreign policy on spin-the-bottle or post-office.

So far, I've been talking about bad arguments when we both know I ought to tell you what a good argument is. I ought to tell you what you should do, not what you shouldn't, like the parent who made his children read every dirty book he could find so that they would know what to avoid. But some of the things that make an argument good can be inferred from the faults of bad arguments.

If the red herring and the straw man and *argumentum ad hominem* don't stick to the point, what does a good argument do?

Rule 1) A good argument sticks to the point.
If arguing in a circle and begging the question start with unproved assumptions, where does a good argument start?

Rule 2) A good argument starts on solid ground.
If the overhasty generalization and the *post hoc* argument rely on insufficient evidence, what does the good argument do?

Rule 3) A good argument uses all available evidence and points out what other evidence hasn't yet come in.

If bad argument is unfair because it deceives either the audience or the writer, what is a good argument?

Rule 4) A Good argument is honest and fair.

Approaching good argument directly, you reach the same kind of description.

A good argument starts at one point and moves to another. It moves from a Premise (starting point) to a Conclusion, travelling en route through such evidence as may be necessary to get from P to C. Evidence that leads in other directions just wastes time. If efficiency is a virtue, Rule 1 above follows.

Since the purpose of arguing is to take somebody with you to your conclusion, you must start on common ground, or you can't travel together. Moreover, you have to start where your audience *really* is, not where he thinks he is. That is, you can't start your argument from his *errors*. That may be where he is, but it isn't where you are. A good argument does *not* start, "Now, we know the moon is made of green cheese, right?" One of the principles of logic is that no conclusions can be drawn from a false premise. You can't start in the thin air of falsehood: you can't pull yourself up by your own bootstraps and get a running start. Rule #2 follows.

Rules 3 and 4 follow from the definition of a good argument as an effort to reach the truth. When you have led someone to agree with you, you don't want him to call you up next day and take it all back. If you think you have led him from P to C, you don't want him suddenly to point out that there are great gaps in the track from P to C, and that he couldn't possibly have made the trip. An unscrupulous politician may slander his opponent on the eve of the election, when there isn't time for the rumor to be disproved. But the next day, all will be revealed. In time, the truth is known. Rule 3 follows.

The truths of human history and human motives are complex and hard to come by. But the world is real, not to be controlled by idle day-dream. Errors are dreams which may become nightmares when the real world intrudes. You may think there is no truck coming down the road; that may be truth for you; but if in fact you are wrong, you will be just as smashed when the truck hits you. Knowing the truth—the truths, if you prefer—as best you may, helps. (Indeed, that is the evolutionary function of human reason—the survival value of keeping belief tuned in to reality.) Human reason is our best guide to the realities of our world. Argument is human reason cooperating. Rule 4 follows: A good argument is honest and fair.

EXERCISE 5: Write an essay proving one of the following to the person named. Use such evidence as you already possess, and follow the rules of good argument. Assume that the audience named will recognize a good argument if you use one, *starting* with assertions the audience will accept.

    a. Convince Archie Bunker that he should treat a Negro courteously.

    b. Convince the Premier of Russia that he should deal peacefully with America.

    c. Convince a failing classmate who has not been studying that he should do his schoolwork.

    d. Convince a miserly employer that he should pay good wages.

The process of logical argument follows rules that apply to most writing. Logical argument sticks to the point. Any good writing sticks to the point in some sense. Good writing coheres; and writing that hangs together doesn't include a lot of irrelevant fluff to pad it out to a stuffy thickness picked in advance. Nothing is unused in good writing—whether for tone or for content, whether to make the basic point or to clarify a supporting detail, everything counts.

As a matter of fact, a minor device that sometimes helps clarify is counting. Number your points: first, second, third—stating in advance how many points there are, and counting each one as you introduce it and perhaps again as you finish it and move on to the next.

There are three main points to consider . . . The first point concerns . . . Although the first point depends entirely on the good will of the shoemakers, the second point takes us to another, where good will is irrelevant . . . Finally, in this review of the three factors affecting the cost of patrolmen's shoes, we must turn to the question of wear and tear. This third point, gradual destruction by use, has perhaps more effect than either of the others.

Counting won't unify an incoherent paper. But if the paper's content coheres, counting points may help make that coherence clearer. If you tell a reader there are three points, and then count out three points, you have fulfilled a promise to him, and he will appreciate it. (But don't start the next-to-last paragraph "fourthly . . .") After all, you want to make sense, doesn't one? It would be bad for the writer if he has shifted tenses, will shift the person of your pronouns, to mix up their verb forms, voice is shuffled, or confused one's indefinite *you* with the definite *you*.

Gibberish? Yes; but why? Start at the end of it: "You" means the person (people) spoken to. That's the definite *you*. But sometimes—often, in fact, in speech—"you" means any old body in the world at large. That's the indefinite *you*. If a man asks me, "How do you get to be president?" I know he uses the indefinite *you*, because I am president of nothing. So:

(1) Don't mix *definite* and *indefinite you.* Don't say, "I want you (definite) to tell me how you (definite or indefinite?) become president," unless you are talking to the candidate himself.

(2) Don't mix indefinite *you* (which like all *you*'s is *second person*) with *third person.* Don't say, "If you (second person) want to become president, one (third person) must campaign with vigor;" don't say, "If a man campaigns with vigor, you must have financial support."

As a matter of fact, any mixing of definite and indefinite is awkward, even if both are third person. *One* is indefinite; it has no antecedent. *He* is definite; it has an antecedent. Don't say, "If one fear not, he will conquer the world;" do say, "If a man be not afraid, he probably doesn't understand the situation." That is, (3) Don't mix the indefinite *one* with the definite *he.*

"Hey, man, you won't believe what happened yesterday. I went downtown, and I'm walking along with one foot in the gutter as usual, see, and up comes. . . ." The shift from past to present is an easy one but usually doesn't go over as well in writing as in chat. Homer shifted tense by twenty years describing Odysseus' scar, but a blind poet who has been dead for 2700 years deserves the benefit of a doubt that most teachers won't extend to a student. In short, (4) Don't mix past with present tense; either may work, but only by itself. UNLESS the times are mixed; perfect writing then requires mixing tenses. If an action is completed by the time spoken of, use the right perfect tense—". . . and up comes this weird cat who has followed me all the way from McCandid's Corner . . ." *comes:* present tense. *has followed:* present perfect tense. (Not: ". . . up comes this cat who followed . . .") "When did you see her? Why hadn't you noticed her before?" *did see:* past tense. *had noticed:* past perfect tense. (5) Use the matching perfect tense (past perfect with past, present perfect with present) for actions already done.

Shifting from active to passive sometimes confuses. "Well, I noticed her when she kissed me, and I didn't know what to say or do, so . . ." Pick one: (a) ". . . I married her. (b) ". . . marriage was performed." (6) Don't shift needlessly from active to passive, especially when the doer is the same in both clauses.

Avoiding incoherence does not create unity, but does make it possible. In the last analysis, the force of good writing comes from a central core— the central idea that began as a seed in a brain-storming session, and now— full grown in the well-finished work—supports and gives life to every leaf and branch, to every paragraph, every sentence, and even every word.

Topics: Write a paragraph on each of the following, labelling the kind of development you used: (a) The candidate to vote for is _____ . (b) A beautiful scene. (c) The first time I met _____ . (d) My favorite chapter in *What's The Usage?* (e) The best class schedule.

Part Five: THE AUDIENCE

15

"Dear Reader": How to be Interesting and Intelligible Without Actually Offending Anyone

ong, long ago, at the beginning of this book, I described a writing as having three elements: the writer, the work he writes, and the audience that reads what he has written. In Part I, I talked about knowing yourself as writer and about the mechanics of the writing process. Parts II, III, and IV discussed the work: what its parts are, how to arrange them, how to fasten them together into a coherent whole. This section considers audiences, and how they affect what the writer writes.

Alors, je suis certain que c'est obvieux que les characteristiques de l'audience font une grande différence au maniere auquel on ecrit. Par example, considerez ma belle-mere, Bess. Un soir, elle m'a dit, "When the dummy came down, he burst out laughing, because I've been promoting everything and his wife says, 'He's laughing because you gave him the fix of the evening.'" Mon Dieu! C'est ridicule! Est'ce que c'est le heroin? le marijuana? Je ne le savais pas. Mais non: c'est le contract-bridge! Quelle vocabulaire![1]

Everyone knows that what language the audience understands makes a difference. Many forget that there are sublanguages within every national language; many forget that people who seem to speak identical languages may understand different words differently. While a student in England, I greeted my English peers with a happy "Hi." After some months, one friend confided to me that at first I had made him a bit nervous, not to say jumpy, with my repeated "Hi's." "Here, you know," he said, "*Hi* is what we say to someone who is just stealing our bicycle—'Hi, stop that thief'—that sort of thing." I then remembered my own experience when I left my native Chicago and moved south; I had been startled by the constant "Hey's" that greeted me, for "Hey!" was what I had shouted when someone stole my marbles. Even interjections like *hey* and *hi* mean different things to different people.

A Bestiary for the Student Writer
V. The Peacock: Mate Selection

The courting invitation of the peacock is one of nature's resplendent aviary displays. Raising his normally trailing tail feathers into a large irridiscent fan many times the size of the bird himself, the peacock invites a passing

---

[1]The illiteracies of this writing are the contribution of the writer; the overall unintelligibility depends on the audience.

peahen into his parlor by a blaze of color—blue, green, tan—accompanied by a shimmering rustle and a treading of the feet which produces the motion and the sound. Such invitations are made only to an appropriate love-mate, apparently identified in general form early during the peacock's youth. Naturalist Konrad Lorenz records the sad plight of a peacock raised during World War II in a reptile house, the only zoo building for which heat was available. During the critical period of mate categorization, the peacock saw nothing but turtles. For the rest of his life, every mating season he put on beautiful displays when a turtle passed—up would go the tail, the feathers rustling, the feet treading. Peahens, paraded before him by the zookeepers, meant nothing to him. Never, alas, did his most enticing displays mean anything to the totally indifferent turtles. He never reproduced.

MORAL: _____

Recall the anecdote about bridge and the fix of the evening. The language was jargon; it was a specialized vocabulary developed by bridge players ("I've got a stiff king and this l.o.l. squeezes me") for bridge players ("I've got a monster fourth hand, my partner goes bye, and East-West are using Stayman—Stayman, for godsake!") and not for poor slobs like me, with glazing eyes and weakly nodding head.

Rule I: Avoid special vocabularies.

Type A: Avoid Jargon

Sub-type 1: Just don't talk about bridge at all.

Sub-type 2: Don't quote a nuclear physicist without knowing what he means; your teacher may not know what he means either, and sometimes he will ask you—if you used the words, you should know what they mean. If you are not a specialist yourself, by using words that you understand you will usually use words that your audience understands.

Answer: Words that the audience will understand.

What is the question?

Type B: Eschew ponderous verbosity, erudite sesquipedalianism, archaisms, and neologisms.

EXERCISE 1: Draw a line through every word in the following statement by a principal to a ninth-grade class which you think the class would not understand:

The iniquitous superabundance of impious castigations prevalent as mural inscriptions in the convenience facilities derogates reflexively their progenitors in a supererogatory self-pejoration. (All those bad words written on the bathroom walls discredit the writers, bad enough already.)

Rule I concerns denotations, the literal meanings of words; if your audience does not understand them, it won't understand very much. Other things besides the literal meaning of the word can affect communication, however, since people often respond emotionally, with a feeling tone, to the connotations of words. To control your vocabulary in the light of who your audience is, you must control not only denotations, but connotations as well.

Controlling your vocabulary can mean dollars and cents. The advertisers obviously think so. Commercials, billboards, and magazine spreads abound with words carefully chosen for appealing connotations, sometimes without regard to accurate or informative denotation.

TEST: The basic function of an advertisement is (pick the one best answer):

1. entertainment
2. giving promising young actors the public exposure that will help their careers.
3. making the audience, one way or another, feel good enough about the product to want to buy it.
4. providing strictly accurate, rigidly controlled, scientifically verifiable factual information.

If you were a grocer, would you label your eggs "small" and "regular," or "regular" and "large"? (Some sell only "large" and "extra large.") At a famous California funeral home and cemetery which has had a tremendous commercial success, the customers don't buy *grave plots,* they buy "spaces." "Spaces" may be bought either "Before Need," "At Time of Need," or "Post Need." Guess what "Need" is.

EXERCISE 2: Copy down the words of two fairly talky T.V. commercials. Bring them to class prepared to identify any words chosen for connotation rather than for denotation, words that sound good but mean little.

Vocabulary can be controlled deliberately in order to have a particular effect; but even if vocabulary is not controlled, it will have some effect. Some words connote (the verb form of the noun *connotations*) ignorance. They ain't no like bad words, but I be hornswoggled effen they ain't some words as makes ary person hears 'em reckon as how they is bein' sassified by a no-count thouten school-larnin.

Most of us already exercise some vocabulary control. Most people, in fact, have several vocabularies that they use in different circumstances. Vocabulary A is used in one context, vocabulary B in another. The difference between the two depends partly on denotations (on whether the listener will know the words) and partly on connotations. Do you talk to children the same way you talk to adults? to a judge the same way as to a bum? to the players and umpires at a baseball game the same way as to the organizers of the church bazaar? to your teachers the same way as to your classmates? Certainly some of those differences depend on what you talk about and what you want to say; but some of them depend on unconscious recognition that connotations need to be controlled. TV's Archie Bunker, for example, was one of the few bigots to call people "spics," "wops," "dagoes," or "niggers" to their faces, and audiences expressed their surprise (in this fictional comic situation) by laughing. If it were real, it wouldn't be so funny; but it would still be surprising. The difference between "nigger" and "Negro" or "black," between "kike" and "Jew," between "Mick" and "Irishman" is not what they denote, for those synonyms denote the same thing. The difference comes with the emotional associations, the memories of past events and attitudes, that they carry with them as their connotations. Using the right words on the right occasion is propriety of diction. Sometimes, propriety of diction may keep you from getting hit right in the mouth.

Using words is a form of behaviour. With words, too, you can behave well or badly. Good behaviour depends, of course, on what you want to accomplish, and on context, just as good writing does; if you want to shock people, the best behaviour for that purpose will differ from the best behaviour for other purposes. If you want to seem rough, tough, and uneducated, you will soak your language in vinegary vulgarisms. And of course what will shock, whether in behaviour or in speech, depends on the audience. Actually, it gets harder and harder to shock people, so many have sought to do so; even running down the center of the street naked doesn't have the impact it used to.

Shock stuns. A stunned mind makes a bad audience. An overshocked mind loses its sensitivity. And a shock that doesn't come off is nothing. Advice: Don't bother trying to shock people.

Both denotation and connotation affect communication.

EXERCISE 3: Make a list of words you would not use when speaking to your grandparents (pretend they are alive, speak English, and live near you, whether they do or not), but that you commonly use in conversation with your friends of both sexes. Indicate for each word whether you wouldn't use it because your grandparents wouldn't know the denotation, or because they wouldn't like the connotation.

Aesop's shepherd boy who cried "Wolf!" because he wanted the villagers to come out and keep him company cried it once too often. What had been an effective communication of emotional tone—for a while, he got across a strong desire to have them come to him—lost its force as he repeated it. Overused, in this case obviously false, his effort to have great impact finally failed, with sad results when a wolf did come but the villagers didn't.

To rely on emotional tone is to manipulate the audience. At a meeting of college professors and some students, I heard a student address the group on American evil. He maintained that American society was the sickest, rottenest society that had ever existed. The audience was annoyed. They objected that America was not the rottenest society that has ever existed, and quarreled hotly. The audience was right, of course, taking the student's remarks as communication, as statement; it takes little knowledge of history to find societies worse than modern America, no matter how much you disapprove of America's faults. In fact, however, the student was not communicating with us; he was manipulating us as a puppeteer pulls the strings of his puppets. He was using a time-honored literary device used often in satire, over-statement. To shock us out of our (supposed) complacency, he said much worse things than were actually true. Now, that manipulation worked, in the sense that he angered a number of people. But no communication took place, and no reforms were begun. Instead, a lot of people who really shouldn't have, lost their tempers.

If that were a bestiary item, what would the moral be? I think one moral would be that if you manipulate people, you are probably going to annoy them. (Another moral might be that a satirist may have to take his lumps.) You will do much better to stay away from both satirical and Madison-Avenue manipulations.

The connotations of words come from their histories. Those histories are public, and should not be ignored. But if you had a pet cat named "Ugly" because of his twenty-three toes and silly grin, the word *ugly* (which sounds an awful lot like the name Ugly) will no doubt have some very good con-notations for you that it does not have for others. Your personal history and the history of a word are not the same.

Choosing the right words is partly a matter of becoming aware of the history of words, reflected in the way they are now used. The only way to do that, in the long run, is to read. And read. And listen. And read some more. But a dictionary will help in the meantime.

In a debate between two people, you may temporarily ignore the history of words, and agree upon your own private definitions, ignoring the usual definitions if you wish to. But if there is an audience, do not let the person you are talking with make up definitions to suit himself. How would you like to discuss your present English teacher with him and the class as audience, making the arbitrary definition that by "incompetent boob" you meant him—nothing about incompetence or boobs, just him, as though you called him by name or "Prof. X"? Unless he is very amiable, you probably wouldn't like it much. You would know, and he would know, that the class was thinking something besides *him* every time they heard *incompetent boob*. He wouldn't like it; and if you are smart, you wouldn't like it because he wouldn't like it. In any argument, therefore, words must be chosen with care, and you should not accept casual definitions that may irritate your audience or weaken your own case.

Respect for an audience is important. Senator Joseph McCarthy used to address the people he was questioning with increasing familiarity: "Tell us your position, Mr. Jones. . . Did you really mean to say, Jones, that . . . Oh, come on, now, Herbert . . . You can't kid us, Herbie. . . ." The effect was to demean the person whose rank slipped little by little with each address. McCarthy's techniques, in front of national television, were demagogic, and he was ultimately censured by the Senate for behavior reflected in a small way in such subtle insults. A good writer decides what his distance from his audience is, and keeps it. Most audiences prefer establishing a relationship with the author whose works they read, and maintaining that relationship.

A Bestiary for the Student Writer
VI. The Stickleback

The stickleback is a small, gaudily covered fish with lovely trailing fins and tail. The male is strongly territorial, and viciously defends his selected territory against intrusion by other stickleback males. In courtship, the male executes a beautiful three-dimensional dance around the female, who in her turn glides and twists around and around the male in a counter-dance of her own. Careful observation reveals that the female's responses to the "steps" of her dance partner have one clear purpose: to keep the male from seeing her flank at right angles. If he sees her side with its stickleback coloration, the male's instinctively violent response to other male sticklebacks will overwhelm him, and—mistaking her for another male—he will tear her to pieces.

MORAL: _____   _____

Rule II: Choose words with the right connotations.

Type A. Don't stir up emotions by mistake.

Type B. Don't try to manipulate your audience's emotions.

So far, I have discussed choice of words and attitude toward the audience. At the end of the last chapter, I noted that a good argument must take the audience into account; it must begin at some point that the audience can accept, some common ground between writer and audience. There, too, I noted two general requirements of all writing: it must be clear (which explains Rule I above) and it must be interesting.

Is this book interesting?

My father once had an interesting operation on an impacted wisdom tooth, he said. It lasted four hours, but the most interesting part began when the anesthetic wore off.

Is this book interesting?

EXERCISE 4: Write an interesting sentence.

What makes a sentence seize the reader's imagination with one rapid swipe and carry it breathless to the final dot?

EXERCISE 5: Rewrite the sentence you just wrote, making it dull.
[Be ready.]
Style helps. Good (that is, clear and interesting) style uses vivid, concrete words.

EXERCISE 6: Rewrite the following sentences, replacing abstract words with concrete words where possible. (See also Rule I, Type B.)

    a. What enables a sentence to arouse the interest and maintain the attention of its audience from commencement to termination?

    b. Deterioration in the quality of present conditions indicates that a reversal of the present trend must ensue.

    c. When one is capable of asserting the position that prevailing circumstances constitute the reprehensible extreme, the reprehensible extreme has not yet been actualized.

    d. The degree of precipitation exceeds normal levels.

Good style varies, too. Instead of one consistent sentence length or one consistent sentence pattern, good style mixes long and short sentences, fast and slow ones, simple and complex ones. Isn't it less dull to read an occasional interrogative sentence in place of a steady, numbing diet of declarative sentences? Try an imperative sentence occasionally, too; but see that you do it right, you dumb clutz, or you'll annoy somebody. [Are you still ready?]

EXERCISE 7: Fill in the blanks in the following account, using the part of speech indicated; try to produce a fairly sensible result.

a. The _____ _____ the _____
        noun subject   verb   noun object

b. That was a simple sentence: one independent clause. Now write another just like *a*.

c. The _____ is _____, and the _____ is _____
     noun   pred. adj. or n.   noun   pred. adj. or noun [2]

d. That was a compound sentence: two independent clauses, joined by a co-ordinating conjunction. Now write another, on the same general topic as your answer to *b* above.

e. _____-ing the _____, the _____ _____
   pres. part.   noun object   noun subject   verb
_____-ly.
adverb

f. That was a simple sentence again, but a more sophisticated one. Now write another, same topic as *b* and *d* above, following the pattern of *e*.

g. Although _____, the _____
         subject + verb + object or pred. adj./noun   noun subject

_____ .
predicate (verb + obj. or pred. noun/adj.)

h. That was a complex sentence, at least one dependent clause plus at least one independent clause. Now write another, the same topic as before (*b, d, f*), following the pattern of *g*.

i. In fact, the _____ _____ until _____ _____ .
         subject   predicate   subject   predicate

j. That was another complex sentence, this time with the dependent clause at the end, but also with an introductory prepositional phrase acting as adverb. Now write another, the same topic as before, imitating pattern *i*.

k. Why _____ _____ _____?
      helper (aux) verb   subject   verb

l. You know what's coming: Write a short question like *k*, same topic as *b, j*, etc.

m. _____ because the _____ _____, the
    same subj. and same verb as k   subject   predicate
_____ _____, and the _____ _____ .
subject   predicate   subject   predicate

---

[2] Reminder: Harry is a *horse*. (Horse is a predicate noun.) The horse is *drunk*. (*Drunk* is a predicate adjective.)

n. That was yet another complex sentence, this time ending with parallel dependent clauses. Write one last sentence on the same topic as *b*, *d*, *f*, *h*, *j*, and *l*, following the same pattern.

EXERCISE 8: Now pull out the seven sentences on the same topic from the preceding exercise (*b*, *d*, *f*, *h*, *j*, *l*, *n*), rearrange them if necessary, put in a few transitions if needed, and you should have a paragraph with a lot of variety in syntax.

Rule III: Vary sentence length and syntactical pattern.

Variety involves novelty, change; for the reader, a discovery is variety and is fun. Make the reader discover things. Tell him, of course; especially those things that he must know. But occasionally involve him directly by making him discover for himself. Any understatement gives the reader a joyous feeling of discovery as he sees more emphasis than you have stated. A classic example of such indirection occurs in Homer's *Iliad*, which makes the reader imagine Helen's great beauty not by describing her but by describing the reaction of a group of old men as she passes.

Rule IV: Let your reader think of a few things himself.

By the way, are you still ready? Expectation is the hope for change; it is an aspect of variety. (If you are ready, now is the time: hurry downstairs and out to the nearest place that sells whatever you like most to drink, buy one, drink it, and hurry back to work refreshed and invigorated.) Therefore, tell the reader you are going to do something, but don't tell all, yet—just hint.

Rule V: Create suspense.

A Bestiary for the Student Writer
VII. The Mocking Bird

The mocking bird has the most varied call of all nature's songbirds. His warbles and twitters, his chirps and tweets, his coos, cries, and catcalls, his whistles and his trills and his turns make him the most interesting of birds to hear.

MORAL: _____

Variety is the spice of life. Alas, too much spice means an upset stomach; too much variety is chaos. If you are too indirect and understate too much, your poor reader won't know what's happening.

Go easy, too, on the number of details. In your search for the concrete detail, don't pile in so many pebbly concretions, so many hard, knobby, rugged, stone-gray solidities with sharp jagged edges to snag the reader's attention, with rugged texture to rub hard on his consciousness, cracked perhaps by the alternating freezes and thaws of your long season of stormy creativity but hard as the granite sunk into the bowels of the earth that shrugs off the freezing flakes of winter that you and your reader forget what the heck you started off to write vividly about.

Don't pack in metaphors so densely, as you search for concrete vividness, that they crowd each other into a quarrel. A mixed metaphor often presents a ludicrous image. One example: keep your eye on the ball, your ear to the ground, and your nose to the grindstone. A former vice-president of the University of Chicago created such classics as, "Let's nail this custard pie to the wall." Both examples are, of course, offered in a spirit of friendly and mutual cooperation, as we skim off the fat and drain the lees to the dregs to see what the old Chinese-fortune-cookie bakers have put in the bottom of our Cracker-Jack box—a golden egg? a diamond in the rough? or just a nugget of solid froth? Such writing creates a kind of chaos that shreds coherence.

Don't overload with details; don't mix metaphors; and don't use clichés. A cliché is a phrase or expression that was original and fresh long ago before many generations of writers and talkers wore it out by using it over and over. If you have had little contact with the language, particularly if you haven't read much, it's hard to recognize a cliché. Apart from asking someone else, about all you can do is keep on reading for the next ten years. In the meantime, you already can spot a few. Don't use them. Using a cliché to gain interest and freshness is like drilling a hole in the bottom of a boat to let the water run out. It is self-defeating. How many clichés can you spot in this passage?

Let's get down to brass tacks. If we don't hit the nail on the head, this is going to be a pretty kettle of fish; you mark my words, because I know what I'm talking about. We won't have the chance of a snowflake in hell if we can't hit it right on the button. I don't care whether it's raining cats and dogs, or pretty as a picture; just shooting the breeze and running around like a chicken with its head cut off will get us nowhere fast. That'll go over like a lead balloon with the boss man, who beyond the shadow of a doubt wants things right as rain. Anybody who says different has his head in the clouds and is chasing a pipe dream—he wants pie in the sky—this is right from the horse's mouth: he's beating a dead horse, and his chances not only aren't as good as gold, they aren't worth a plugged nickel.

EXERCISE 9: List five clichés in addition to those you just marked. Hint: clichés often are comparisons (similes); many of them deal with very common things, such as being hard, soft, smart, slow, fast, rich, poor, hot, cold, etc.

Using clichés doesn't make writing incoherent; it just makes it dull at the very moment you are trying to make it vivid. "Student nurse Jones, what's that perfume, you sexy creature?" "I got it from the supply room; it's called ether." "Zzzzzzzz. . . ." "Do you like it, Doctor Handmussen . . . Doctor . . . Doctor, wake up!"

Rule VI: Don't kill interest trying to rouse it.

Type A. Don't smother your meaning in too much detail.

Type B. Don't mix metaphors.

Type C. Avoid clichés.

Inexperienced writers often weaken their writing unintentionally by over-using passive voice. When passive voice is used, a sense of passivity, of inactivity, is communicated, and the reader's sense of motion is retarded and finally is stopped altogether. In contrast, verbs in the active voice move vigorously, imply activity, and communicate a sense of energy and motion. Contrast, for example, these two accounts:

I: And he was spoken to by them, this being said: "No; but you will be bound fast by us, and you will be delivered into their hand: but surely you will not be killed by us." And he was bound by them with two new cords, and was brought up from the rock.

And when he was found to be in Lehi, he was shouted against by the Philistines; and the Spirit of the Lord was mightily presented upon him, and the cords that had been put upon his arms were changed like flax that was burnt with fire, and his bands were loosed from off his hands.

And a new jawbone of an ass was found by him, and his hand was put forth, and the jawbone was taken by his hand, and a thousand men were slain therewith.

And the following was said by Samson, "With the jawbone of an ass, heaps upon heaps, with the jaw of an ass have a thousand men been slain by me."

II: And they spake unto him, saying, "No; but we will bind thee fast, and deliver thee into their hand: but surely we will not kill thee. And they bound him with two new cords and brought him up from the rock.

And when he came unto Lehi, the Philistines shouted against him: and the Spirit of the Lord came mightily upon him, and the cords that were upon his arms became as flax that was burnt with fire, and his bands were loosed from off his hands.

And he found a new jawbone of an ass, and put forth his hand, and took it, and slew a thousand men therewith.

And Samson said, "With the jawbone of an ass, heaps upon heaps, with the jaw of an ass have I slain a thousand men."[3]

---

[3]*Judges* 15: 13–16.

Sentences describing physical actions such as Samson's come more naturally, as well as more vigorously, in the active voice; but abstractions seem to be presented more naturally in the passive voice (that is, presenting abstractions in the passive voice seems to be more natural). When an abstract topic has been assigned, passive voice is used more than active. (That is, when a teacher assigns an abstract topic, students use passive voice more than active. Note that to write in the active voice you have to say who does the action; that specificity makes your writing more concrete.)

Since verbs are action words, the right verb can inject a good deal of adrenalin into a sentence. Active voice does more than passive voice; also, verbs of action do more than verbs of being. Linking verbs—particularly the forms of *to be: is, are, was, were*, etc.—do little. They affirm being, and they *are* useful, but they lack pizzazz. They look like passive verbs, and have much the same effect. A passive verb, after all, is a linking verb (is, was, etc.) plus a past participle (verb + ed) acting like a predicate adjective. (He is defeated; the effort to write well has been abandoned; no active verbs were found.) Transitive verbs carry more energy than any others, pushing, as they do, their verbal message from subject to direct object. Wherever possible, therefore, don't use linking verbs, do use transitive verbs.

Rule VII: Write vigorously.

Type A. Use active voice more than passive voice.

Type B. Use transitive verbs more than linking verbs.

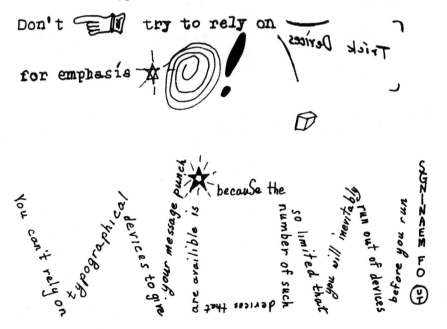

Moreover, they provide the wrong kind of emphasis: they divert. A probably apocryphal teacher is supposed to have leaped onto his desk and crowed like a rooster. "There," he said, "now you will never forget what I have just told you, because you will always remember that when I told you, I jumped on this desk and crowed like a rooster." It's a long story, because it was twenty years later at a school homecoming that an alumnus said to the teacher, "Say, I'll never forget that day when. . . By the way, what was it. . ."

Rule VIII: Emphasize the material itself.

Interest comes from variety: variety of sentence length, variety of sentence pattern (syntax), variety of discovery and expectation. Interest comes from vigor. But most of all, interest depends on significance.

Take the end of the world, for example. Do you believe in it? If you do, then it should be an interesting topic (rather like the interest of my father's dental operation, although on a somewhat larger scale). Some things are important.

More significantly—after all, how many times will you write about the end of the world, whether an eye-witness account or not?—meaning lives in your topic. I have already said that your topic is the most important thing in your essay; to keep interest by writing meaningfully, you must write about your topic. An essay on "How to Use a Can-opener"—that's the topic, re-member, not just a trick title—cannot gain significance by including a discussion of the end of the world. Such an essay generates as much interest as it can support by dealing with everything that matters about can-opener use. That is where the meaning of the essay with that topic lives—right there between the crank and the cutter, between the lip and the lid; between the pressing hand and the waiting pan, between the empty grocery shelf and the empty plate, between the economics of production and the hunger that consumes, between efficiency and incompetence, between impatience and speed.

When writing a narrative, for example, constantly ask yourself why the story deserves telling. What does it mean? Vivid details are not enough by themselves, if they do not come together meaningfully. During a riot a few years ago a man looting a case of beer was shot by a policeman when he did not halt on command. The reporter describing the event for *Life* magazine commented casually in an earlier paragraph, about events 15 minutes before, that the policeman accepted the offer of a can of looted beer and drank some of it, laughing and chatting happily. That is a meaningful detail. It says something about the usefulness and ultimate justice of death in the streets, something about law and order and what happens when law meets disorder.

Suppose you are writing, more frivously, an account of a milkman spilling a case of milk bottles when bitten on the ankle by a dog one rainy morning. What will the point of your narrative be? That accidents are part of life? Then you may describe the confidence of the milkman as he steps from the van and swings out the metal, milk-laden crate (that detail goes in as preparation for the big spill), strong and confident master of the sidewalk. Such a description will prepare for contrasting details, as he sits a few moments later in a rain-splashed pool of milk and cream, surrounded by crumpled cardboard, holding his ankle and cursing. If you find meaning in the events themselves, you will hold your audience's interest.

Rule IX: Stick to the topic and develop it thoroughly.

Topic: Tell how you offended someone (or someone offended you) without meaning to; OR how someone's vocabulary blocked communication because the audience didn't know the words; OR how a commercial meant to tempt you actually turned you off. Point out in the margin what Rules (I-IX) you are following.

LETTERS

Published writing is remote. I, writer, do not so much as know the name of you, reader, although I may know some things probably true of you. You would hardly be reading a discussion of *The Reading—A Line You Can Model* if you weren't a model railroader. Even there, as we have seen, the writer must have some concern for the audience, for its likes, dislikes, prejudices, fears, interests, and needs; even there the writer must have some idea of how he relates to the reader, and stick with it.

In a much more direct way, some forms of writing pass between people who know each other personally, perhaps well. Particularly, letters depend very directly on personal knowledge. Whom you write means how you write.

The Murchison File

Letter #1

8 February 1973

The Honorable Percival Featherbed
The House of Representatives
Washington, D.C.

Dear Sir:

I commend you for your recent strong stand against
the crosstown throughway. Your high-minded opposition
to the local power structure and the selfish policies
of a few financiers will not be forgotten by the common
voters next autumn.
I join with you: no crosstown throughway!

Very truly yours,

William Delbratt

William Delbratt
Citizen of Urbanburg

Letter #2

8 February 1973

First Federal Savings & Loan Association
Urbanburg

Dear Sirs:

Temporary business reversals prevent me from meeting
the original due date on my note. If I can pay the
interest now, you will I hope find it possible to extend
the note another thirty days.
Thank you for your consideration in this matter.

Very truly yours,

William J. Delbratt

William J. Delbratt
69 Green Lane
Urbanburg

Letter #3

```
    THE G-D REAL ESTATE COMPANY          INTER-OFFICE MEMO


    from the desk of:  William J. Delbratt

    to:   Harvey Grimbold

    date: 9 Feb.

    Harv: I think the x-town t-way is dead, but unless the public
    believes it we'll never unload that Murchison property at a
    profit--everyone knows the t-way route would wipe it out.
    Check w/ some of yr buddy-boys in PRO to see if they can
    whip up a gimmick we could advertise personally---in the
    public interest, of course--to prove the X-town won't go through
    the Murchison sub.

                            WJD
                                   Bill




         WRITE IT DOWN AND YOU'LL REMEMBER IT
```

Letter #4

```
                                    11 February 1973

      Mr. Robert Wordbetter
      Editor's Office
      Daily Blare
      23 Skiddor Row
      Urbanburg

      Dear Mr. Wordbetter:

           Sally and I are having a small group for dinner--
      informal, of course--next Friday, the 17th, and wonder
      if you and Mrs. Wordbetter would find it possible to
      join us. Cocktails at seven, and we will sit down to the
      table about seven-thirty.
           It was a real pleasure to meet you at Harvey Grimbold's
      and I hope we can spend a little time together.

                              Sincerely,

                              William Delbratt
```

Letter #5

24 February 1973

Billing Department
Daily Blare
23 Skiddor Row
Urbanburg

Dear Sirs:

    I believe there is some mistake in connection with
the bill I have just received, dated 23 February, for
advertising space in the Sunday Supplement. Although
my firm was mentioned in the spread about the demise of
the crosstown thoughway project for which you have billed
me, I believe this very large bill ought not have been
sent to me. Please check with Editor Wordbetter to
confirm my impression.

Very truly yours,

William Delbratt

William Delbratt

Letter #6

28 February 1973

Citizens Trust Bank
100 Cashkill Road
Urbanburg

Dear Sirs:

I am at a loss to account for your action in refusing
to honor my check, slightly overdrawn by clerical error
on my part. I have maintained an account--#543 2032720
3660I Q80--in your bank for twelve years, and in all that
time I have never experienced such an embarassing and
disgraceful affront.

May I have some assurance from you that this conduct
on your part does not reflect the indifference to
customer welfare which it so strongly implies.

Very truly yours,

William J. Delbratt
69 Green Lane
Urbanburg

Letter #7

28 February

Miss Benoria Glust
Murchison Mansions
Apt. 3-B
Urbanburg

My beloved,

How can you ask? My heart aches at the thought that you
could suspect my affection, my need for you, of having
changed in the slightest. Don't you remember that night
on the sofa with the embroidered lamp=posts, with
"I Can Hear It Now" on the stereo, and the firemen had
to chop the door down with their axes because we hadn't
heard them knock? And you ask whether I care?!
Lambie, I really am sorry about the mink coat, but
there has been some incredibly stupid mistake at the
bank about the check; I am trying to get them to straighten
things out right away, and it shouldn't be long before
you have that super sleeping-coat you've always wanted.
I think we have a customer for the Murchison property,
so I may have to ask you to humor your old Daddykins and
move to another and of course better, apartment, but
shopping for it will be fun.
And you won't call me at home again, will you?

Kisses,

Billyboy

Letter #8

5 March 1973

Sally K. Delbratt
The Pebbles
Reno, Nevada

Dear Sally,

My God, Sally, what are you doing? You don't think
that woman meant a thing to me! She was just window dressing
to make the apartment building seem more attractive--sort
of a hostess, to show it to prospective customers; even
cities have welcome girls, at the airport, for heaven's aske.
It's all a mistake.

Sall, please come home. I don't know what's going on
around here without you--breakfast isn't the same at all;
the house seems empty; there's this stupid nonsense about
your signature on our joint properties; the checkbook is
all fouled up; the maid is quitting; and Sal, I'm so
lonely. What do you say, hon? Give the old guy one more
chance?

Your loving and
faithful husband,

Bill

EXERCISE 10: Write a short paragraph explaining the relationship of William Jenkyn Delbratt to each of the following; explain too how the vocabulary and general tone of Mr. Delbratt's letters to each person reflects his relationship.

    a. Congressman Featherbed
    b. First Federal Savings and Loan Association
    c. Harvey Grimbold, III
    d. R. Aloysius Wordbetter
    e. The Billing Agent of the Daily Blare
    f. Citizens Trust Bank
    g. Benoria "Moue-Moue" Glust
    h. Sara Kensington Delbratt

Pedagogic Comments on the Murchison File

Letter #1:
    A manual on business correspondence would point out the placing of the date, the inside address, the salutation—followed by a colon because formal, the formal closing salutation; a guide to letters that most people might write will content itself by pointing out that a letter of political opinion should be brief, precise, and definite.

Letter #2:
    Mr. Delbratt didn't know his bankers very well, and so could neither call them by name nor begin, "Hi, guys!" Since he is in fact asking a favor of these strangers, he thanks them for granting it—as he hopes they will—at the end of his letter.

Letter #3:
    Mr. Delbratt never knew it, but this memo deeply offended Mr. Grimbold. Mr. Grimbold always regarded the Public Relations Office with contempt; he mistakenly saw in Mr. Delbratt's reference to "yr buddy-boys in PRO" a slighting equation of him—Mr. Grimbold—with public relations employees. Without actually lying to anyone, he made arrangments with Mr. Wordbetter that were quite different from what Mr. Delbratt believed them to be. The tragic repercussions of this misunderstood insult (the bill strained his finances and therefore his most intimate personal relationships to the breaking point) all arose because Mr. Delbratt overlooked the basic rule of memo writing: Don't get cutesy with people who may misunderstand the tone of your words.

Letter #4:

Eagerly rushing to his own destruction, Mr. Delbratt pens a gracious letter of invitation to a relative stranger, Mr. R. Aloysius Wordbetter. His informal reference to his wife by her first name and the informality, too, of his closing salutation express his wish—for motives of his own—to talk closely with a man who will hear only what Mr. Grimbold has led him to expect to hear. Wisely, Mr. Delbratt states the time of the event very precisely.

Letter #5:

The clouds of doom are gathering, but Mr. Delbratt—as yet unaware that there is no way out—still retains control of himself. The tone of this letter seeking an adjustment is very sensible: courteous, taking it for granted that some little, easily correctable mistake has been made, which the firm in question will be very happy to set right just as soon as it is pointed out to them. Alas, no mistake has been made; but that was not the fault of Mr. Delbratt's letter.

Letter #6:

At this point, Mr. Delbratt's correspondence loses some of that polish which has graced it heretofore. The hostility of his assault—a counter-assault in his eyes—upon the Citizens Trust cannot have endeared him to the Head Teller who first read his letter, to the Account Supervisor with whom he discussed it, or to the second Vice-President to whom they showed it. Lips tightened. Mr. Delbratt's account was red-flagged. A good letter would: 1) apologize for Mr. Delbratt's error; 2) state unemotionally that he had been inconvenienced; 3) assume that the bank had not meant to inconvenience him; 4) express confidence that the bank wouldn't do it again.

Letter #7

The content of his letter will interest few; but note the use of the comma after the informal salutation, the use of direct address within the letter itself, and the generally conversational tone.

Letter #8:

Once again, we may note the marks of a letter to one known intimately: informal salutation, personal closing salutation, casual use of conversational contractions. Perhaps we may note that as literary composition, both this and the preceding letter do not end well; the emphasis that naturally falls on the end of any writing would better have been directed to other topics, considering the audience to which each was addressed. Whether or not Miss Glust did call the Delbratt home again is not public information; certainly, Mrs. Delbratt, prior to the granting of her divorce, signed no documents associated with the joint properties; and I myself heard the third teller at Citizens Trust comment with cryptic bitterness on Mr. Delbratt's apparent inability to add two and two.

EXERCISE 11:

    a. Assume that you met one of the people mentioned in the correspondence (your choice) at a party and chatted for ten minutes. Now you want to invite that person to your house for a social event (your choice). Write a letter of invitation to that person.

    b. You understand that the Delbratt's furniture is being put up for sale. Write a letter to Mrs. Delbratt to find out how you can buy some of it.

A Portfolio of Model Letters for Every Occasion

July 12, 1973

4-2-U Enterprises, Inc.
Old 999 Railway Avenue
Chooton, Uruguay

Dear Sirs:

    Enclosed you will find a check in the amount of
$5.99 as payment in full for your World Wide Weenie Widget,
as per the special introductory offer advertised in the
May issue of <u>West</u> magazine. Please ship by Railway Express,
charges collect.

                        Very truly yours,

                        Thelma Knox

                        Thelma Knox
                        Box 1, Route 83
                        Middleway, Virginia 93208

1 incl: check

Note that Mrs. Knox lists her inclosure, to help the incompetent clerical help at 4-2-U Enterprises keep from losing it. At least they will know it was there to start with. Her special instructions are quite clear, if hopeless, since Railway Express service does not extend from Chooton to Middleway.

August 1st, 1973

Mr. Tom Throwback
Herculean Efforts, Co-ordinated
10 Spot Lane
Chicago, Illinois

Dear Mr. Throwback:

   I write in reply to your recent want ad calling for
experienced masseurs. Although my present position pays
well, it does not offer the opportunities for advancement
I would find at a more dynamic enterprise such as your
own. For your convenience, I enclose on a separate sheet a
resumé of my professional experience.
   I look forward to your reply.

                                   Very truly yours,

                                   Cuthbert Twiddleton
                                   Cuthbert Twiddleton
                                   3 The Mews
                                   Milltown, Illinois

1 incl: resumé

The resume is a chronological table listing Mr. Twiddleton's jobs, giving employer's name, length of service, ranks held, promotions, and any special recognitions (e.g., Steam-Room Stamp of Excellence, 1963), and names and addresses of several references—people Mr. Twiddleton checked with before writing, who said they would be willing to recommend him if asked; personal information—age, marital status, etc.—is grouped at the end of the career data. Mr. Twiddleton made a serious error in his application for a position with Herculean Efforts, Co-ordinated: he used perfumed stationery. This was even more tasteless than writing a letter of condolence on Peanuts stationery with Snoopy dancing at the top of the page. Some attention to the actual paper used, its appearance, and its odor may have practical consequences.

                                                March 1, 1972

Professor Henry Thwachem
Alluvial State College
Riverbed, Illinios 10987

Dear Professor Thwachem:

       I have been nominated by a committee from my hometown,
Riverbank, for the Steamboat Memorial Scholarship.
I write to ask if you would be willing to write a letter
recommending me for this award.
       Next fall, I will enroll at the Center for Legal
Studies to begin my graduate preparation for the career
I plan as a lawyer. The S.M.S. award will pay half my total
expenses, as the enclosed brochure explains. Letters of
recommendation go to the addresses on the front of the
brochure and are due March 30th.
       For your convenience, I enclose a transcript of my work
at Alluvial, including the three courses I took with you,
Eh I--Freshman English, Eh 297--The Nineteenth Century Novel,
and Eh 387.5 sum q--The Literary Criticism of Thomas Rymer.
       I hope that Mrs. Thwachem and Sandringham Prancer of
Thwachem or "Old Spot," as we used to call him, are both
well.

                               Sincerely,

                               Isabel Zelstrom

                               Isabel Zelstrom
                               3, The Orchard
                               Riverbank, Illinois 10960

Miss Zelstrom, writing to ask for a letter of recommendation, very properly includes the following:

1. A brief statement of what she plans to study, where, when, and why.

2. The address and due date for the recommending letter. (Remembering Professor Thwackem's reputation for absent-mindedness, she puts the due date in the letter itself.)

3. A transcript, which will tell the professor her overall grade average and her grades in his courses.

4. A reminder of which courses she took from him (he has been known to forget).

5. A brief social greeting.

6. In a *later* letter she will tell him he was her favorite professor; in this one she does not.

                                                    1 April 1973

Grist-Mill Publishing House
101 Stern Street
Megalopolis, New York

Dear Sirs:

     Helloooo! Is anybody there? Anybody at all? If you can
read this, please write in longhand.
     On 31 June I received, with my August issue of <u>Blurt</u>,
a notice that my subscription would expire in two months.
     About 1 week later, I wrote you that I subscribed in
July of last year, which would have made my subscription
expire in June (not two months from June) <u>except</u> <u>that</u> I
paid in advance for a two-year subscription.
     In the third week of July I received a reminder that
my subscription expired in two months. In the last week of
July I received a form letter thanking me for my inquiry,
and enclosing a subscription blank.
     In the first week of August, I wrote again, this time
enclosing a copy of the cancelled check paying for the two-
year subscription.
     In the second week of August I received two copies
of the June issue of <u>Blurt</u>, an apology for the confusion
over my bill for <u>Blitz</u>--a magazine I have never heard of and
do not want to receive, and a copy of the October issue of <u>Blurt</u>
with a warning that my subscription had expired and the false
statement that I was getting the October issue without
having paid for it as an expression of good-will from
Grist-Mill towards all of their subscribers.
     I do not want good will. I just want the magazines I
paid for. I also do not want to talk to any more machines.
Either you write me longhand or I am not replying. Envelopes
addressed by machine will be returned unopened, delivery
refused.
     Do you hear me? Is anyone there?

                              Very truly yours,

                              Jane Plainne
                              Jane Plainne
                              62 Moor Street
                              Pillsburg, Ohio

This letter is not the usual request for adjustment. For example, Mrs. Plainne's rejection of typed correspondence is whimsical. On the other hand, there is a plaintive quality to her cry for human contact that may touch the heart of someone at Grist-Mill. In general, when writing to ask someone to do something—whether it is something he ought to have done anyway or even something that only the most ghastly fiend would not do—the best procedure is to assume his good will and reasonableness and explain clearly and simply (as, in fact, Mrs. Plainne does) what the problem is.

The marked page, 256, is for you to practice correspondence of your own. Write your letter to Messrs. Colwell-Knox on the blank side; fold as marked; and staple. The form is addressed and requires 8¢ postage if mailed within the continental United States.

In writing this letter, it will be necessary for you to decide just how chummy you wish to be, and to maintain that relationship throughout the letter. Suggested topic: what you think of this book.

Note that this page serves double-duty. It may also be used as a crumple page. If, after the letter is written, you find that it has relieved a good bit of your pent-up hostility, but if you also find upon second thoughts that the contents make you liable for libel; then you may at your discretion destroy the letter, thereby venting further hostility. Correspondence received in time will be acknowledged in the second edition.

With all of these rules for writers, it seems unfair not to have at least one rule for audiences. The rule is brief.

Rule for Audiences: Listen

Listening means concentrating on what the speaker or writer tries to get across. Language is like window-glass—the less you see it, the better it is. Listening is like trying to see through that window-glass to the human being on the other side. If the glass is a little smudged, or a color you don't like, don't get hung up looking at the glass instead of through it. When you read or listen to words, don't get hung up on the words apart from what they mean. If a speaker is profane, don't close your mind to his meaning because you react against dirty words. If he is a southerner who softens his vowels and says "Nigra," don't stop listening because he doesn't say "Neegrooh." If he uses long words, don't stop listening because he talks like a high-brow; if he uses short words, don't stop listening because he talks like a low-brow. If he says "Mrs." and "Miss" instead of "Ms." don't stop listening because he talks like a male chauvinist. The speaker, the writer may mean well but choose his words badly. Before you punish or reject or educate him try to understand what he is saying.[4]

In this section, I have tried to make the point that correct writing and good writing are not identical. Correct writing puts participles and periods, clauses and commas, in the right places. Good writing communicates. An act of communication starts and ends with a person. Unless you're doing crumple-page writing (which has its virtues), the person communication ends with is different from the person communication begins with. The person who begins had better know what the difference is, or the connection will be cut.

Some of my examples have been frivolous. But communication, like charity and the ability to laugh at ourselves, is in the last analysis a serious matter. Language theorists now surmise that verbal communication is a human instinct. It may be a human need in that sense; certainly, it is a human need if we are to survive in harmony. Respect language, as a medium of human communication. But most of all, respect the people you communicate with. "With" is a good word.

---

[4] THEN punish or reject or educate the stupid son of a gun.

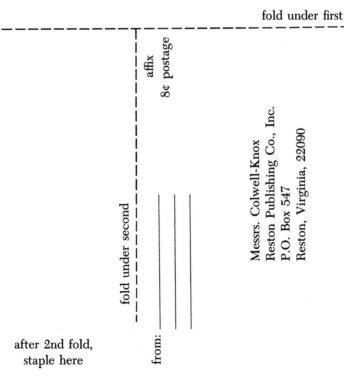

fold under first

affix
8¢ postage

Messrs. Colwell-Knox
Reston Publishing Co., Inc.
P.O. Box 547
Reston, Virginia, 22090

fold under second

after 2nd fold,
staple here

from:

Dear Messrs. Colwell-Knox:

(when letter is completed, fold under according to instructions on p. 255, leaving address panel showing, staple, stamp, and post one day later)

RESEARCH PAPER

16

The Research Paper: New Wine in an Old Bag

I t's called by many names: a Term Paper, a Library Paper, a Research Paper. But to most students, it is not a rosy assignment and, whatever you call it, it doesn't smell so sweet. Yet, like love and buried treasure, the more you dig it, the sweeter it is! There is satisfaction in knowing a lot about a little—more, possibly, than knowing a little about a lot. It is rather nice to be an authority on something, on anything. To uncover information; to select the most important parts of what you have uncovered; to organize these parts into a coherent whole; to write them down in the most interesting way you can; to know, finally, that you have communicated with a reader and given him facts, varied viewpoints, and interpretations about a subject he may have known little or nothing about before reading your paper—there is sweet satisfaction in that. Believe it!

You may have heard of Gertrude Stein: she was an American writer who lived most of her life in Paris, was a counselor and friend of Fitzgerald, Hemingway, Dos Passos, and many other famous writers. She is probably best known because of the people who knew her—and for one phrase: "a rose is a rose is a rose." A bit repetitious, we would say; not much reason to say it and obviously true, we would say. Okay, so she was a talkative and repetitious person in her life. As she died, however, she was divinely precise. Her last six words, as I have read, were these: the first three, "What's the answer?" the last three, "What's the question?"

Questions lead to answers that lead to questions that lead to answers that lead to questions. Answers are temporary; questioning is eternal. Each is part of the other; each engenders each. They live together; they can't live apart. T. S. Eliot in his "The Hollow Men" pronounced in the last lines of this poem:

> This is the way the world ends
> This is the way the world ends
> This is the way the world ends
> Not with a bang but a whimper.[1]

[1] ((text page 260: I believe the permission source here is the same as for the first Eliot quote. That source—for couplet from "The Lovesong of J. Alfred Prufrock"— is poem title—here, "The Hollow Men" in *Collected Poems*, 1909–1962 (New York: Harcourt, Brace, Jovanovich, and London: Faber and Faber, Ltd.) But you have the separate permission letter for the "Hollow Men" quote, which my memory tells me contains some instruction from them as to what info. should be cited.))

But maybe when that fated moment comes, the last dying man will cry out—as Gertrude Stein did—"What's the question?"

You should be asking by now, "What's all this stuff about?" What does writing a Research Paper have to do with these profoundly morbid reflections on life and death—of a woman or a world? Only this: What's the question? What is there that I want to know about? Is there something I know something about but not enough? What answers do I want that I'm curious enough to search for—through encyclopedia volumes, periodicals, books on the humanities, tomes on the sciences, myriad after myriad of sources and resources, many dry as dust? It can be worth it to you *provided* you can find that interesting question and *provided* that it's not of such a cosmic nature that a short paper could scarcely breathe on its scope and *provided* that your instructor agrees with you that the question is worth investigating and the answer worth knowing.

From this point on, I am going to assume that you and your instructor have shaken hands on a subject. But both of you think it's probably too much to handle in a paper of one thousand to two thousand words. And there are other things to check out, also, before you put down on paper or a note card that first magic, immortal word. For example, does your library or another local library have the reference works you need? For this is not to be "creative writing," the burning issue of your teeming brain. That vivid imagination must, for a time, be stilled. This is not the time and place for flashing flights of fancy. For this assignment, disciplined freedom; ordered initiative. This assignment, though independent study, demands dependence on other studies— on the facts, the insights, the interpretations, the conclusions of many former researchers who have touched your subject only lightly or who have hit it hard. You will even read material that you thought might be of help but turns out to be as barren as a solitary mule. You count these minutes or hours as necessary to a thorough investigation. So, to sum up: your job in writing a research paper is to find and select the facts, the information, the ideas, that focus on your subject and to combine, contrast, criticize, reflect—and then to capsule all you have learned and all you have concluded as a result of what you have learned into a tight, organized, logical, interesting paper following certain standard rules for its preliminary preparation and for its final form. To learn these rules or procedures and by them be guided through the throes of writing an acceptable research paper, read on.

As in eating any whale, you can divide the process of the writing of a research paper into a number of small steps. To write a research paper:

1. Select a subject.
2. Make a preliminary survey.
3. Define the topic.

4. Prepare a working bibliography.

5. Browse.

6. Narrow the topic: write a tentative thesis sentence.

7. Take notes

$7\frac{1}{2}$. During step 7, make topic headings (a rough, rough outline).

8–12. From this point on, the process corresponds to the preparation of any paper: 8. rough outline; 9. rough draft; 10. final outline; 11. final draft; 12. final copy.

Note that all of this falls into two halves. In steps 1–6, you are clarifying your topic (1, 3, 6,), soaking up a little background (2, 4, 5,), and staking out your prospector's claim area (4), the area you will dig through, seeking nuggets of information.

THE LAST THING FIRST

I want to talk first about what you'll actually be doing last: that is, the format of your finished paper. Of all the assigned written work you'll be doing, the research paper is the one that should be most "proper." While, obviously, it is the content that basically counts, yet there is a way to put down the content on the paper you will proudly turn in to your instructor. He may have given you certain special instructions, but he will, in general, expect you to follow a standard form.[2]

1. Type, on one side of good white bond paper, $8\frac{1}{2} \times 11$. (If you must write the paper in long hand, use lined paper.) *Double space* the **body** of the paper, but *single space* the **bibliography** and **footnotes**. If you copy a **long quotation**—maybe, of one hundred words or more—*indent* and *single space* the quotation without quotation marks. **Short quotations** in the paper itself should be *double-spaced* and *enclosed with quotation marks. The MLA Style Sheet* recommends that you leave *margins* of from 1 to $1\frac{1}{2}$ inches on both sides and at the top and bottom. Margins of $1\frac{1}{2}$ inches are preferable—especially on the left hand side of the paper to allow room for your instructor's comments. Naturally, you will *number* your **pages** in consecutive order: but do not number the title page or the first page of the manuscript; that is, the first numeral (placed five or six spaces below the top right hand corner) will be on the second page and, of course, will be number "2."

2. The **title page** can vary to a degree, but it should include the *title* of your paper, *your name,* the *course name* and *number* and *section.* The *date* the paper is submitted and, often, the name of your instructor is also on the

---

[2] See *The MLA Style Sheet* in your library if you feel you would like more information than I will provide here. Many of their suggestions are included here.

title page. Your instructor's wishes, if they differ from these, I would advise you to follow. A suggestion: let your first page be a blank one—to cover and protect the title page.

3. More than is usual in most of the papers you write, *italics* are often needed in the body of the paper, in the bibliography, and in the footnotes. In either handwritten or typed material, *underlining* is used to indicate italics. So always underline the following, wherever they may appear in your Research Paper or in any other formal paper you write: the **titles** of *complete publications—books, newspapers, magazines, plays, operas, record albums, pamphlets,* and *long poems.* (The guide is *complete publications.*) Italics are also used to indicate foreign words, and to call special attention to a part of a sentence or to certain words and phrases that you want to emphasize. Do not use italics to set off chapters in a book, short stories or short poems, magazine articles, etc.; for these, use quotation marks.[3]

4. *Parentheses, ellipses,* are often appropriate to use in the Research Paper—and sometimes brackets are, too. Check for the uses of these punctuation marks in Chapter 13.

5. **Footnotes** are essential to a Research Paper: they are essential because credit must be given where credit is due (more later about this and plagiarism); and to point out to the reader, who might be interested in further information, where it can be found. There are several ways to handle notes: they may be placed at the bottom of the page[4] or you may place all your notes on one page at the end of the paper—numbered consecutively, of course, as they appear in the text. Your instructor's preference, again, I feel sure you will follow. As for the mechanics of it: if placed at the bottom of the page, as I do in the sample paper in the next chapter, separate the text from the footnotes by a line that is three-quarters to one inch long, extending from the left margin of the paper toward the center.

One hundred footnotes out of one hundred and one will be like one listed here; if you happen to use the one hundred and first source, which doesn't fit these patterns, check the *MLA Style Sheet* or other library reference as your instructor says.

Basic footnote form for a book: Author's Name, *Book Title: With Complete Subtitle* (Place of Publication: Publisher's Name, year of publication), page reference.

[1]C. Carter Colwell, *The Tradition of British Literature* (New York: G. P. Putnam's Sons, 1971), p. 99.

---

[3] See the section dealing with quotation marks in Chapter 13.

[4] A number placed slightly high in a line of the text indicates a footnote.

Add the following, if necessary: names of other authors; names of editors (ed. John Smith) and translators (trans. Jane Smith) after the title.

An encyclopaedia article: "Title of Entry," *Name of Encyclopaedia* (date of publication), volume number in capital roman numerals, page reference in arabic numerals.

²"Labour Law," *Encyclopaedia Britannica* (1970), XIII, 533–52.

A magazine article: Author's Name, "Title of Article," *Name of Magazine,* volume number in capital roman numerals, issue number or season if given (date), page reference.

³Harold W. Russell, Jr., "Magnetic Couplers for 0 Scale," *Model Railroader,* XXXI (August, 1972), 58–59.

A newspaper article:

⁴*Winchester Evening Star,* August 21, 1972, Sec. 2, p. 15, col. 3.

Add the following if available: Author's Name, "Title of Article," in front of newspaper's name. (Place of Publication), if not obvious, follows newspaper's name in parentheses.

An essay in an anthology: Author's Name, "Essay Title," in *Book Title,* ed. Name of Editor(s) (Place of Publication: Publisher's Name, date), page reference.

⁵F. W. Dillistone, "The Atonement," in *Christian History and Interpretation: Studies Presented to John Knox,* ed. W. R. Farmer, C. F. D. Moule, and R. R. Niebuhr (Cambridge: Cambridge University Press, 1967), pp. 35–56.

If you are using a **casebook,** a textbook collection of materials dealing specifically with your topic, check with your instructor as to whether he wishes you to make reference to the original source or to the casebook as an anthology.

Second reference to a work:

If the author's name was given in the first note, then the second can refer simply to that name:

⁶Russell, p. 59.

Add the title (shortened, if a long one) if you have already cited two works by that author. If the author's name wasn't given, cite the title alone.

Ibid., the most useful of many abbreviations, means "in the same place." Use it to refer to the same source as the footnote right above it (on the same page of your paper), with a page reference if that is different.

[6]Russell, p. 59.
[7]Ibid.
[8]Ibid, p. 58.

  6. The **bibliography**—the list of books you have used in the preparation of your paper—should be listed in alphabetical order, surname first. Each item should be single-spaced, but use double spaces between them. The bibliography is the last page of your paper. With your instructor's consent, divide your bibliography into three separate lists: 1. Works Cited; 2. Other Works Consulted; 3. Additional Bibliography. 1. Works Cited: This list contains only those books and articles whose content appears in your paper; all of the works listed here also appear in footnotes. 2. Other Works Consulted: This list names dead ends—works you checked, but useless for your purposes. 3. Additional Bibliography: This final list is those works whose titles you found, but which you could not lay your hands on. If your instructor does *not* consent, your whole bibliography will consist *only* of items in list # 1. Here are the bibliographical entries for the footnotes above:

1. Works Cited

  Colwell, C. Carter. *The Tradition of British Literature.* New York: G. P. Putnam's Sons, 1971.

  Dillistone, F. W. "The Atonement." *Christian History and Interpretation: Studies Presented to John Knox.* Ed. W. R. Farmer, C. F. D. Moule, and R. R. Niebuhr. Cambridge: Cambridge University Press, 1967.

  "Labour Law." *Encyclopaedia Britannica* (1970), XIII, 533–52.

  Russell, Harold W., Jr. "Magnetic Couplers for 0 Scale." *Model Railroader,* XXXIX (August, 1972), 58–59.

  Winchester Evening Star, August 21, 1972, p. 15.

2. Other Works Consulted

  Knox, James. *Sunday's Children.* Boston: Houghton Mifflin Company, 1955.

  Prentice-Hall Author's Guide. Englewood Cliffs, N.J.: Prentice-Hall, Inc., 1962.

3. Additional Bibliography

  Nyensky, Vladislav Grigorievich. *British Literature, Christian History, Labor Law, and Model Railroading.* Trans. J. Hervey Orr. Reston, Virginia: Reston Press, 1979.

FIRST THINGS NEXT:

Step Number 1: Select A Subject

Earlier in this chapter I said, "I am going to assume that you and your instructor have shaken hands on a subject." It—he—is Oliver Wendell Holmes, the jurist, not the author. You are curious about him; you've heard of him; you have vague questions about who he was and what he did. But no answers. Your instructor is glad you're curious—and wouldn't at all mind knowing more about him, too. But both of you know that your paper can't bear the heading, "Oliver Wendell Holmes: His Life and Work": hundreds and hundreds of pages would be required to cover that subject, and while you wouldn't mind writing them, your instructor says he just doesn't have time to read that much. So, while your general subject has been decided on, the specific topic of your paper has not been. How to find a fraction of the man—not the whole integer—I *will not* say: that is the question.

Steps Number 2 & 3: Preliminary Survey; Define the Topic

The point of the preliminary survey is getting enough information so that you may define the topic better. You have to know something in order to define a topic. Topics like "The Digestive Habits of the Sea-Cucumber" are not produced like rabbits out of the hats of people who have never heard of sea-cucumbers or their digestive peculiarities (they eat everything they can swallow, and vomit their stomachs when something unhealthy goes down). So make a preliminary survey. For most topics, an encyclopaedia provides the best (broadest, clearest, most easily available) introduction.

Go to your library and find the *Encyclopaedia Britannica Index.* On page 269, you will find:

Holmes, Oliver Wendell (jur.)

11-603d

There will be other notations under his name: Am. law. 1–759d; Brandeis 4–97c; and other special references. But the general reference, first noted, is the one you should look into first. You find volume 11, p. 603 and see that several pages are devoted to a brief summary of his life. The article begins with his birth and early life, continues with his schooling, his religious beliefs, his Civil War record, his decision to make a career in law, his travels, his marriage; many, many other items are there about the man and his work. Among them is one that interests you and which appears narrow enough in scope to serve as the topic of a brief Research Paper: Holmes served on the supreme judicial court of Massachusetts from 1883 until 1902, the last three years as chief justice.

Step Number 4: Prepare a Working Bibliography

A working bibliography (biblio=book; a *biblio-graph*-y therefore is a
_____ - _____ , or the Research-Paper Writer's Bible) tells you two things:
where you are going to look; where you have looked. The first leads you finally
to a pile of note cards; the second provides your footnotes and the bibliography
listing at the end of your paper, and saves you time—it keeps you from
checking the same source twice.

Where do you get a working bibliography?

At the end of the article on Holmes there is a bibliography: eight books,
written by others about him; and ten other books that refer you to Holmes'
own writing that include his legal opinions and decisions, personal letters,
etc. From the *Encyclopaedia Britannica* alone you now have a wealth of
material with which to begin to compile your bibliography cards and, later,
your note cards. And there are other available encyclopaedias that you might
want to refer to: *Collier's Encyclopaedia, Encyclopaedia Americana, World
Book Encyclopaedia,* and others, too. There are dictionaries, also, that you
may want to consult: The *Biographical Dictionary* which contains information
about people in all fields may be of help. And there are specialized dictionaries
devoted to one area: chemistry, music, etc.

While encyclopaedias and dictionaries contain the facts you may want
to use directly in your paper, there are also *indexes, digests,* and *abstracts*
whose main purpose is to refer you to other relevant material. Digests and
abstracts are slightly different from indexes: they do attempt in a few words
to tell you the essential information you will find in the book or article to
which reference is made; *indexes* do not make this attempt: they simply refer
you to parts of books, periodicals and other publications.

The index most used is the *Readers' Guide to Periodical Literature*—although there are many others, many others in particular fields. One
that often proves to be especially useful to the researching student is the *Social
Sciences and Humanities Index*. The first of these refers you to information
of a more general and popular nature; the second, to more scholarly periodicals. It is in the second that you will probably find, for example, the references
that will point you to the periodicals containing information about the legal
career of Justice Holmes. Don't get turned off when you first peek at an index
because of the mass of abbreviations; they're all explained in the front pages.
No problem. And remember, when in the agonies of doubt and frustration,
you have two ready and willing friends near you: the warm, friendly librarians
and the cold but helpful card catalogue.

By this time in your academic career, you have consulted the *card
catalogue* many times. You know that this is where you go to find where to
go to know what you want to know. Also, you know that what you want

to find may be listed by the name of the author—the originator of the work; by title, the title of the work; and by subjects, the subjects treated in the work. You may look under the "R's" for Roberts, David Everett; you may look under the "p's" and find *Psychotherapy and a Christian View of Man;* you may continue to look under the "P's"[5] and find PSYCHOLOGY, PASTORAL, which tells about other subjects treated in that book. Having located the card that lists the book you want, you make a note of the *call number* found at the left hand top of the card.

Consider the working bibliography developed by the author of the research paper on Blaustark (a country which you have never heard of until this second), reproduced as the next chapter. The author of the paper is writing it for a history class; he is interested in this never-known Blaustark; he has followed the procedures outlined so far and has narrowed the subject of his paper to one critical event in that nation's history: The Battle of Simica Creek.

Our student author has used the card catalogue in his college library and in the much larger university library near him and in the local library. In addition, he has found a history buff who happened to have a few books about Blaustark. He has checked *The Reader's Guide* and other resources and has found ten sources that he sees can be of help to him—and he makes—on separate index cards—a list of these. They represent his *working bibliography.* Certain information is needed on each card. For example, on a **bibliography card** for an entire book, he has written down

1. The author's name with the last name first
2. The title of the book
3. If it isn't the first edition, the edition it is
4. City of publication
5. The name of the company that published the book
6. The date of its publication
7. The card catalogue call number (maybe, upper right hand corner)
8. Often, it helps to write a sentence about the general or specific content of the book
9. Where he found it
10. The number of the student's card

Here are some of his bibliography cards:

---

[5] Often a library will keep these different types of cards in different catalogue files.

920.112
B28

Gutterschimdt, Hans

A <u>Brief</u> <u>History</u> <u>of</u> <u>Blaustark</u>

Boston, Northsouthern Univ. Press, 1871

Observations about McCrutch:criticism
College Library card catalogue

 721.01
H740

McCall, Samson

"Blaustark Revealed"

The Goliath Review, VIII (1965),pp.24-33.

College Library periodical index

 940.05
B12

McCrutch, George Bart

<u>The</u> <u>Last</u> <u>Hundred</u> <u>Days</u> <u>of</u> <u>Blaustark</u>

New York: Pierpont Press, 1869

College Library card catalogue.
OUT due April 1st.

Every time you find the name of a book (or other work) that you want to look at, make a bibliography card. Put on it, in ink, all the information you may need. Be sure to include where you found the title—library card catalogue, periodical index, encyclopedia article, what have you; otherwise you may forget whether you have checked that source for titles. (In fact, keeping a separate list of such bibliographical sources as you check them, whether you find anything or not, will save absentminded repetition. When you checked the MLA Annual Index two weeks ago, did you check back through 1950 or just through 1960?)

Step Number 5: Browse

With bibliography cards in hand, go to the shelf—it's easily found; libraries make sure of that with identifying signs—and start picking out books. Libraries use one or the other of two systems: the Library of Congress Classification or the Dewey Decimal Classification. The first is identified by letters of the alphabet to designate twenty categories; the second is identified by numerals and is divided into ten basic categories.

The Library of Congress Classification

A	General Works	M	Music
B	Philosophy, psychology, religion	N	Fine Arts
		P	Languages and literature
C	History, auxiliary sciences	Q	Science
D	History and topography (except America)	R	Medicine
E and F	American history	S	Agriculture, plant and animal industry
G	Geography and anthropology	T	Technology
		U	Military science
H	Social Science	V	Naval science
J	Political Science	Z	Bibliography, library science
K	Law		
L	Education		

The Dewey Decimal Classification

000	General works	500	Pure sciences
100	Philosophy	600	Technology (applied sciences)
200	Religion	700	The arts
300	Social sciences	800	Literature
400	Language	900	History, geography, biography

These basic groups are divided and subdivided into more specific categories. The Dewey system divides each of its ten major divisions into ten subdivisions:

800–809	General Works	860–869	Spanish Literature
810–819	American Literature	870–879	Latin Literature
820–829	English Literature	880–889	Greek and Classical Literature
830–839	German Literature	890–899	Literature of Other Languages
840–849	French Literature		
850–859	Italian Literature		

So you should be able to find some of the books on your bibliography (cards).

You have collected a number of books; but you still are not quite ready to begin the basic labor of note-taking. The more you know, the better the notes you will take. Also, your topic may still be too big, in which case you will take many more notes than you will finally be able to use. (You're bound to take some extras anyway, but you surely want to keep the number down.) Therefore, browse a bit. That is, skim rapidly through several of your sources, the ones that look most promising for whatever reason, reinforcing the overview you began with an encyclopedia article. This browsing prepares you for

Step Number 6: Narrow the Topic: Write a tentative thesis sentence.

You have taken a few hours or parts of a few days for preliminary reading. You undoubtedly have in the front of your mind what each source might say about your topic: Holmes years between 1883 and 1902 when he was on the Massachusetts Supreme Judicial Court. But you have found that altogether too much is said. Although you had narrowed your subject already (from *Oliver Wendell Holmes: His Life and Work* to *Oliver Wendell Holmes: His Years on the Supreme Judicial Court of Massachusetts*) you see, after some preliminary reading, that this topic, too, is not narrow enough for a 2000 word research paper. What it had better be, you conclude, is *Oliver Wendell Holmes: His Three Years as Chief Justice of the Supreme Court of Massachusetts*. Usually, the longer the title, the narrower the topic.

The baby steps you have taken are not like that at all: you have taken giant strides. The way you felt a few days before when you had reluctantly shaken hands with the prof has almost insensibly changed. While the initial depression hasn't lifted, it has lightened. A clutter of nothingness is beginning to assemble into an order of something. You have a topic; you have absorbed something of the aura of your character and of the long days and years of his life (94 of them!) and can direct your thoughts and energies to only three of them. So buckle down to investigate, like some academic private eye, the activities of Mr. Holmes in that miniscule 3.2 percent of his life (that reminds you, it's time for a beer) and then to write a tentative thesis sentence.

You have to write a thesis sentence because you can't find anything if you don't know what you're looking for. The thesis sentence is your main point; what you are looking for is evidence that supports it, explains it, proves it. On the basis of your browsing, you draft one: Under the leadership of Chief Justice Oliver Wendell Holmes during the years from 1883 to 1902, the Supreme Judicial Court of Massachusetts rendered many decisions that effected changes in laws throughout the United States. But your thesis statement must be *tentative,* because most of your research is yet to come, and you must be willing to modify your first statement in the light of later discoveries. These discoveries occur during

Step Number 7: Take notes.

With the thesis sentence written to direct and control you, you're ready to begin writing note cards that will, in a few weeks, constitute the text and the footnotes of the finished chapter. But wait! You're finding too much! That Supreme Judicial Court of the Commonwealth of Massachusetts under Chief Justice Holmes must have worked like hell during that three years. Decision after decision, interpretation after interpretation, infinitum after infinitum. Fifty pages might cover your thesis sentence, not ten pages. You'll take one of them, the one most interesting to you, and that one will be your topic: *Oliver Wendell Holmes: His Interpretation of the Illegal Purpose Doctrine during his Service as Chief Justice of the Supreme Judicial Court of Massachusetts.*

Congratulations, fellow student! You have done it! Now rephrase your thesis sentence—"tentative" no more—and apply the seat of the pants to the seat of the chair. You carefully read your sources to find what is relevant to your topic—don't drift away from it. Every time you find a fact, statement, or idea that you may want to use in the paper, write it down on a note card. Each note card is labeled only with the number of the bibliography card for the work it comes from (that's why #10 on the bibliography card was your numbering) plus page number (s). Some of the note cards you write, you will find are not needed—their information would distract you from your topic. Some of the notes will be direct quotations; most should not be. While your paper is based necessarily on facts that happened—actual events—and interpretations and recountals of these facts by other writers, yet the paper is yours.

Note cards do not contain the detailed information that bibliography cards do. You will refer to the source of your note (a code number for where it came from, plus page number or numbers) but the meat of it is what you think will, in effect, when all the cards are put together in a coherent order, turn out to be your research paper. Remember that only one item of information (of course, from one source) goes on each card.

THE WORM IN THE SALAD

By the time you have been admitted to college and are assigned your first Research paper, you certainly have heard the word plagiarism. But you may have a notion of what the word implies without knowing the full meaning of it, how bad the practice of plagiarism is, or how, sometimes, the crime can be committed without your knowing you are committing it. What it is, in plain talk, is stealing: a special kind of stealing that applies to all writers who swipe the ideas, expressions, words of another and try to palm them off to the reader as their own. The crime rate for this felony soars among students writing term papers: after all, these papers are *supposed* to use the thoughts of other writers. But you are to use the thoughts and words of others only if, in *every instance, you identify their rightful owners in the text of your paper or in footnotes.* The hypocritical Iago in Shakespeare's *Othello* says to him, "But he that filches from me my good name/Robs me of that which not enriches him/And makes me poor indeed." If you plagiarize, you are robbing yourself of your good name, which makes you "poor indeed."

I believe, as I think many instructors believe, that most plagiarism is unintentional. When a direct quotation is written into your paper—enclosed in quotation marks as it is—it is practically automatic to say who said it. This is not confusing to the average student; almost without thinking, he makes the proper identification of the author of the quote. The confusion comes—and the crimes are committed—when you attempt to paraphrase or think you can get away without paraphrasing. To "paraphrase" is to put another's words into your own words, at the same time duplicating his thought, and crediting that thought to him in a footnote. If you use his own words or switch around a few or use a synonym or two and think this is okay because you have footnoted it—you are wrong! You have plagiarized. If you have used his thought, really have put it into your own words in your own style and also have footnoted it, you're clean.

My wife and I have a little plagiarism problem. She keeps claiming that some of my best stories happened not to me, as I tell them, but to her; she claims that I have simply absorbed these stories and now wrongly claim them as my own experience. Well, we struggle along pretty well. But your instructor won't. Neither will any public audience, any audience larger than an understanding wife or husband. Written work is public speech. Public speech should be honest. It cannot afford the well-meant errors of casual conversation. When writing a research paper, errors must be headed off at the pass (prevented while taking notes).

A suggestion to avoid unintentional plagiarism: As you write the note cards which will become the essential content of your paper, either put every passage you copy in "quotes" or, if you plan to use the passage paraphrased, paraphrase it—thoroughly reworded—right then. That is, at that point put the passage in your own words—*or* copy the author's words as they are and make a note on the card to yourself, "change to my own words."

I hope that I have said enough about plagiarism so that you will avoid it like the plague in your research paper and in all the themes you write in school and in all the necessary written work you may need to do in your after graduation work. Each of us has varying writing talents as we have varying talents in other fields. While the hope is always alive with your English instructor that during the course of a semester or a year your themes will become more literate and more interesting (why else have a composition course or this book, for that matter) yet each student does have either an excellent or an average vocabulary; either a sense of language and its subtleties or not much feeling for words and style—your instructor soon knows what, in general, is *your* style. Marked changes from it glare at him like a sore typewriting finger.

Steps 7½ to 11: Outlines and drafts.

The steps up to the final copy follow the general procedures for good writing suggested in Chapter One of this book. There is one exception. Begin the rough outline while taking notes.

As soon as you have some idea what shape your paper may take, as soon as you know what some of the topic headings are likely to be, make a rough, rough outline, and label your notes as you continue to take them according to where they will probably go. You can do this either with words (for example, "Background to 1805") or with symbols (for example, "II A"). Symbols are shorter, but words are easier to rearrange.

This whole process must seem very complicated. It is. What makes it especially hard is that you, like every freshman, must feel your way—you don't know where you're going until you're almost there. So you must constantly narrow your topic, constantly revise your thesis statement, constantly revise your outline. When you have written a term paper once, how much better a job you can do writing the same paper over again!

But cheer up. That applies to everything you learn. If I went back to school now, I would learn so much more as a freshman than I did the first time. And remember: "Every little bit helps," as the man said spitting into the ocean.

17

The Affair at
Simica Creek

ote that unlike 3½% of his fellow students, Mr. Hervey did not forget to put his name on the paper. Unfortunately, he misspelled the name of Mr. Phuller, who was rather sensitive.

THE BATTLE OF SIMICA CREEK:
ITS HISTORICAL AND POLITICAL BACKGROUND

by
James Hervey

English 101 Section 6
Mr. Fuller
May 25, 1972

OUTLINE

<u>Thesis:</u> George Bart McCrutch abandoned his role of objective historian and became an active participant in the war between North and South Blaustark because he believed the nation should be unified under Reston I.

I. The two questions to be answered
    A. Why was Colemann defeated?
    B. Why did McCrutch fail to report the details of the battle?

II. Historical Background of Blaustark
    A. From its founding in 1248 to 1805
    B. From 1805 to 1815
        1. Conquest by Sapoleon I
        2. Attempts to establish new laws and customs
            a. In the southern valley
            b. In the northern mountains
    C. From 1815 to 1860
        1. Sapoleon's defeat at Vasserlaut
        2. Civil war and anarchy in Blaustark
    D. From 1860 to 1864
        1. The political and military situation as of April 1, 1860
            a. South Blaustark and its ruler, von Reston der Moste
            b. North Blaustark and its ruler, Colemann
        2. The emergence of and involvement in the affairs of Blaustark by
            a. Rosa de Chambre
            b. George Bart McCrutch

3. The contrasting ambitions of Reston I and Colemann
4. The von Reston–McCrutch conspiracy and its successful implementation
5. Plan of battle
   a. The main bridge over Simica Creek
   b. The underwater bridge and its critical importance
     (1) von Reston anticipates Colemann's plan
     (2) What von Reston and McCrutch planned

III. The Battle of Simica Creek, August 7, 1864
  A. Colemann
   1. Disposes his forces as von Reston had anticipated
   2. Loiters with Rosa
  B. The battle: von Reston's ambush works
  C. Conclusions: see thesis
  D. Aftermath

Checking the outline against the opening paragraph reveals that it is misleading. The outline implies that there will be two major topics covered: A. Why von Colemann was defeated; B. Why McCrutch was silent. But those are in fact just two items listed as questions, treated together, not separate subdivisions. Indeed, very little is said of von Colemann. He and his unusual activity—or inactivity—appear too abruptly. Who is he? What did he do—or not do? The word "then" implies that the sentence follows from what was said before; but nothing was said about von Colemann. The effect may be suspenseful, but it is not enlightening.

```
memo:            I          McCrutch, pp 380-90
                            Gutterschmidt
                            Cynicovitch

Two questions to be answered:

1. Why did Colemann act as he did at
the battle of Simica Creek.

2. Why did McCrutch skip in his book
the details of the battle.
```

This card is a note to himself, made by the student probably while reviewing his own notes, as an idea to be included in the paper. Because of its generality, and the fact that three writers play with it, no specific reference or footnote is required for the idea. While developing his outline, to some extent a matter of shuffling cards, the student marked on each card where it would go. This card comes in part I of the outline.

THE BATTLE OF SIMICA CREEK:
ITS HISTORICAL AND POLITICAL BACKGROUND

Through the many years since the publication of
George Bart McCrutch's The Last Hundred Days of
Blaustark,[1] scholars and interested readers, alike,
have wondered about the curious events at Simica
Creek on the morning of August 7, 1864. McCrutch's
explanation is, at the best, lame. Yet it must be
assumed that he knew intimately and exactly the details of the affair: his precise account of what immediately preceded that morning and of what immediately followed it, makes that assumption, in fact,
a certainty. Two questions, then, are involved:
what caused General von Colemann to act—or rather
not act—in such an uncharacteristic way, and (2)
why did McCrutch at this important—indeed, critical—juncture break the smooth flow of his story
with what the eminent German historian, Hans Gutterschmidt, calls "" limping away from a challenging
problem rather than charging into it, as McCrutch
in his unswerving (often, almost ruthless) quest
for the truth always did."[2] Gregor Cynicovitch,
one of the first of the Russian historians to write
a penetrating study of Blaustarkian politics, said
of McCrutch: "He never evades an issue; the issue
tries to evade him—and fails."[3] This paper will
concern itself with examining and explaining the

---

[1]George Bart McCrutch, The Last Hundred Days of
Blaustark (New York: Pierpont Press, 1869).
[2]Hans Gutterschmidt, A Brief History of Blaustark
(Boston: Northeastern University Press, 1871), p.
128.
[3]Gregor Cynicovitch, Blaustark: A Nation Divided
(New York: G. D. Stimpson, 1865), p. 92.

This passage is plagiarized. Although Mr. Hervey has altered the wording slightly, he still follows exactly the sequence of thought and the sentence structure of the original, keeping most of the phrases intact.

IIA

"Although the curious history of Blaustark is, in large degree, known by the scholars of the period, a rather lengthy mention of x£it must be made here as a necessary introduction to the immediate subject of our study. It is even more needed as background for the reader whose memory of this small monarchy may have grown dim. No modern map traces its wavy boundary lines; no name identifies the massive mountains and verdant valleys blending so beautifully together that for centuries this tiny kingdom was known as the "Belle of the Balkans'". p.124.

IIA

"But the rose harbored an invisible worm that, unknown to the rest of the world and even to itself, was feeding on it and destroying its very essence. Blaustark was born in agony; lived in ecstasy; and died inignominy." p.34

The circled number on this and other note cards identifies the bibliography card for the book the passage came from. Any convenient code of abbreviations would serve as well. The card above, from p. 124 of book 3 (Germaine's *Blaustark*), was so long that it took two cards to hold it; the second card was identified "p. 124, card 2."

strange incidents of the morning of August 7, 1864
at Simica Creek, and examining and explaining the
reasons why George Bart McCrutch chose to ignore or
conceal them.

Although the curious history of Blaustark is,
in large degree, known by the scholars of the period, mention of it is a necessary introduction to
our study. It is even more needed as background for
the reader whose memory of this small kingdom may
be dim. No modern map traces its boundary lines; no
name identifies the massive mountains and lovely
valleys blending so beautifully together that for
centuries this tiny kingdom was known as the "Belle
of the Balkans."[4]

"Blaustark was born in agony; lived in ecstacy;
and died in ignominy"[5] are the words that might best
become the gravestone of this forgotten nation.

Born in the blood of the devastating invasion
of Central Europe by Christopher XI in 1248, it was
established to serve as a buffer state between Vampiria and Necturia--which had been at each other's
throats for hundreds of years. Throughout the years
from the middle 1200's to the early 1800's, Blaustark was at peace with the world and within itself.
Sapolean the First was to change all this: not recognized at the time, it was his conquest and occupation of Blaustark that made inevitable--we see now--
the disaster of Simica Creek and the end of an era.

Sapoleon I attacked Blaustark in 1805. He followed his usual procedure with conquered countries:

---

[4]René Germaine, Blaustark: La Belle Patrie, trans.
W. B. Baum (New York: V. S. Green & Co., 1901),
p. 124.
[5]Samson McCall, "Blaustark Revealed," The Goliath
Review, VIII (1965), p. 34.

he appointed one of his lieutenants as the ruler;
established the code of law which prevailed in his
own nation, Francisca, under a constitution which
he had, himself, created for it. Whether, eventu-
ally, this totally new and strange form of government might have worked in Blaustark, we don't know.
Cynicovitch observed that during the interval between its occupation by Sapoleon and its evacuation
by the Franciscans after Sapolean's total defeat at
the battle of Vasserlaut (September 15, 1815), some
changes toward a more republican form of government
had been achieved.[6] Gutterschmidt, however, in his
article of July 8, 1866, in Heures Perdues[7] stated
that only in the capitol of Blaustark, Babiche, and
the valley surrounding it, was this the case. The
people of the mountains, he states, had scarcely
been touched by the new regime and lived their
lives of hardy independence as they had for centuries. McCrutch agrees with Gutterschmidt.[8]

Their mutual viewpoint appears to be the correct one, as the events of the years from 1815 to
1865 undoubtedly show. As usual, when there is no
one government, there were many. For forty years—
from 1815 to 1860—Blaustark was a slaughterhouse,
as faction fought faction in open battles, in raids,
in secret murders. By 1860, indifference might be
the word that best describes the condition of the

---

[6]Cynicovitch, p. 246.
[7]Hans Gutterschmidt, "Vasserlaut et Apres:
L'Histoire d'une Occupation," Heures Perdues,
July 8, 1866. Trans. Annette Coulet, Sunshine Re-
view, XI (1930), 8.
[8]George Bart McCrutch, "Blaustark: The Interval
Between," Publications of the Balkan Bibliographical
Society, LI, Winter, 1866.

". . . by surviving . . . it was his eyes . . ." A dangling modifier; awkward to say his eyes survived; also awkward to say his eyes opened by surviving—by surviving they were there, but surviving is not how they opened.

people of Blaustark and its administration. This in-difference was born of desperation, and in this state there was stability for a short time. It was to last only four years. "The morning of this pe-riod of calm came without warning: deep into one night, there was chaos; by the next dawn there was (sic) order and peace, as if a raging giant had suddenly and inexplicably sighed, shrugged his shoulders, and walked away to sleep."[9]

The political situation at this moment in Blau-stark was as follows: There were two separate states: South Blaustark, the valley region with its capitol, Babiche; North Blaustark, the mountain re-gion, with its capitol, Brotschrift. Mention must be made of the two rulers, who, by chance, happened to reign on this strange morning of April 1, 1860. The king of South Blaustark was von Reston der Moste. He was the last of a long line of von Restons who had never really managed to achieve their desires—not because of lack of ambition and energy but chiefly through a lack of intelligence and directed effort.[10]

Unlike his ancestors, he was intelligent and cunning and conniving, and by surviving for nearly five years through bribery and deceit, it was his eyes that opened in the royal bed on this weirdly quiet morning.

At the same time, a hundred or more miles away, a vastly different leader surveyed the misty moun-

---

[9]Horatio Hobbs, Bart. Blaustark: The Philpott Lec-tures, 1861. (rpt. London: Psmith and Smith, 1865), p. 3.
[10]Hermann Schlink, The Uncertain Peace (New York: Handover, 1863), p. 89.

The student has properly paraphrased this direct quote, marked as such on the note card to prevent unintentional plagiarism. His wording differs enough from McCrutch's to make no quotation marks necessary. The necessary footnote identifies the source of the information even though different words have been used.

NOTE CARD
IID1

"A leader was critically needed; Colemann quickly became that leader. He was decisive, courageous, aggressive. Yet, strangely enough, he seemed to hate the carnage of the battlefield and tried, as much as possible, to protect the life of every individual soldier under his command. His compassion for his men engendered their loyalty to him."
p.298

From this point on, the paper draws exclusively from one source, Carlier and Kyart's "Cherchez la Femme." This is a major weakness in the topic chosen: the last half of the paper is pure summary of one article.

Footnote #11: This second reference to McCrutch's *The Last Hundred Days of Blaustark* needs less information than the first reference: it contains only his last name, a shortened form of the title (to avoid confusion with his article, "Blaustark: The Interval Between," also cited earlier), and the page number.

tains surrounding--like enclosed parentheses--the
fortress of Brotschrift. His name was Errol Colemann.
Little is known of his family's history or of his
own before Colemann appeared in Brotschrift at a
time when North Blaustark was being assaulted by Vampiria on its left and fighting off guerrilla attacks
by South Blaustark on its right. Colemann, who was
brave and decisive, took over leadership when leadership was desperately needed. Since he hated blood-
shed and tried, whenever possible, to save the
lives of his men, he was loved and trusted by them.
These positive qualities and one other which represented a weakness were to combine to cause his defeat four years later at the Battle of Simica Creek.
We owe to Charles Bart McCrutch these descriptions
of von Reston and Colemann: he made his headquarters in Babiche but often visited Brotschrift
and knew both leaders equally well. It was he who,
in one short sentence, summed up the men and their
manners: "Von Reston was to Colemann as Octavian
was to Anthony."[11]

One other person (her name is never mentioned
in the histories by Gutterschmidt, Cynicovitch or
McCrutch) whose activities played so essential a
role during the last days of Blaustark is Rosa de
Chambre. Her participation in the affairs of Blaustark did not become apparent until either 1863 or
1864. This would explain why Gutterschmidt and Cynicovitch ignored her: neither was close to the internal affairs of Blaustark during the 1860's. But
it was during these very years that McCrutch was
most closely associated with the two regimes in Blau-

---

[11]McCrutch, The Last Hundred Days, p. 298.

This sense of *man* is not special enough to call for quote marks.

The second sentence of the next paragraph ("The history of the next four years . . . ") sounds like an idea (not wording) taken from Carlier and Kyart. Not only all direct quotations, but also all information that comes from a particular source must be annotated, must have a footnote identifying where the student learned that fact. This statement is a judgment rather than a fact, but it is Carlier and Kyart's judgment, not the student's, and should be so labeled. If a whole paragraph paraphrases a source, put the footnote at the end and work in such phrases as "Carlier and Kyart feel . . . They go on to say . . ."

stark. But McCrutch's silence—rather secrecy—is understandable now due to the recent publication in the <u>Journal Historique</u> of Carlier and Kyart's monograph, "Cherchez la Femme."[12] The world can now know what really caused the defeat of Colemann on the morning of August 7, 1864.

For the history of Blaustark from its formation in 1248 to its invasion by Sapoleon in 1805 we are chiefly indebted to Hans Gutterschmidt and to Gregor Cynicovitch. Most of our knowledge of Blaustark from 1815 to 1860 is due to the painstaking research and on-the-spot reporting of George Bart McCrutch. However, because of what is now known through the work of Carlier and Kyart, we must totally discredit McCrutch's recountal of the years from 1860 to 1864: during those four years, the objective scientist, the detached observer and recorder, changed into a subjective, emotional "man."

The last mention made, in this paper, of von Reston I and General Colemann was at that moment on April 1, 1860 when an unnatural peace replaced the violence of the previous forty years. The history of the next four years must be thought of not as the political or military history of a nation but rather of the personal history of von Reston I, Colemann, McCrutch and, to a lesser but important degree, Rosa de Chambre.

Von Reston was determined to unite Blaustark; Colemann and his mountain people had no such ambition: to be left alone in peace and security was

---

[12]Georges Carlier and P. Kyart, "Cherchez la Femme," <u>Journal Historique</u>, XVI (1959), 26–42, trans. Jean Paul Paul and rpt. in <u>Listen</u>, VI (December 1960), 735–749.

```
Ⅱ D 3                              (11)

Reston was determined to unite Blaustark;
Colemann and his mountain people had no
such ambition: to be left alone in peace
and security was all they wanted. So for
four years von Reston thought and schemed
while Colemann, satisfied with things as
they were, enjoyed the beauties of North
Blaustark's hills and streams and women
                                    p. 21
```

This note is a paraphrase; Mr. Hervey has chosen to include it verbatim in the text. Only because he has been careful to put quotation marks around all direct quotations in his note cards can he use the note confident that he is not plagiarizing.

Like footnote 13, notes 14 and 15 are second references: the full information about Carlier and Kyart's article has already been given. Therefore, these notes give only authors' names and a page reference. Since 14 is one the same page as 13, "Ibid.," in the same place, and the right page number are enough.

all they wanted. So, for four years, von Reston thought and schemed while Colemann, satisfied with things as they were, enjoyed the beauties of North Blaustark's hills and streams and women. Rosa de Chambre, enjoying the castle of Babiche and the occasional arms of its ruler, was not passionately devoted to von Reston, the man, but was devoted to von Reston, the ruler, and willingly obeyed his wishes. McCrutch, according to Carlier and Kyart, believing sincerely that Blaustark should be reunited under one strong king and that king should be von Reston I, had, by 1862, abandoned his role of historian and become the court counselor.[13] "It is probably he who proposed to von Reston the plan that was, a few years later, to unite the separate parts of Bluastark. The plan was a simple one based on the weakness—the flaw—in Colemann's character: his compulsion to conquer women and his pride in his sexual virility."[14] The very qualities—his aggressiveness on the battlefield and his pride in military conquest—which had saved North Blaustark in time of war were to prove to be his and his country's loss in a time of peace. McCrutch proposed to King von Reston that he and Rosa de Chambre pretend to join the enemy; that each use his respective talents to convince Colemann of their loyalty to him and that a united Blaustark under one ruler, Colemann, was actually what the people of South Blaustark desperately desired.

---

[13]Carlier and Kyart, p. 21. All subsequent events recorded in this paper are taken from the article in _Journal_ _Historique_.
[14]Ibid., p. 24.

"The plan worked out just as McCrutch envisioned it; Colemann welcomed them—body and soul. From the bed chamber to the council chamber was a short step and, within a few months, Errol Colemann, through the assorted arguments propounded in each place, was persuaded that a decisive battle should be waged against von Reston and that it would be won."[15]

In the valley of South Blaustark ran a creek that, fed by scores of mountain streams from N. Blaustark, was very deep but, because of the high banks on each side of it, was narrow—at its widest point not more than one hundred yards across. There was, of course, a bridge across it which in the old days was used equally by the mountain and valley people of Blaustark. If any attack was made by either side, this bridge must be taken. Many battles had been fought there and the result had always been the same: heavy casualties—and that was all! For offensive purposes, this bridge was useless. Here, again, the difference in the characters of the two men was decisive: Colemann abandoned any notion of forcing a crossing of Simica Creek; von Reston did not. He came up with an idea that was so simple that neither he nor any of his predecessors had thought of it: to find a place in the creek where the water might be only five or six feet deep and build an under-water bridge, an invisible and unknown road between the banks. During the summer months of 1863, using a small corps of engineers whom he could trust completely, this was accomplished. There was now an invasion route.

---

[15]Carlier and Kyart, p. 25.

This paraphrased note, with one short quote marked, was further altered by Mr. Hervey for stylistic reasons as he prepared his final draft.

IID 5

Of course, what von Reston and McCrut planned was exactly the reverse: Reston and what appeared to be his main force would defend his side of the bridge but actually it would be deployed in the heavy forests thru which the enemy must march after the N. Blaustarkians had crossed the creek. They would be "engulfed from both sides and from the front and rear" and be so badly damaged that any remnants of the army would not be able to complete their mission.

"fool-proof": Quotation marks should not be used apologetically.

Before McCrutch joined Colemann, he and von
Reston had carefully worked out their strategy:
after gaining the confidence of General Colemann,
McCrutch would tell him about the secret road
across the creek. They assumed that Colemann would
design the logical battle plan: that he, with what
would appear to be the major part of his army,
would pretend to attempt the crossing of the bridge
but that, actually, his main strength would be at
the ford ten miles below the bridge. His army would
cross it at dawn, sweep around the flank of von Reston's army which would, they thought, be concen-
trated at the bridge, and attack von Reston from
the rear.

Of course, what von Reston and McCrutch planned
was exactly the opposite: von Reston and what
seemed to be his main force would defend his side
of the bridge but actually von Reston's army would
be hidden in the forests through which the enemy
must march after they had crossed the creek. They
would be surrounded and unable to complete their
mission. Then, the forces of von Reston would ford
the creek, attack Colemann from the rear, and destroy him. The plan seemed to them "fool-proof."
But there was one aspect of it that troubled them:
Colemann was a brilliant general, a courageous man
who had often turned what seemed to be certain defeat into victory or stalemate. To be absolutely
sure of success, von Reston and McCrutch knew that
he must in some way or other be diverted and de-
ceived. McCrutch would be in a position to deceive
him; Rosa de Chambre would be in a position to divert him. The Battle of Simica Creek or, as it is
sometimes referred to, "The Affair at Simica Creek"
is history.

There seems to be no particular reason for quoting this paragraph directly. Direct quotes should be used only when the original's wording, its exact phrasing, matters, as in the next quotation, at the end of the following paragraph. That quote not only plays deliciously with three parallel -ities combined in a fourth (sagacity, duplicity, amorous amorality, unholy trinity), but also expresses a judgment—"destroy not just a man but a nation"—whose meaning might be subtly changed if reworded. (For example: "They killed von Colemann, of course, but more significantly, they had killed North Blaustark." In fact, von Colemann survived the battle; he was "destroyed" in a different sense, which this rephrasing lost.)

Note that since note 17 refers to the same location as 16, "Ibid." with no other reference can be used.

General Colemann determined to attack on the
morning of August 7, 1864. He made no secret of his
intentions: it was important that the enemy know of
his apparent massive assault at the bridge so that
von Reston would assemble his forces there to defend
it. The night before, under the command of his most
trusted and capable aid—Colonel Ira Vederci—
20,000 battle-tested veterans assembled at the ford
for the dawn invasion. Colemann's headquarters was
a tent on a hill overlooking the bridge. "He was
supremely confident of the outcome of the next
day's battle; he had every reason to be. After all,
the dawn battle at the bridge was only a feint; it
would be noon or later before the real battle would
begin—after Vederci had crossed the ford, flanked
von Reston's army, and attacked its rear. Then, he
would take active command of his divisions and
charge the bridge. Meantime, the beautiful Rosa de
Chambre was waiting for him in the tent."[16]

By noon, as General Colemann mounted his horse
and prepared to lead his forces to a glorious victory, he had been disastrously defeated. The cream
of his army, the divisions under Colonel Ira Vederci,
who early in the battle had breathed his farewell
to this life, were dead or dying; the victorious
battalions of South Blaustark—whose casualties had
been light—had crossed to the north bank and were
within a mile or two of the bridge hurrying to attack Colemann's rear.[17] There was nothing left to do.
"The sagacity of von Reston, the duplicity of Mc-
Crutch, the amorous amorality of Rosa de Chambre com-

---

[16]Carlier and Kyart, p. 31.
[17]Ibid.

NOTE CARD
IIID

McCrutch spends two chapters on Vampiria's and Necturia's simultaneous attack on Blaustark, defeating it in 1864.

ch. 17 and 18

bined in an unholy trinity to destroy not just a man but a nation."[18]

George Bart McCrutch in his last book, The Last Hundred Days of Blaustark, devotes one sentence to the Simica Creek "Affair": "The army of General Colemann was decisively defeated by King von Reston I in the Battle of Simica Creek."[19] We know now why McCrutch chose to conceal the details of the battle. We know now what caused General Colemann to act—or rather, not act—in such an uncharacteristic way at this same battle. The questions posed at the beginning of this paper and that motivated its writing are answered.

McCrutch did, however, describe in cruel detail—as it must have been for him—the death of his adopted kingdom. In the months following the end of the war, Vampiria and Necturia made an alliance; one attacked Blaustark from the north; the other from the south. The end of 1864 was also the end of Blaustark; its name no longer proudly marks its former wavy boundaries. It has joined that legion of the nearly-forgotten lands whose names may be vaguely remembered only by a few.

---

[18]Carlier and Kyart, p. 33.
[19]McCrutch, The Last Hundred Days, p. 301.

1. Works Cited

Carlier, George and P. Kyarts. "Cherchez la Femme." Journal Historique, XVI (1959), 26–42. Trans. Jean Paul Paul and reprinted in Listen, VI (December 1960), 735–749.

Cynicovitch, Gregor. Blaustark: A Nation Divided. New York: G. D. Stimson, 1865, p. 92.

Germaine, René. Blaustark: La Belle Patrie. [1781] Trans. W. B. Baum. New York: V. S. Green & Co., 1901.

Gutterschmidt, Hans. A Brief History of Blaustark. Boston: Northsouthern University Press, 1871.

Gutterschmidt, Hans. "Vasserlaut et Apres: L'Histoire d'une Occupation." Heures Perdues, July 8, 1866, pp. 18–24. Reprinted in Sunshine Review, XXXI (1930), 118–121. Trans. Annette Coulet.

Hobbs, Horatio, Bart. Blaustark: The Philpott Lectures, 1861. Reprinted London: Psmith and Smith, 1865.

McCall, Samson. "Blaustark Revealed." The Goliath Review (1965), pp. 24–33.

McCrutch, George Bart. "Blaustark: The Interval Between." Publications of the Balkan Bibliographical Society, LI (Winter, 1866).

————, The Last Hundred Days of Blaustark. New York: Pierpont Press, 1869.

Schlink, Hermann. The Uncertain Peace. New York: Handover, 1863.

2. Other Works Consulted

"Blaustark: political leaders." <u>Encyclopaedia Columbianna</u> (1962), III, 121-123.

Hall, Peter. <u>The</u> <u>Mountain</u> <u>People</u>. London: Stilwell & Sons, 1902.

Additional Bibliography

Nyet, Petrovich. "The Geo-politics of Blaustark." <u>Studies</u> <u>of</u> <u>Eastern</u> <u>European</u> <u>Politics</u>. Ed. C. F. Carter, B. D. Brill, and U. T. Cole. London: Packitin Press, 1867.

Appendix I

More Work

Here are forty (and it could be more) incorrect expressions used by millions of people in America. Although common in conversation they are not suitable for standard writing.

Substandard	Standard
1. There is little doubt *but what* he'll be at home.	
2. Between you and *I*.	
3. I don't like *those kind* of cars.	
4. *Irregardless* of the circumstances, it's your fault.	
5. She told me to buy nails, a hammer, *and etc.*	
6. I was *suppose* to go, but I didn't.	
7. If he *would of* seen me, he *would of* said hello.	
8. The woman in the apartment *hadn't ought to* play the stereo so loud.	
9. *Most all* the actors were miscast.	
10. The mail *can't* come *only* on Mondays.	
11. The rain was *real* bad on Wednesday.	
12. *Being as* I wasn't there, how can you blame me?	
13. There was a *large amount* of pigs in Mr. Clay's yard.	
14. She is different *than* me.	
15. The man was *setting* on the sofa.	
16. The house *lays* between two mountains.	
17. The problem is *when* you don't know how they live.	
18. He was a little *a head* of his time.	
19. The *modern* world *of today in which we live.*	

Substandard	Standard
20. The setting is *where* two men are on a deserted island.	
21. He had a nervous breakdown *of which* he never recovered.	
22. Try *and* come to the party.	
23. The team didn't look too *well* in the second inning.	
24. The *concensus of opinion* is that the incumbent will be elected.	
25. The theme of the story is *where* evil fights against good.	
26. He didn't feel *like* it was worth doing.	
27. It hurt *terrible*.	
28. The man *left* him off at the corner.	
29. Both you and *her* are invited.	
30. It is *me*. (Included as a point of personal privilege by J. H. Knox).	30. It is *me*. (Included as a point of personal privilege by C. C. Colwell, who has the *American Heritage Dictionary* editorial staff on his side.)
31. *Her* and I went to the movies.	
32. *Us* citizens should write our congressman.	
33. If *anyone* will search carefully *they* will find the proof.	
34. The reason is *because* he's sick.	
35. It was *like* it was a bad deal.	
36. She feels *badly*.	
37. There's *alot* to be done to make it *alright*.	
38. *Between* the four of us, we ought to find a solution.	
39. The story is about *this* man who had a big dog.	
40. She is prettier than *me*.	

Appendix II

Glossary

Absolute: Applies to phrases or constructions that modify a whole clause without being linked to it by any specific word, as in *"The war being over,* everyone came home," or *"The job done,* everyone left."

Active Voice: A verb form used when the subject does the action (in contrast to passive.)

Adjective: A part of speech. Describes (modifies) a noun or pronoun. "A *good* boy keeps his teeth *clean."*

Adverb: A part of speech. Describes (modifies) a verb ("He ran *well."*), an adjective ("The *very* tall boy . . ."), an adverb ("He ran *very* well."), or a whole clause (*"Frankly,* I doubt it.") Many end in -ly.

Agreement: The matching of inflected forms in a sentence, especially number. "The *boy says* to let *him* know." All three words, being singular, *agree* in number.

Antecedent: The word or words a pronoun stands for. "The *man* shrugged and said *he* had no explanation." *Man* is the antecedent of *he.*

Appositive: A noun standing beside another noun to give more information about it: "Have you met my son, *the doctor?"*

Article: *a, an,* or *the.* A and *an* are indefinite, *the* is definite.

Auxiliary: Also called helper verb. Used with main verb to show tense (I *will* go) or voice (It *was* done): shall (should), be (is, am, was, were), have (has, had), ought, will (would), can (could), do (does, did).

Case: Changes in noun or pronoun form (inflection) to show role as subject (they) or object (them), or possession (their, theirs).

Clause: A subject and its predicate. "[1] Until it grows, [2] we have a tree [3] which has no leaves" is a sentence with three clauses.

Collective Noun: A grammatically singular form that sometimes has plural meaning. "The *jury* were divided among themselves;" used in a plural sense. "Here comes the *jury* now;" used in a singular sense. Note the plural verb *were,* the singular verb *comes.*

Colloquial: Conversational, informal; not used much in formal writing.

Comma splice: Two independent clauses joined by a comma (no conjunction). "He walked happily, the weather was fine." Corrected: "He walked happily; the weather was fine," or "He walked happily, for the weather was fine."

Complement: Part of the predicate that completes the verb's statement. Includes direct objects ("She kissed *him."*), predicate adjectives ("The test was *hard."*), and predicate nouns ("This book is a *gasser."*).

Complex sentence: Includes at least one subordinate clause. "He tried, although he really didn't care."

Compound adjective: Two words, at least one not an adjective, used together as an adjective, usually with a hyphen (the *hard-working* boy).

Compound sentence: Has at least two independent clauses. "He came and he conquered."

Conjugation: Changes (inflection) in verb forms.

Conjunction: A part of speech. Joins words, phrases, or clauses. Clause-joiners are co-ordinating (*and, or, but, for,* etc.) or subordinating (*if, until, unless, whether, that,* etc.)

Conjunctive adverb: An adverb showing relationship to a previous sentence or clause; not a conjunction, so cannot correctly link two independent clauses. *However, therefore, moreover, nevertheless, furthermore,* etc.

Coordinating conjunction: Links independent clauses; implies equal importance. *And, or, for, but, nor,* etc.

Dangling: A modifier or participle not clearly tied to one word in the sentence. "Working all night, the task seemed impossible." Corrected: "Working all night, I thought the task was impossible."

Declension: Changes (inflection) in noun form.

Demonstrative: Pointing out; *this, that, these, those,* as pronoun or as adjective.

Dependent clause: Cannot stand alone as a complete sentence. Introduced by a subordinating conjunction or a relative pronoun. "Until he gets well . . ." and ". . . who came to dinner" are dependent clauses.

Direct object: Who or what the action of a transitive active verb is done to, as in "I see *it,*" or "John loves *Mary*": *it* and *Mary* are direct objects.

Direct quotation: The exact spoken or written words of someone else (or yourself at another time.)

Expletive: *It* or *there* used with no meaning, as a grammatical subject; as in "*It* is lucky *there* were some."

Fragment: Less than a sentence punctuated as though it were a sentence. Usually a subordinate clause; sometimes a phrase.

Function word: Words that show grammatical relationship (conjunctions, prepositions) rather than representing some real thing, action, or quality.

Fused sentence: Two independent clauses joined without punctuation or conjunction. "I came I saw." A run-on sentence. Corrected: "I came. I saw." Or "I came; I saw." Or "I came and I saw."

Future tense: A verb form to show time after now: "Tomorrow we *will die.*"

Future perfect tense: A verb form to show that the action will be completed before a future time: "Tomorrow we *will have died.*"

Gender: Whether masculine, feminine, or neuter; matters in deciding whether to use, *he, she,* or *it* and in the form of some nouns (*poet, poetess; hen, rooster; etc.*)

Genitive: Possessive (our; ours; women's rights; two books' price).

Gerund: Verb + ing used as a noun. "Parting is such sweet sorrow. . ."

Helping verb: Used with main verb to show tense ("I will go") or voice (it was done)—shall (should), be (is, am, was, were), have (has, had), ought, will (would), can (could), do (does, did). Also called auxiliary.

Idiom: An expression that tends to lose its meaning when translated word for word into another language.

Imperative mood: Verb form used for orders. The subject (you) is generally understood, although appositives may be used: "John, go home."

Indefinite: Not saying exactly which or how many; applies to *each, some, many, more, etc.,* used as adjective or pronoun, and the articles *a* and *an.*

Independent clause: Can stand alone as a complete sentence; subject + predicate, not preceded by subordinating conjunction or relative pronoun. Every nonfragmentary sentence has at least one.

Indicative: One of the moods of verbs (and therefore sentences): makes a statement. (For many grammarians, includes questions.)

Indirect object: To or for whom an action is done, as in "Bring *me* the book"; usually comes before a direct object.

Indirect quotation: The meaning of what someone else (or yourself at a different time) said or wrote, in different words; often introduced by "He said that . . ."

Infinitive: To + verb, as noun or, less often, adjective or adverb. (Occasionally, as with *make* and *let,* may appear without to: "Make me *go*" = "Force me *to go,* you brute.") Sometimes has subject and object, as in "For *John to enjoy the movie,* he must have buttered popcorn."

Inflection: A change in word form to show number (singular or plural), case (subjective, possessive, objective), person (first, second, or third), comparison (e.g. happier, happiest), tense (past, present, future, perfect, etc.), mood (indicative, *etc.*), voice (active, passive), *etc.* The inflection of nouns and pronouns = declension; of verbs = conjugation.

Intensive pronoun: An emphatic form, ending in *-self:* "Do it yourselves."

Interjection: A part of speech: an exclamation unnecessary to the rest of the sentence, as in *"Hey, wow!"*

Interrogative: Asking a question; applies to pronouns (as in "Who?"), to *which* and *what* as adjectives or pronouns; and to mood of verb (or whole sentence; for some grammarians an interrogative sentence is in the indicative mood).

Intransitive: Describes a verb with no direct object. The two main types are linking verbs (especially *to be*) and verbs of motion.

Irregular: Not following the usual pattern of changes.

Linking verb: Equates the subject with a predicate noun ("War *is* hell") or describes it with a predicate adjective ("She *seems* weak.") Especially the verb *to be* (*is, am, was, were,* etc.), verbs like *taste, smell,* and *feel* when followed by an adjective ("I feel good.") and verbs like *appear.*

Main clause: One that can stand alone as a sentence. = independent clause.

Modifier: Word, phrase, or clause describing another word; an adjective or adverb.

Mood: How a verb relates to the facts. There are four moods: indicative or declarative, claiming truth; interrogative, asking what the truth is (included with indicative by some); imperative, ordering that something be done; and subjunctive, expressing doubt.

Nominative: = subjective, or like the subject ("*Who* killed whom?")

Non-restrictive: Describing something already identified, as in "The Empire State Building, which is in New York, was climbed by King Kong." Could be removed without materially affecting sense of sentence.

Noun: A part of speech: the name of someone or something in the broadest sense, e.g. *John, boy, love, abstraction, home, DeLand.*

Noun clause: A clause used as a noun, as in "*Whether you like it* doesn't matter."

Number: Whether singular (one) or plural (more than one). Nouns (man, men; boy, boys), pronouns (I, we), and verbs (runs, run) inflect—change—to show number.

Object: Three kinds: direct object, can follow a transitive verb, as in "I kick *the cat*"; indirect object, can be preceded by "to" or "for" as in "Bring *me* the body"; and object of a preposition, follows a preposition, as in "The fuzzy object on *the ground* has once been a cat."

Objective: Like an object; pronouns have an objective case, as in "He gave *him* his dead cat." "Who killed *whom?*"

Parellelism: Words, phrases, or clauses of the same form that attach to the sentence at the same place, as in "I love *to play, to sing,* and *to dance.*"

Participle: Verb + ing = present participle; regular verb + ed = past participle. (Irregular past participles take many forms, such as *bought, run, stunk.*) "*Wondering* about his *destined* end, he died."

Passive voice: A way of turning a direct object into a subject, as in "The cat *was kicked*"; the verb action is done to the subject, not by it.

Past Participle: Regular verb + ed (*walked, wondered*) and the various irregular equivalents (*struck, built*). Used as an adjective or with a helper verb, as in "The *staggered* steps had *confused* him."

Past tense: A verb form to show that action took place before now. "He *saw* that I *walked* well."

Past perfect tense: Verb form showing that action was completed before a time in the past. "I *had quit* by the time you arrived."

Person: The speaker (first person), the one spoken to (second person), or someone or something else (third person). Pronouns (I-we, you, he-she-it-they) and a few verbs (am, are, is) inflect—change—to show person.

Possessive: Showing ownership or a similar relationship, as in *"his* book," "a *dog's* life," *"its* future."

Predicate: Part of a clause excluding the subject: verb (with its modifiers) and complement (direct object or predicate adjective or predicate noun, with its modifiers).

Predicate adjective: Describes the subject of a linking verb, as in "He is *strong.*"

Predicate noun: Equals the subject of a linking verb, as in "God is *love.*"

Preposition: A part of speech that relates a noun in a certain way to another word (*in, by, after,* etc.)

Prepositional phrase: Preposition + noun (pronoun) with any modifiers. *"For the very handsome man,* hair-combing was *among the essentials."*

Present participle: Verb + ing. Typically used as an adjective or as part of a verbal construction: "The *falling* man was *screaming* loudly."

Present tense: A verb form to show that action occurs now or habitually. "I *say,* do you *jog* often?"

Present perfect tense: A verb form to show that action was completed before now. "You *have been* to the well once too often."

Progressive verb: Helper + verb + ing; shows continuous action. "I was singing while it sank."

Pronoun: Stand-in for a noun (*I, you, him, many,* etc.)

Pronoun adjective: A pronoun used as an adjective. *"Which* boy made *this* mess?"

Proper noun: A specific person or thing; capitalized. "The town *John* lives in is *Chicago.*"

Reflexive Pronoun: Pronoun ending in -self that shows identity with the subject: "I could kick *myself.*"

Regular verb: Past and past participle end in -*ed.*

Relative pronoun: A pronoun with an antecedent introducing a dependent clause. "The boy *who* stood on the burning deck said that was his thing, *which* surprised me."

Restrictive: Necessary to identify fully. Removing a restrictive modifier changes the sense. Compare: *"War that prolongs a hopeless situation is futile,"* with *"War is futile."*

Run-on sentence: Two independent clauses joined without punctuation or conjunction. "She went to town she bought a gown." A fused sentence. Corrected: "She went to town, where she bought a gown."

Sentence: A grammatically complete thought. Contains at least one independent clause, subject + predicate.

Simple sentence: One (independent) clause.

Squinting: A modifier between two elements with no clue as to which it modifies. "He swore *viciously* striking the counter." Corrected: "He swore viciously, striking the counter," or "He swore, viciously striking the counter."

Style: A recognizable quality of writing, affected by diction, syntax, and content.

Subject: What does the action of the verb (or has the action of a passive verb done to it). The answer to the question "Who or what (verb)?" The subject of every imperative sentence is "you," usually understood, not stated.

Subjective: Like a subject. Some pronouns have a distinctive subjective case. "*He* gave him his last dollar." = nominative.

Subjunctive: A mood; a verb form showing doubt, especially an untrue hypothesis. "If this definition *were* not here, you *would be* just as happy."

Subordinate clause: = dependent clause. Introduced by a subordinating conjunction or relative pronoun; used as noun, adverb, or adjective. "*Until you came home,* I hadn't known the man *who was with you.*"

Subordinating conjunction: A joiner of two clauses that makes one of them dependent. "I waited *until* the cows came home."

Substantive: Anything used as a noun.

Syntax: The way word order affects meaning; meaningful order.

Tense: Verb form showing time (past, present, future, perfect, progressive).

Transitive: Taking a direct object; can be used in passive voice. "I *wrote* the book. It *was written* well."

Verb: A part of speech. An action word, the center of a predicate (*climb, am, continue*).

Verbal: Like a verb. Often applied to participles, gerunds, and infinitives.

Voice: Verb form to show whether the subject does the verb action (active) or receives it (passive). "I took it" (active), "I was taken" (passive).

Index